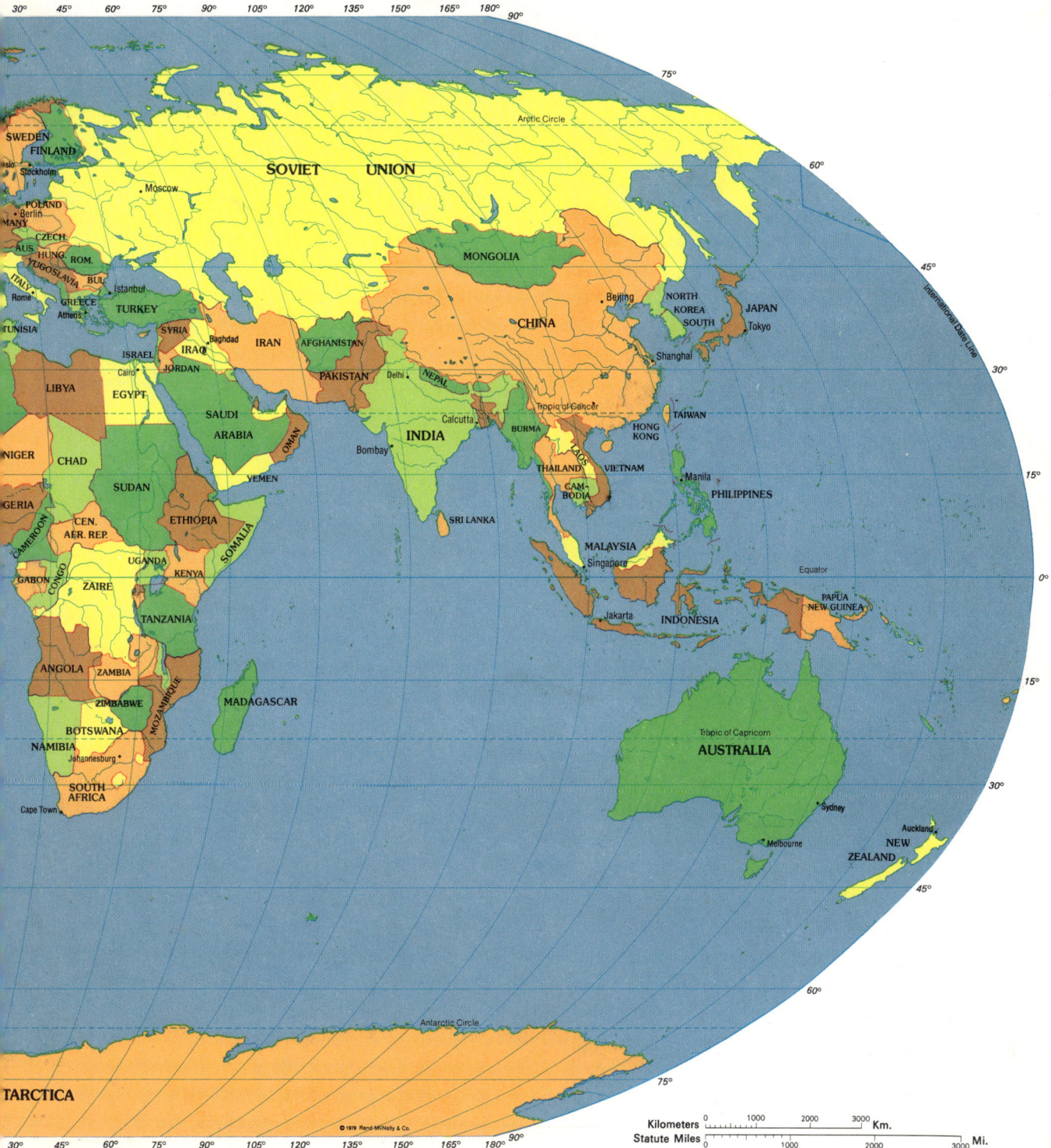

30° 45° 60° 75° 90° 105° 120° 135° 150° 165° 180° 90°

75°

Arctic Circle

60°

SWEDEN
FINLAND
Oslo
Stockholm
Moscow
SOVIET UNION

POLAND
Berlin
MANY
CZECH.
AUS HUNG ROM.
YUGOSLAVIA BUL
ITALY
Rome GREECE
Athens
TURKEY
Istanbul
TUNISIA

45°

MONGOLIA

Beijing
NORTH
KOREA
SOUTH
JAPAN
Tokyo

CHINA

Shanghai

SYRIA Baghdad
ISRAEL IRAQ IRAN AFGHANISTAN
Cairo JORDAN
PAKISTAN
Delhi NEPAL

30°

LIBYA
EGYPT

Tropic of Cancer

Calcutta
TAIWAN

NIGER
CHAD
SAUDI ARABIA
OMAN
YEMEN

INDIA
Bombay

BURMA
HONG KONG

GERIA
SUDAN

THAILAND LAOS
VIETNAM

15°

CEN. AFR. REP.
CAMEROON
ETHIOPIA
SOMALIA

SRI LANKA

CAM-BODIA
Manila
PHILIPPINES

UGANDA
GABON CONGO ZAIRE KENYA

MALAYSIA
Singapore

Equator 0°

TANZANIA

Jakarta
INDONESIA
PAPUA NEW GUINEA

ANGOLA ZAMBIA
ZIMBABWE
MADAGASCAR
MOZAMBIQUE

15°

BOTSWANA
NAMIBIA
Johannesburg
Tropic of Capricorn
AUSTRALIA

SOUTH AFRICA
Cape Town

Sydney
30°

Melbourne
Auckland
NEW ZEALAND

45°

60°

Antarctic Circle

75°

TARCTICA

© 1979 Rand McNally & Co.

30° 45° 60° 75° 90° 105° 120° 135° 150° 165° 180° 90°

International Date Line

60°

45°

30°

15°

0°

15°

30°

45°

75°

Kilometers 0 1000 2000 3000 Km.
Statute Miles 0 1000 2000 3000 Mi.

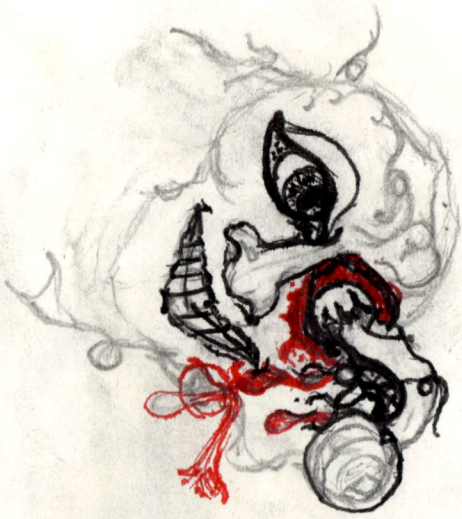

Young Students World Atlas

Weekly Reader Books

Middletown, Connecticut

Contents

PHOTO CREDITS:

Satellite photographs on pages 10 – 15 from *Images of the World* ©
1983 by Rand Mᶜ Nally & Company. Originally published in German under the title of DIERCKE WELTRAUMBILD-ATLAS.
Copyright © 1981 by Georg Westermann Verlag, Braunschweig/
Federal Republic of Germany.

Revised Edition, 1991, 1988

Copyright © 1982, Rand Mᶜ Nally & Company

All rights reserved

ISBN 0-8734-6030-1

Library of Congress Catalog Card Number: 87-51144

The *Young Students World Atlas* has been prepared especially for
Weekly Reader Books by Rand Mᶜ Nally & Company

Young Students Learning Library is a federally
registered trademark of Field Publications.

Printed in the United States of America

The Earth in Space

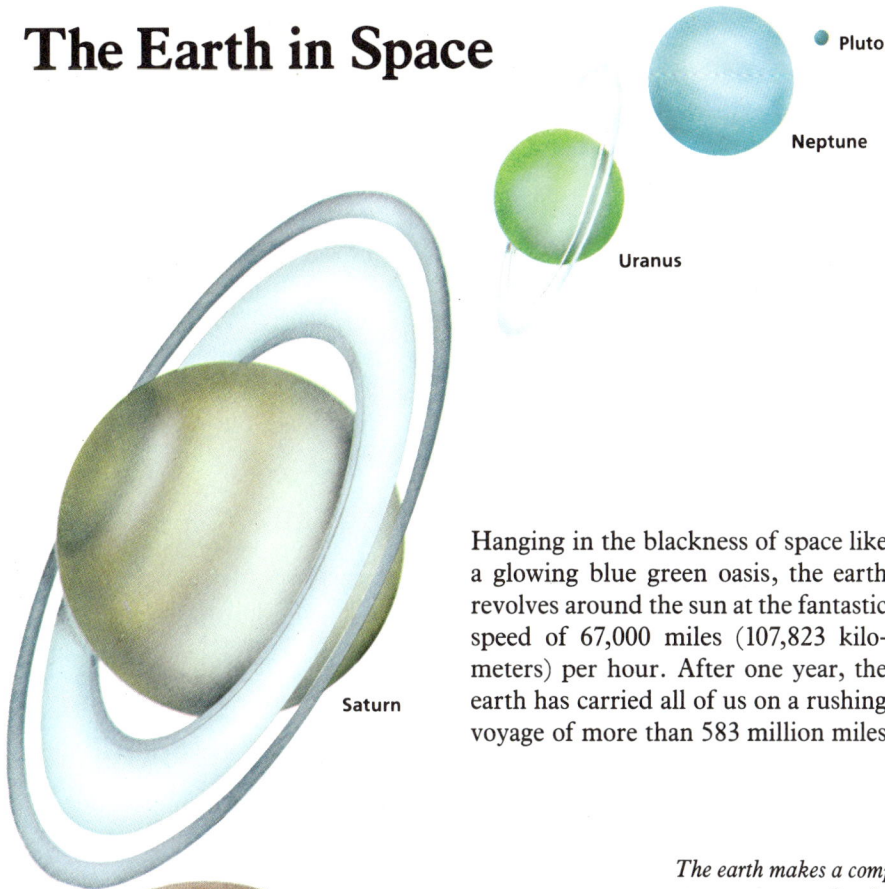

Pluto

Neptune

Uranus

Saturn

Hanging in the blackness of space like a glowing blue green oasis, the earth revolves around the sun at the fantastic speed of 67,000 miles (107,823 kilometers) per hour. After one year, the earth has carried all of us on a rushing voyage of more than 583 million miles

(938,221,900 kilometers)! The earth is a spacecraft taking us on a journey around the sun.

In addition to orbiting the sun, the earth makes a rapid rotating movement on its axis. Each earth day is a result of one rotation. Once every twenty-four hours, the earth turns completely around. As it does so, the sun seems to slip across the sky, rising in the east and setting in the west. But the sun is not moving. It is the earth whirling itself about like a merry-go-round that causes what seems to be the sun's motion.

The earth makes a complete turn every twenty-four hours. This eastward movement is a help in launching spacecraft. A rocket shot eastward from Cape Canaveral gets a boost of nearly 900 miles (1,448.37 kilometers) per hour from the earth's spin.

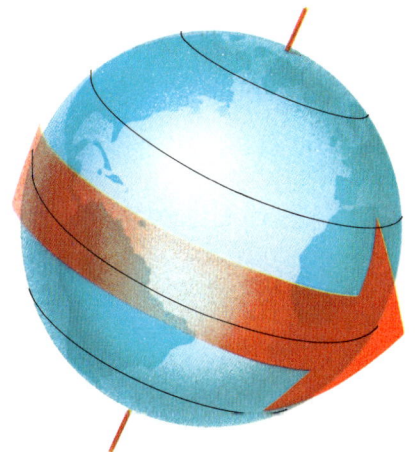

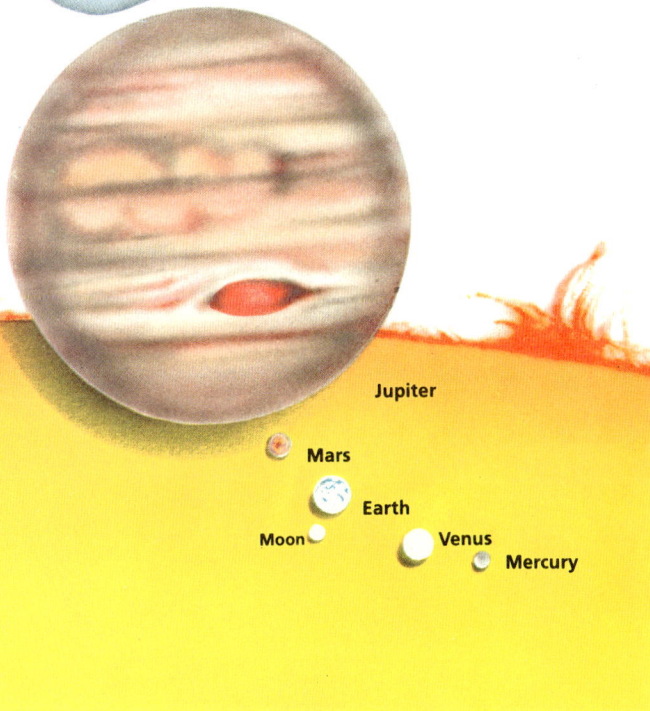

Jupiter

Mars

Earth

Moon   **Venus**

Mercury

34,555,475 kilometers
145,750,000 miles
91¼ days

Spring

Summer

Winter

Fall

The 23½° tilt of the earth's axis and the earth's yearly trip around the sun cause the seasons. In summer, the northern part of the earth is tipped toward the sun, receiving more heat. In spring and fall, both parts of the globe receive equal amounts of sunlight. In winter, the northern part is tipped away from the sun and therefore receives less heat. It is all a matter of angles, not distance. In fact, the earth is a little closer to the sun when January blizzards howl across Europe and North America than when the July thermometer pokes past 100°F (38°C).

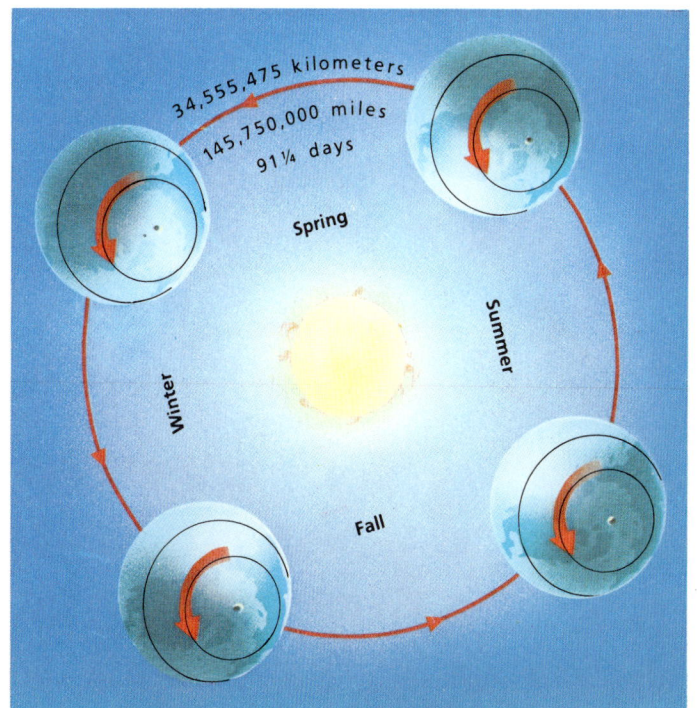

NEPTUNE
Dia. 27,700 mi.
44,600 km.
Rot. 18.5 hrs.
Dist. from Sun 2,794,190,000 mi.
4,496,600,000 km.
Rev. 164.8 yrs.
Moons 2

JUPITER
Dia. 88,700 mi.
142,700 km.
Rot. 9.92 hrs.
Dist. from Sun 483,700,000 mi.
778,400,000 km.
Rev. 11.86 yrs.
Moons 16
Rings 1
Dia. 160,300 mi.
258,600 km.

EARTH
Dia. 7,926 mi.
12,756 km.
Rot. 23.93 hrs.
Dist. from Sun 92,960,000 mi.
149,600,000 km.
Rev. 365.26 days
Moons 1

Comet

MERCURY
Dia. 3,032 mi.
4,878 km.
Rot. 58.65 days
Dist. from Sun 35,980,000 mi.
57,900,000 km.
Rev. 88 days

MARS
Dia. 4,213 mi.
6,778 km.
Rot. 24.62 hrs.
Dist. from Sun 14
228
Rev. 1.88 yrs.
Moons 2

SUN
Dia. 865,000 mi.
1,392,000 km.
Rot. 25.4 days
Surf. Temp. 5,800° Kelvin
Cen. Temp 15,000,000° Kelvin

VENUS
Dia. 7,520 mi.
12,104 km.
Rot. 243.1 days
Dist. from Sun 67,240,000 mi.
108,200,000 km.
Rev. 224.7 days

M-33 Galaxy

PLUTO
Dia. 1,860 mi.
      3,000 km.
Rot. 6.39 days
Dist. from Sun 3,706,780,000 mi.
                  5,965,200,000 km.

Rev. 247 yrs.
Moons 1

URANUS
Dia. 32,600 mi.
      52,400 km.
Rot. 16 hrs.
Dist. from Sun 1,783,170,000 mi.
                  2,869,600,000 km.

Rev. 84.01 yrs.
Moons 5
Rings 9
Dia. 59,700 mi.
      96,000 km.

Map of Outer Space

Our solar system is part of the
Milky Way galaxy, which is represented on the map by the blue
area. The yellow lines show each
planet's path of orbit, and the small
light-colored spheres found near
most of the planets are moons.
The purplish bodies below Jupiter
are asteroids.

ABBREVIATIONS

Dia. :   Diameter of planet
Rot. :   Planet rotation time
Dist. from Sun :
         Distance from the sun
Rev. :   Revolution time around
         the sun

SATURN
Dia. 75,100 mi.
      121,000 km.
Rot. 10.67 hrs.
Dist. from Sun 886,740,000 mi.
                  1,427,000,000 km.

Rev. 29.46 yrs.
Moons 21, possibly 23
Ring System
More than 1,000 ringlike
features in 6 distinct bands
Dia. 177,100 mi.
      285,000 km.

Andromeda Galaxy

)00 mi.
)00 km.

On its voyage around
the sun, the earth is ac-
companied by eight other
planets—plus asteroids,
comets, meteoroids, and
dust. The sun and the
bodies revolving around it
make up the solar system.
Our solar system is a tiny
part of one of the millions of
galaxies, or groups of stars,
that form the universe.

The center of the solar
system, the sun is actually
a star. Its gravitational pull
holds the solar system
together. It keeps the earth
and the other planets from
flinging themselves
into the starry reaches
of outer space.

Our planet is a pygmy
among the giants of the
solar system. Mighty Jupiter
could form more than 300
earths! But the earth is far
more solid than the bigger
planets. Neptune and
Uranus are little more than
thick gas balls. Saturn is so
light it could float in water.
Jupiter is only a little heavier
than water.

None of these other
planets can support life as
we know it. Most contain
choking gases. The planets
closest to the sun, such as
Mercury and Venus, are
sizzling hot. The planets far
away from the sun, like
Neptune and Pluto, are cold
as tombstones. On a hot day
on Venus, temperatures can
reach 900°F (482°C), and
the surface of Saturn is
−285°F (−176°C).

Our planet is neither too
close nor too far from the
life-giving sun. The earth
alone has scarlet flowers and
swaying trees and creatures
that laugh and cry and care
for one another. It is the
jewel of the solar system.

Mapping the World

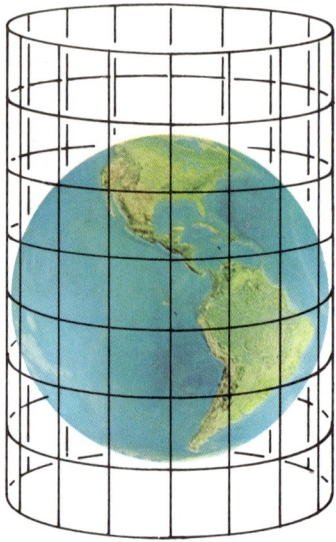

If a globe is projected onto a cylinder, it is called a cylindrical projection.

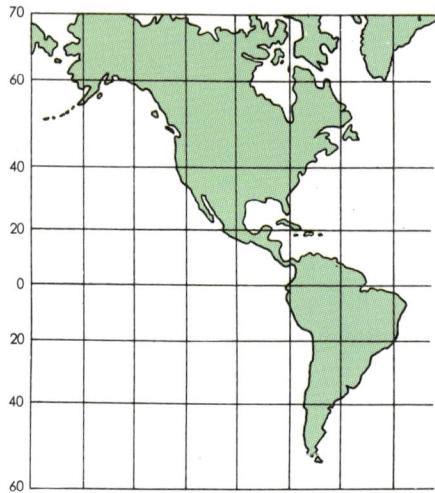

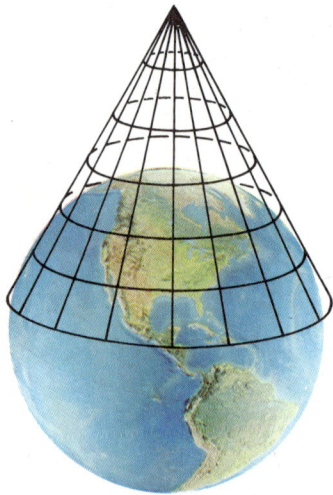

Projection of the globe onto a cone results in a conic projection.

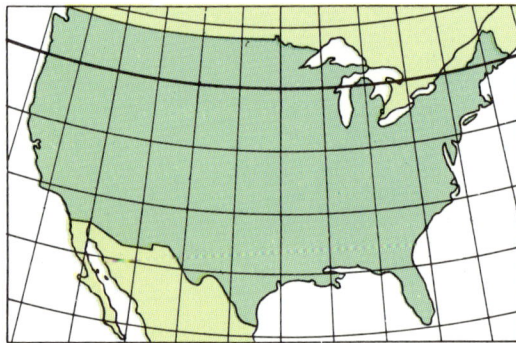

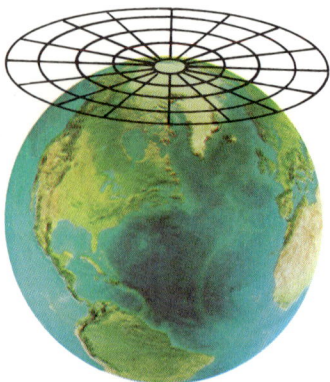

Plane-surface projection is based upon the projection of the globe onto a disc.

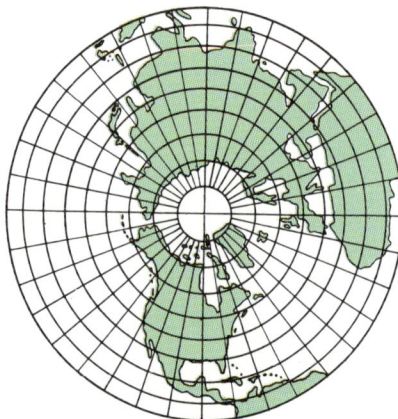

Where in the world am I? Have you ever looked at a map to discover just where you are in the world? And why a map?

A map makes it possible to understand where we are in relation to other people and places. Without maps, our understanding of the world would be limited to what we can see. A map is the best way to communicate information about the earth's surface.

The most accurate model of the earth is a globe. However, a globe doesn't show much detail of the earth. Nor is a globe easy to store in a drawer or carry around in your pocket. A flat map can have many details and is easy to carry or store. And a map can show large areas on a single piece of paper, making it easy to compare cities, countries, and other places.

But how can the curved surface of the globe be transformed into a flat map? Cartographers have found the answer, called map projection.

Map Projections

Most maps contain lines that cross to form a grid. These lines are called parallels of latitude and meridians of longitude. (For a more detailed description of latitude and longitude, see the section "Using the Atlas.") Transforming the round earth into a flat surface is done by projecting this grid onto a simple shape, such as a cylinder, a cone, or a plane shaped like a disc. The surface is then flattened, and the transformation has taken place. The round earth is on flat paper.

This is done in much the same way as a picture is projected onto a movie screen. Or think of a light inside a transparent globe, projecting the grid lines of the globe onto paper, where they can be traced.

However, each projection has some distortion. On a flat surface, it is impossible to represent the angles, distance, direction, and area that only a globe can faithfully show.

Experiment with this yourself. Peel an orange carefully and lay the orange peel on a flat surface. The peel will distort as you flatten it out.

While there is distortion in map projections, the places in the world are always in the right location on a map. The grid of latitude and longitude guarantees this accuracy.

There are many different kinds of map projections, and each is used to show specific features for a specific purpose. Often the type of projection is listed somewhere on the map. At the bottom of the physical-political maps and the environment maps in this atlas, the type of projection is stated.

But once the outline of the earth is on flat paper, how does the cartographer get information to fill in the map? One way is through satellite imagery.

Imagery and Maps

For thousands of years, people have been trying to get a bird's-eye view of the earth. At one time, they climbed trees or hills to get a better view of the terrain around them.

Modern technology has found a way for us to see more of our world than we can with the naked eye or a telescope. Today, there are satellites and airplanes circling the earth, equipped with cameras and electronic equipment acting as "remote sensors."

From a distance, remote sensors gather and record information about features on the earth. The cameras' sensitive film and the electronic instruments are so highly developed that they can detect things that our eyes cannot see. The pictures and information gathered by these satellites and airplanes are used by cartographers to create detailed, up-to-date maps.

Some of the best examples of remotely sensed imagery are the pictures gathered by the Landsat satellites. These satellites were launched in 1972, 1975, and 1978. As the Landsat satellites pass over the land taking pictures, information about water, soil, vegetation, and crops is sent back to earth. Every eighteen days, each satellite orbits over the same area, so that changes in the terrain can be detected. As a result, the satellite images show changes in crop, vegetation, and farming patterns; damage resulting from hurricanes, earthquakes, floods, and fires; erosion patterns; desert sand movements; and other changes that

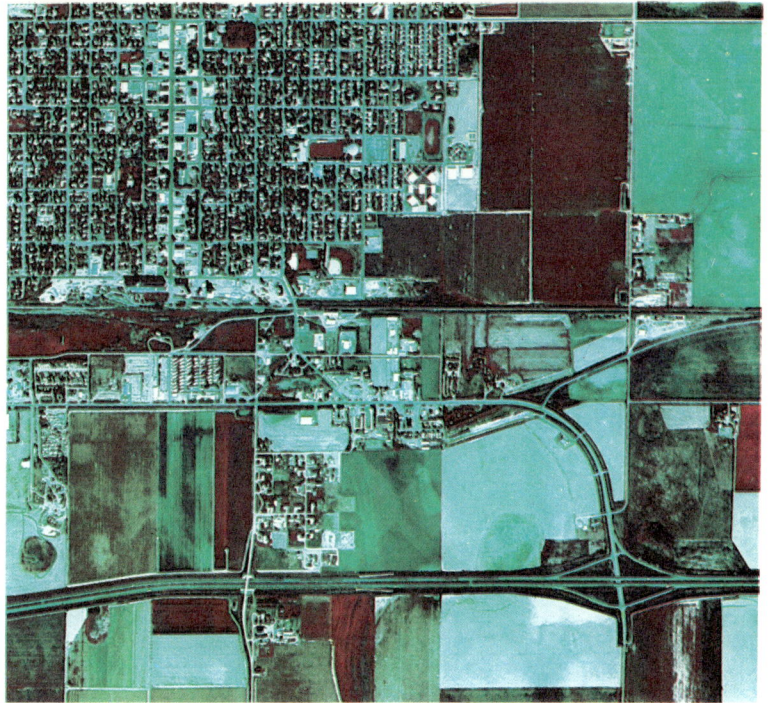

An aircraft-mounted camera produced this high-altitude photograph of the Goodland, Kansas, area.

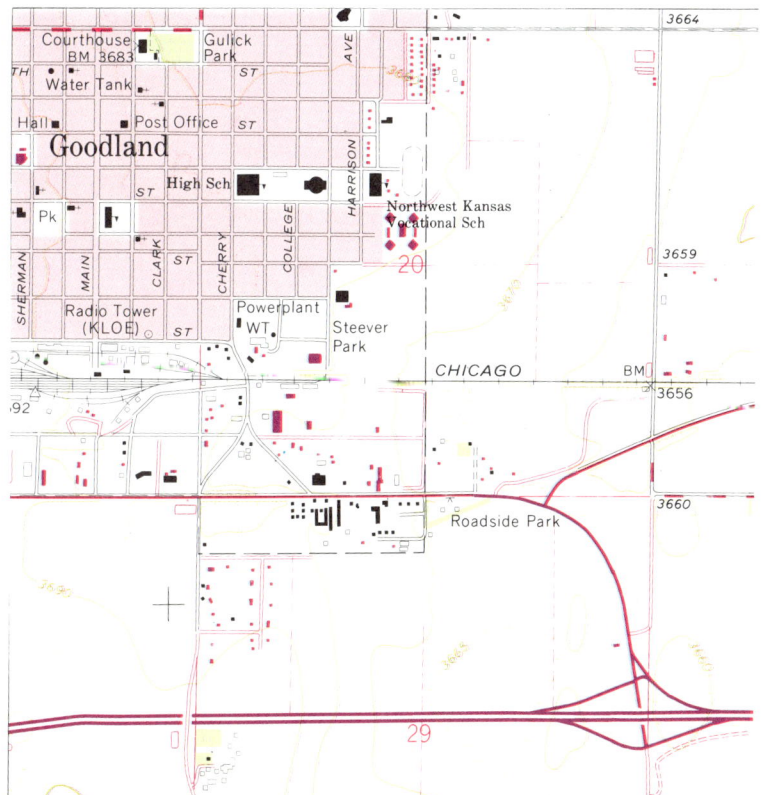

Using the information on the high-altitude photograph, cartographers made this detailed map of Goodland, Kansas.

make it necessary to update maps. In this way, technology provides mapmakers with the latest, most accurate information about the world.

Cartographers also make use of pictures taken by cameras mounted in aircraft. Very detailed maps can be produced from these high-altitude photographs, because all the roads and other features can be seen.

Because of advances in satellite technology and high-altitude photography, more details about the earth are constantly being discovered.

Geographic Features

The study of geography is the study of the people and the land, and any feature found on the surface of the earth can be called a geographic feature. Geographic features are either natural or human-made. They are a result of natural or human activity.

About 5,000 million years ago, our planet came into existence. Millions of years passed, air and water developed, and the shaping of the earth's crust began. Continents collided, thrusting up mountains. Erupting volcanoes created islands. Glaciers passed over the land, depositing rocks and soil and leaving lakes in their wake. Water, wind, and sand cut away at rock.

Humans shaped the land in a different way. They cut down trees to plant crops for food. They blocked the rivers with dams and built reservoirs to bring water to dry land. Mountains are rugged and difficult to farm, so people settled mostly in the valleys and on the plains, where the soil was rich and easy to cultivate. They built cities along coastlines and rivers, because transportation routes were available there. Soon developments were found even in the deserts, where irrigation gave life to the dry land.

This drawing shows some of the different kinds of geographic features on the surface of the earth. It is easy to see the difference between the human-made and natural features. Humans mark the land with bold, even shapes, such as squares and triangles. Nature, however, is not so uniform, and mountains and rivers often cut a jagged line across the earth.

The word list at the right defines some of these land and water features. The pages that follow show pictures of geographic features taken from satellites and aircraft. These pictures, called satellite images and high-altitude photographs, show what the land looks like from above. Satellite images and high-altitude photographs give cartographers the information they need to create maps.

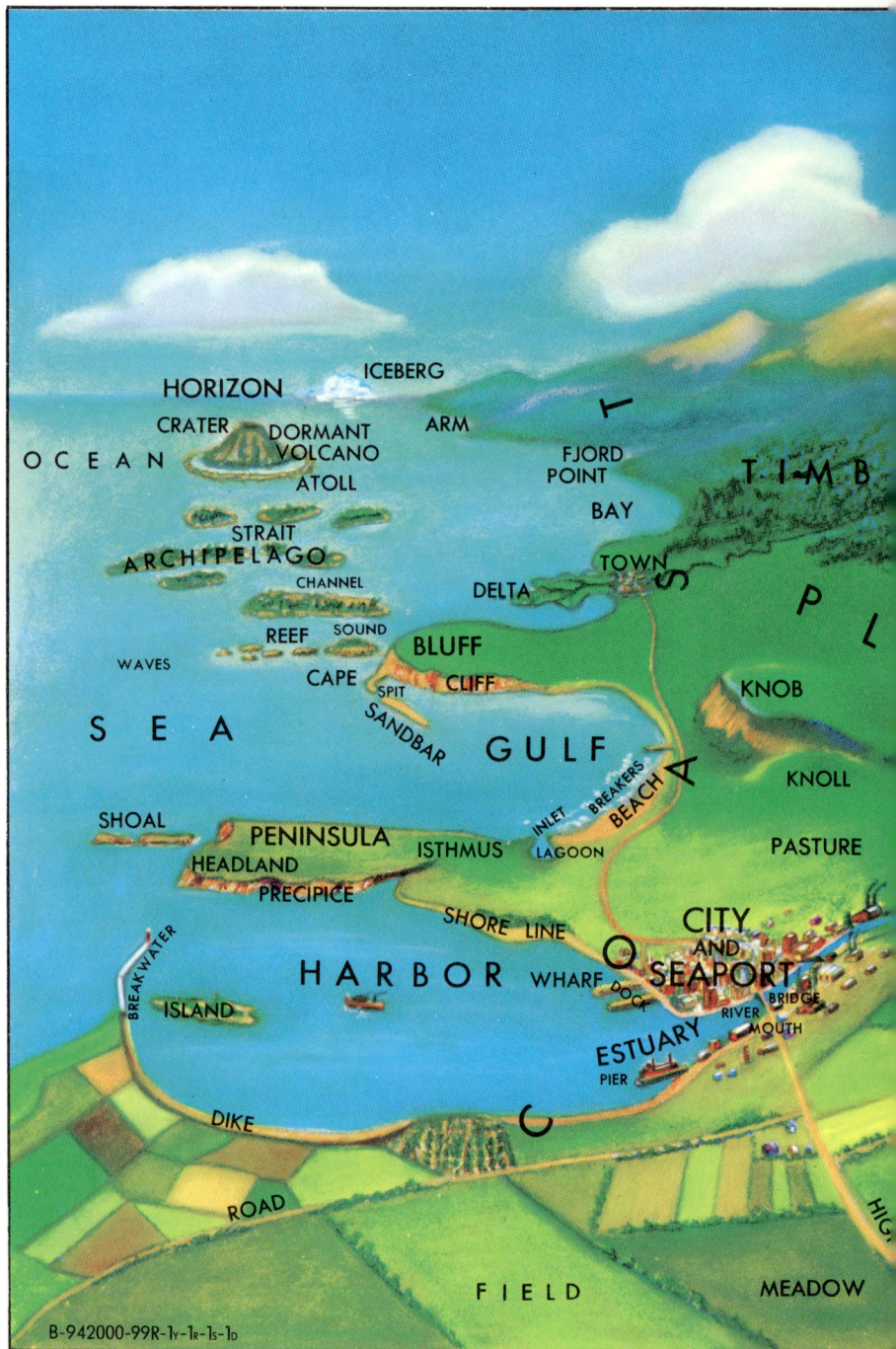

B-942000-99R-1v-1r-1s-1o

archipelago — A group of islands.

bay — Part of a lake or sea that is partly surrounded by the shore land.

canyon — A deep, narrow valley having high, steep sides or cliffs.

cape — A narrow part of land that sticks out into the water along a shore.

coast — Land along the sea.

delta — Land made by soil that drops from a river at its mouth, the place where it meets a larger body of water.

desert — A large land area in which there is little or no rainfall. Few plants can grow on this dry land.

divide — The high land that separates two river basins. A river drains the water from land, and that land is its basin.

fjord — A deep, narrow inlet of the sea, between high, steep cliffs.

forest — A large area of land where many trees grow.

gulf — A large area of the ocean or sea that lies within a curved coastline.

harbor — A sheltered body of water where ships anchor and are safe from the winds and waves of storms at sea.

hill — A small area of land that is higher than the land around it.

inlet — A small strip of water that

reaches from a sea or lake into the shore land.

island — Land that is surrounded by water and smaller than a continent.

isthmus — A narrow piece of land that joins two larger bodies of land.

lagoon — A pool of shallow water linked to the sea by an inlet.

lake — A body of water, usually fresh water, that is surrounded by land.

mountain — Land that rises very high, much higher than the land at its base. Mountains are much higher than hills.

mountain range — A row of mountains that are joined together. A mountain range makes a giant natural wall.

oasis — A place in a desert where people can get water. Water in an oasis comes from underground springs or from irrigation.

peninsula — A land area with a narrow link to a larger land area. It is almost surrounded by water.

plain — A large, flat land area.

plateau — A large land area that is high and generally very flat.

river — A large, moving body of fresh water that starts at a source in higher land. It drains the water from an area called its basin. The river moves from higher to lower land, and it carries the water to its mouth, where it ends. That mouth is at a lake, ocean, sea, or at another river.

sea — A large body of salt water nearly or partly surrounded by land. A sea is much smaller than an ocean.

sound — A long and wide body of water. A sound connects two larger bodies of water or separates an island from a larger body of land.

strait — A passageway of water that connects two large bodies of water.

tributary — A stream or small river that flows into another river or stream.

valley — The lower land between hills or mountains.

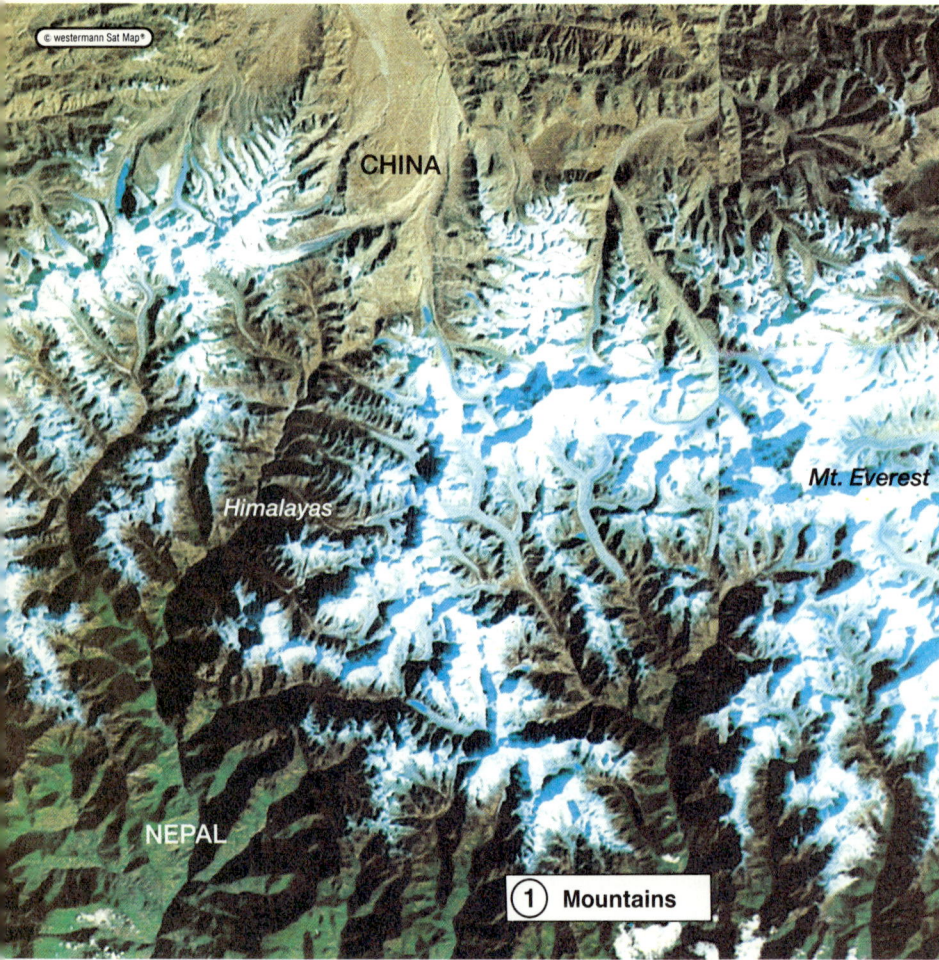

© westermann Sat Map®

CHINA

Mt. Everest

Himalayas

NEPAL

① Mountains

Mountains

High mountains arose millions of years ago, created by great collisions between the earth's "plates." Despite its appearance, the earth's crust, or outer layer, is actually made up of huge slow-moving plates. These plates are like rafts floating on the earth's mantle, the layer of the earth below the crust. Mountains are formed when these gigantic plates collide, thrusting one part of the earth high above the other.

One of the world's most rugged mountain systems is the Himalayas ①. Mount Everest, in the Himalayas, is the highest mountain in the world, rising to a height of 29,028 feet (8,848 meters).

Canyons

Canyons are deep, narrow valleys with steep sides. Most canyons were formed by streams or rivers that cut into rock. Water following the same path over a period of many years has the power to erode the land, carving a canyon in the earth's surface.

The Grand Canyon ② in Arizona is the largest canyon in the world and is

② Canyons

Colorado River

Grand Canyon

ARIZONA

© westermann Sat Map®

© westermann Sat Map®

WASHINGTON

Mt. St. Helens

③ Volcanoes

an example of how canyons form. Over a period of 10 million years, the Colorado River slowly cut into the earth's surface as it traveled to the sea. As the land was cut away, the canyon walls showed the different layers of colored rock that make up the earth. In the satellite image you can see the canyon and its river winding across the land. The dark brown and olive green areas are forests.

Volcanoes

The earth consists of three layers: an outer crust, a middle rock mantle, and an inner core. A volcano erupts when hot, molten rock, or magma, rises from the earth's mantle to its surface. Here it spews forth as lava. There are two kinds of volcanoes, shield volcanoes and cone-shaped volcanoes.

A shield volcano, or lava plateau, is formed when magma finds its way to the earth's surface through fissures, or openings in the earth's crust. The lava flows out gently to form these slightly arched volcanoes.

Cone-shaped volcanoes are formed by magma that contains water and gases. With explosive force, the magma erupts through central openings in the earth, shooting gas, ash, and lava into the air. In time, the layers of lava and ash form the cone shape of the volcano.

Mount Saint Helens ③ is a cone-shaped volcano in western Washington State. It erupted with a fiery blast on May 18, 1980. The satellite image shows gray blue lava flows from the volcano that have covered forested land.

Deserts

Deserts are dry lands with low rainfall and sparse plant and animal life. Not all deserts are hot, sandy, and sunny. Deserts can also be cold, rocky, or snow and ice covered. In a polar desert, cold air keeps moisture from forming.

In some deserts, months or even years may pass with no rain. Then the sky darkens, and the rain comes in a short, violent storm.

The Makrān coastal region ④, which extends from Iran to Pakistan, is a desert off the Arabian Sea. The satellite image shows a dust storm in the desert. Dust clouds, heading out over the sea, appear along the lower edge of the picture.

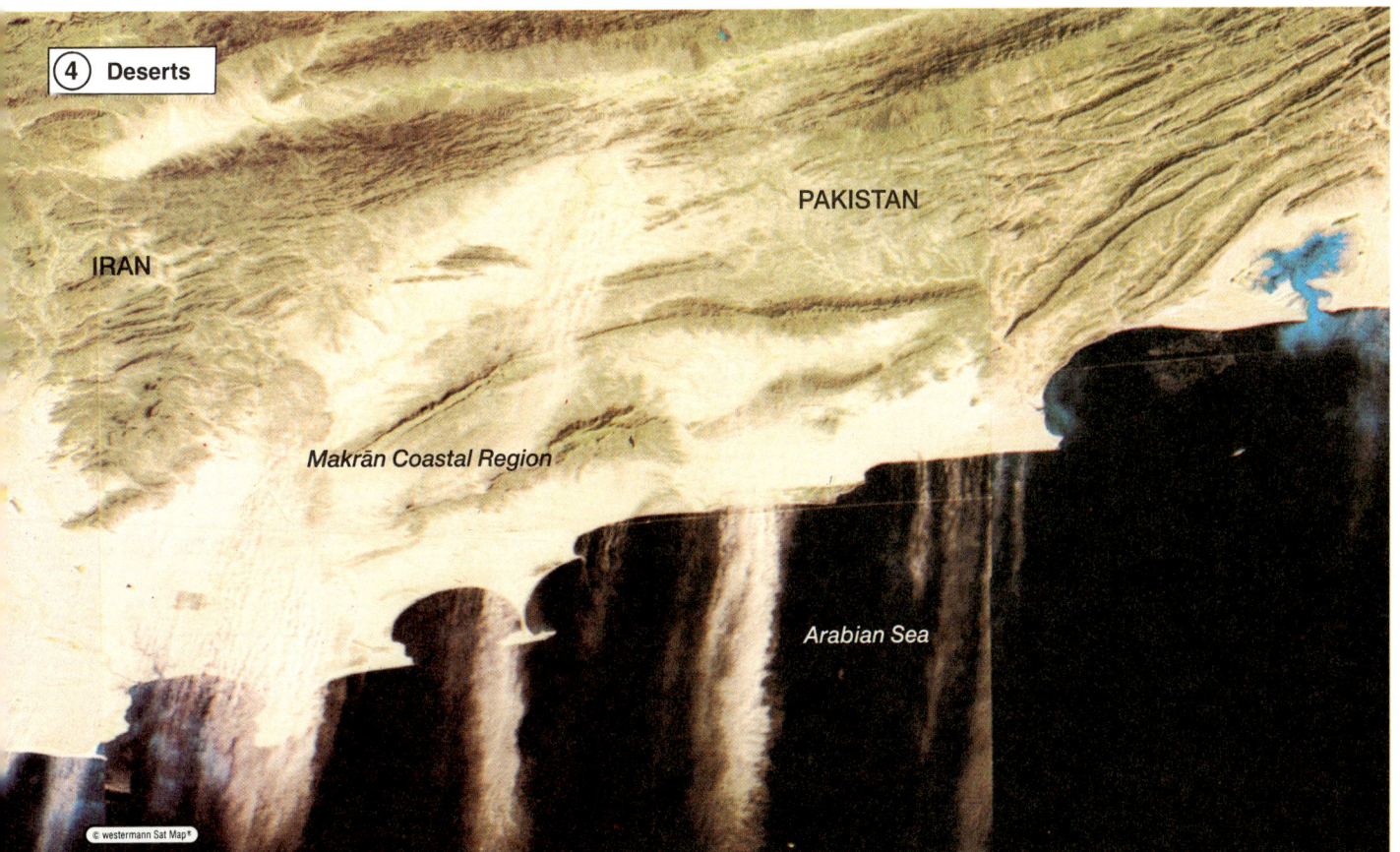

④ Deserts

PAKISTAN

IRAN

Makrān Coastal Region

Arabian Sea

© westermann Sat Map®

⑤ **Coastlines**

Saronic Gulf

GREECE

Gulf of Argolis

© westermann Sat Map®

Coastlines

The land along the sea is called the coast, and the coastline is the boundary between land and water. This boundary is always changing. Some changes occur slowly as the water carves out the land and fills in bays. Other changes occur daily. These are the tides that pull in and out, sifting and moving sand and sediment.

The satellite image of the Gulf of Argolis and the Saronic Gulf in Greece ⑤ shows the jagged line where the water meets the land.

Deltas

A delta is land that forms at a river's mouth, the place where the river meets a larger body of water. Here, the river slows down, and the clay, silt, sand, and gravel it has picked up on its journey drops to the bottom. In time, these deposits rise above the water to form a delta.

The Mississippi River ⑥ forms a delta where it meets the ocean near New Orleans. In the picture, the lighter blue around the river's mouth shows deposits that are slowly extending the delta into the Gulf of Mexico.

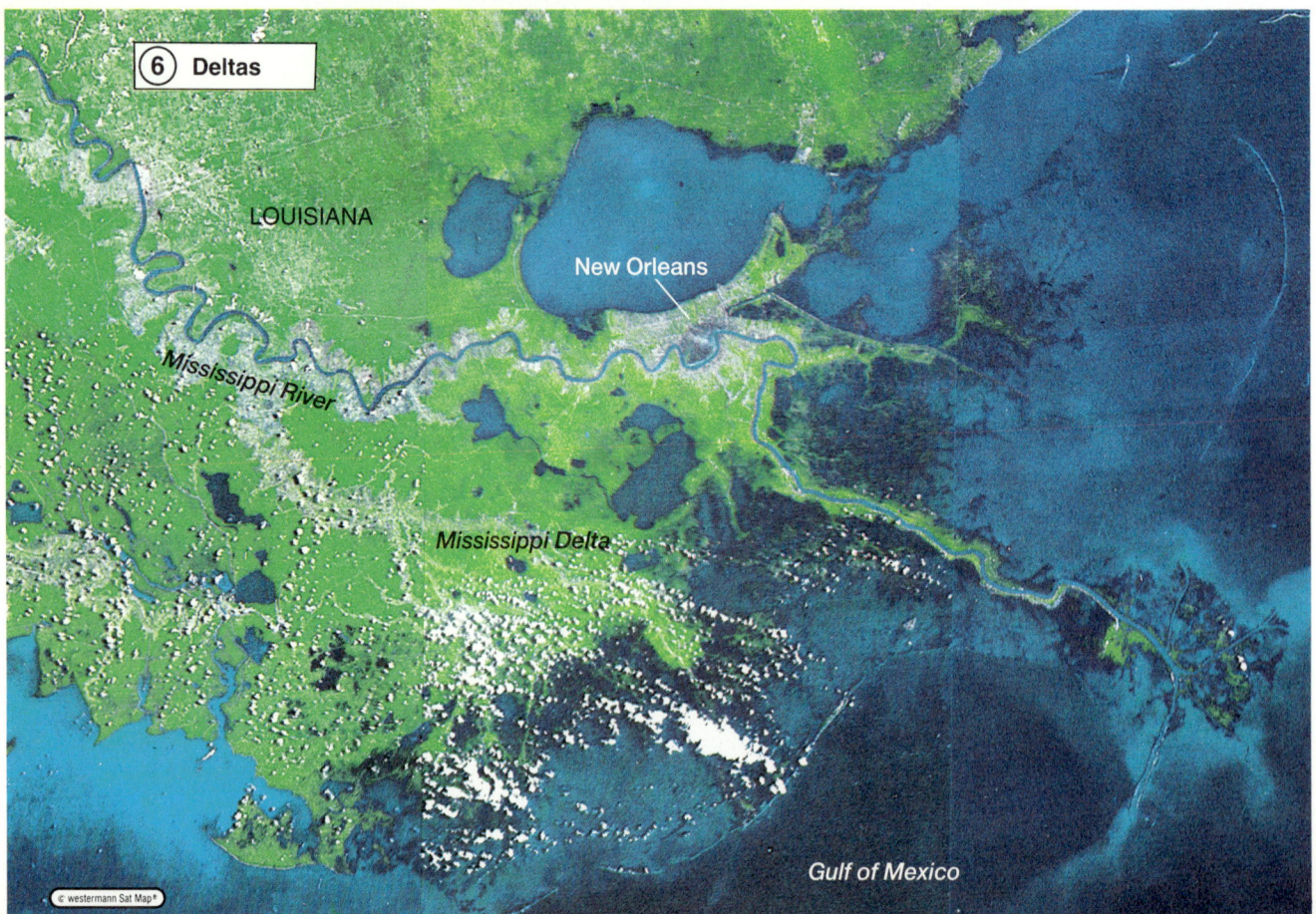

⑥ **Deltas**

LOUISIANA

New Orleans

Mississippi River

Mississippi Delta

Gulf of Mexico

© westermann Sat Map®

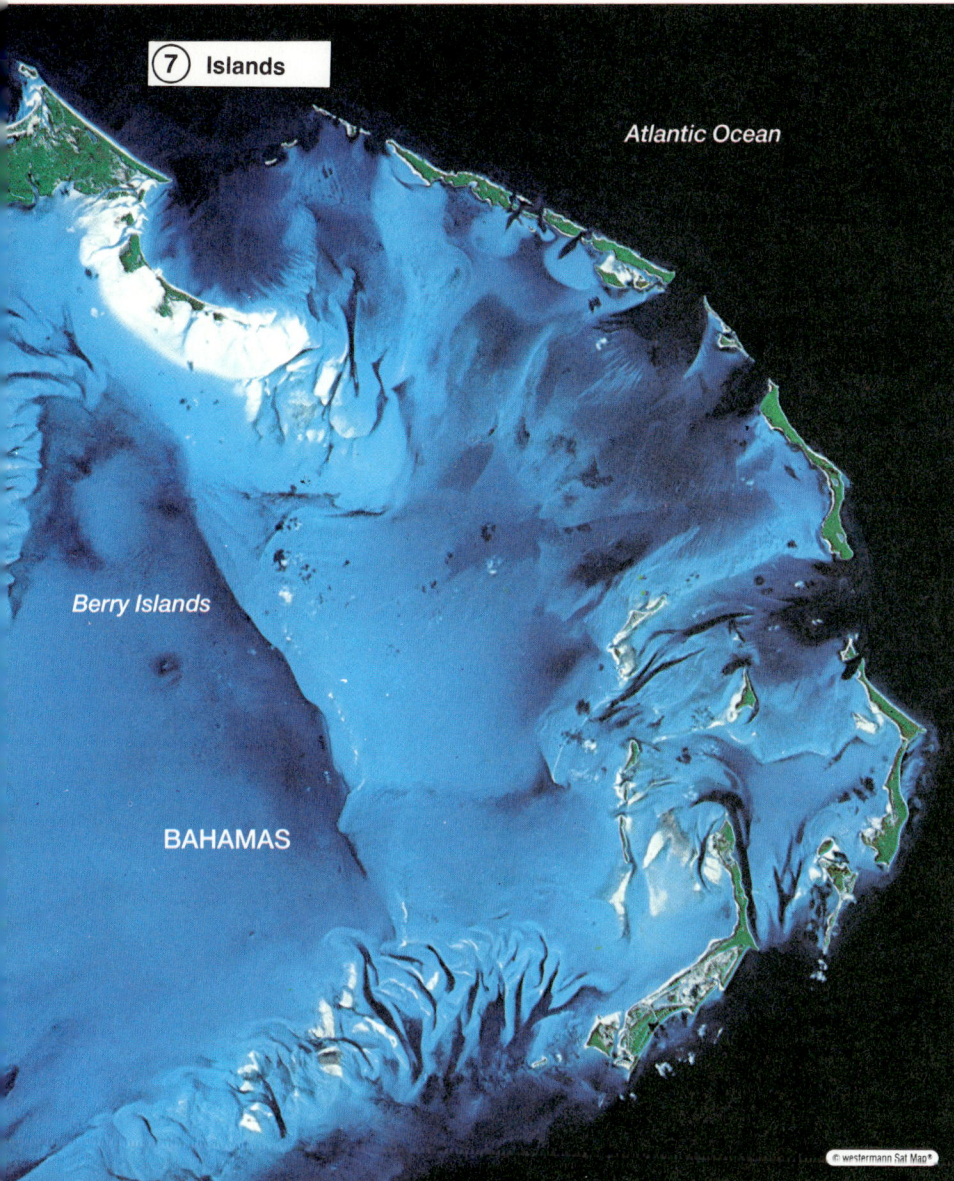

(7) Islands

Atlantic Ocean

Berry Islands

BAHAMAS

Islands

An island is a body of land that is smaller than a continent and completely surrounded by water. Islands are formed in different ways. Sometimes water crosses a peninsula or continent, cutting off a section of land as an island. Some islands are volcanoes or mountains resting on the ocean floor and extending above the water. Cays are low islands built from coral, sand, and algae reefs.

The Berry Islands (7) in the Bahamas are cays built upon a huge underwater limestone base. The green areas on satellite image are the cays, and the blue shows the reef that lies under the water.

Glaciers

A glacier is a slow-moving mass of ice found in high mountains and polar regions. Glaciers are formed when snow builds up year after year. The weight of the snow compacts it into glacial ice. As snow continues to fall and ice continues to form faster than it can melt, the glacier grows.

Many glaciers move only a fraction of an inch per day, and others move several feet. Some have moved up to 330 feet (101 meters) in a single day.

Glaciers are found in the St. Elias Mountains (8), which extend from Alaska into Canada. The mountains' Malaspina Glacier is larger than the state of Rhode Island.

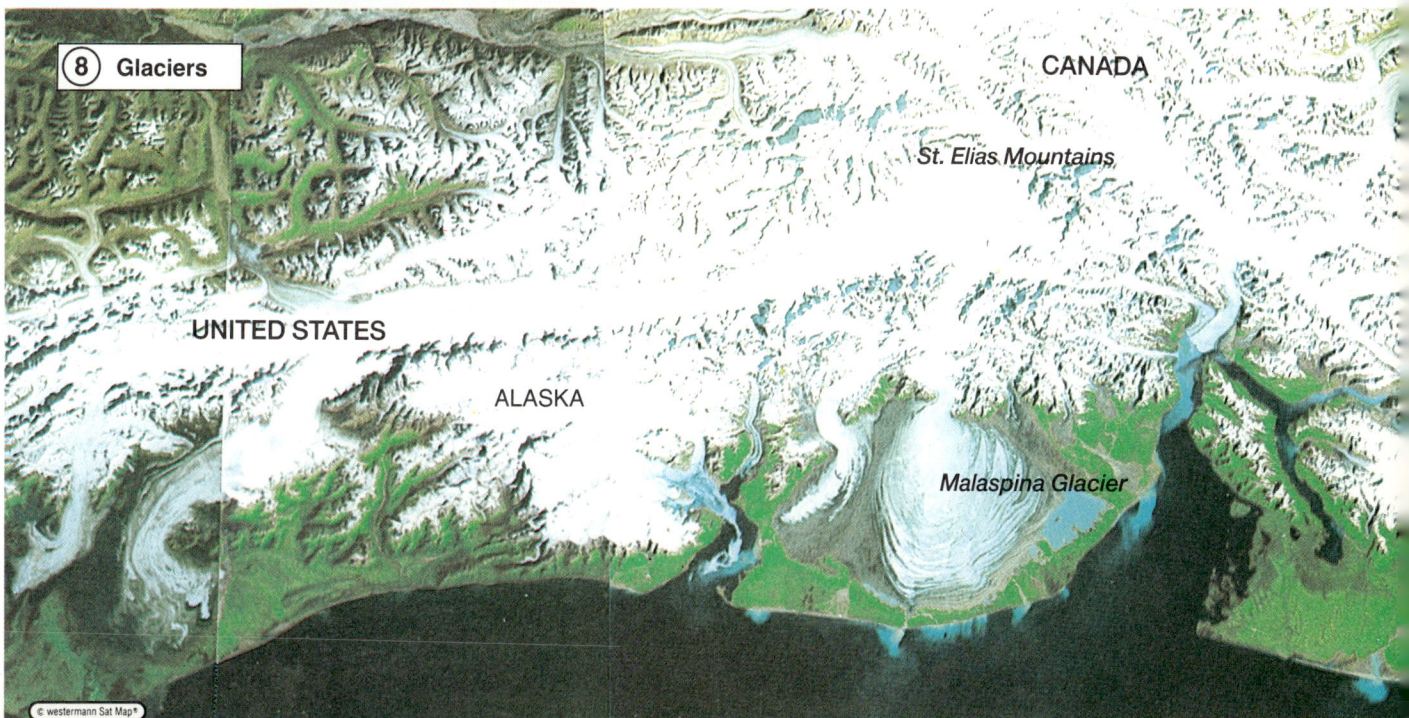

(8) Glaciers

CANADA

St. Elias Mountains

UNITED STATES

ALASKA

Malaspina Glacier

⑨ Cultivated Land

OKLAHOMA

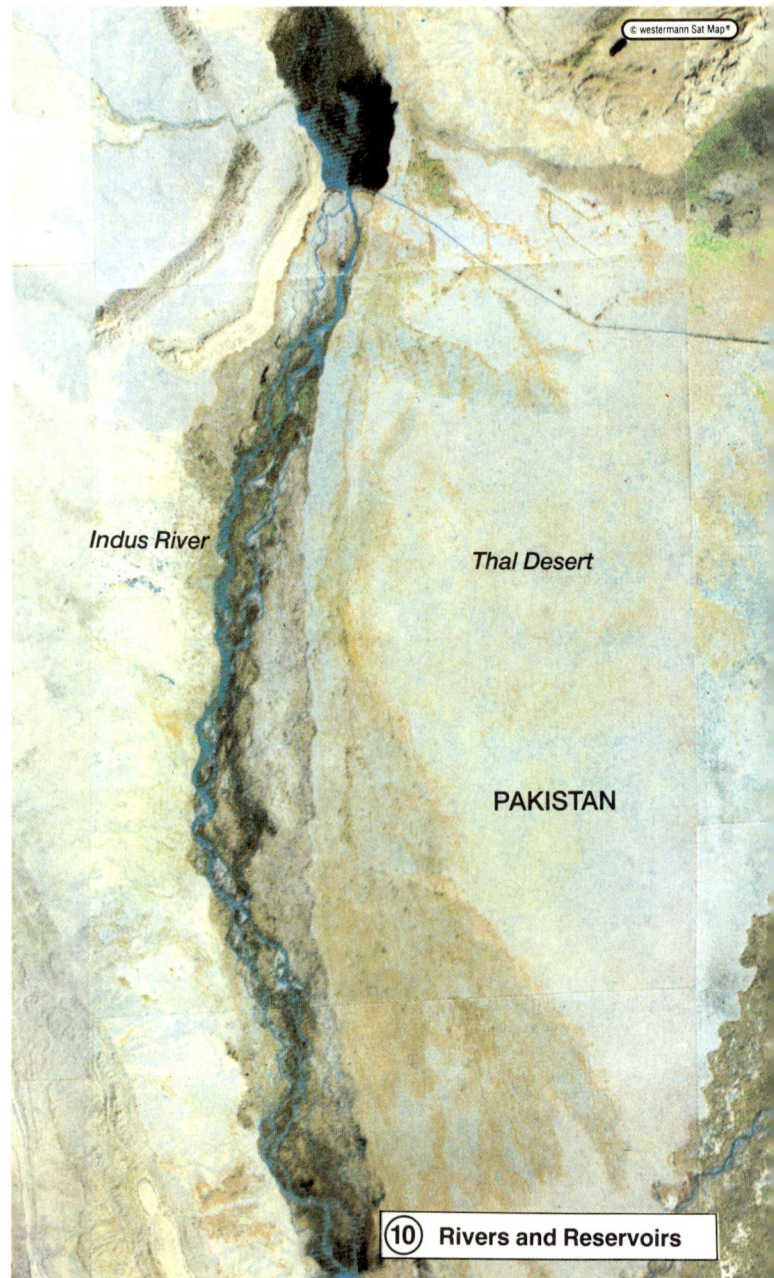

Indus River

Thal Desert

PAKISTAN

⑩ Rivers and Reservoirs

Cultivated Land

Agriculture is the science of producing crops and livestock. It provides the food that sustains human life, and so can be considered the most important of all employments. Land that people have altered to produce crops and feed livestock is called cultivated land.

The cultivated land of western Oklahoma ⑨ is an example of agriculture in the United States. Rectangular fields are bordered by country roads and highways. Tan areas in the image show cropland planted with wheat, which has just been harvested. Green areas are meadows and pastures used for livestock. The darker green sections are forests.

Rivers and Reservoirs

Water is essential for life, but water is not distributed evenly on the earth. Sometimes people shift water from lakes and rivers to dry land in order to help crops grow. This is called irrigation. Windmills, sprinklers, dams, reservoirs, and canals are some of the methods used for irrigation. People also use dams and reservoirs to block rivers and to obtain water for their daily use.

The Indus River ⑩ in Pakistan brings life to the surrounding land. In certain places dams block the river to control its flow. Reservoirs store water for irrigation and other purposes. And canals direct water away from the main

path of the river to bring water to the dry lands.

Cities

In settling the land, people were influenced by geographic factors. Some areas were too dry or too wet, subject to droughts or floods. Other places were hard to get to, blocked by mountains or far from the rivers used for transportation. So people settled in valleys, near mineral resources, and on fertile plains. They built their homes close to rivers and along harbors and bays. As time went on, more people were drawn to these population centers, looking for work and an easier life than farming could provide. Goods

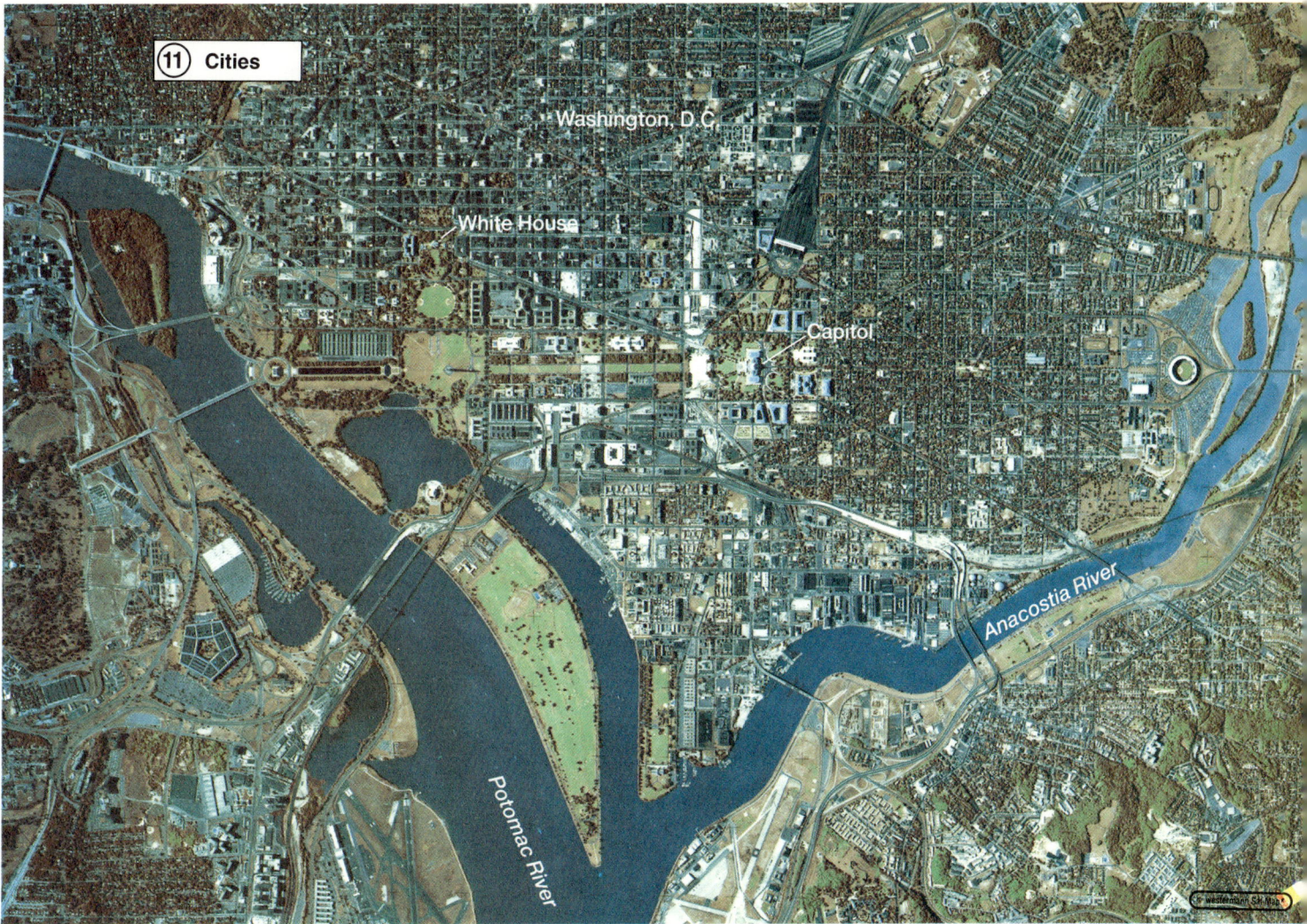

11 Cities

Washington, D.C.

White House

Capitol

Anacostia River

Potomac River

were shipped in and out of busy ports, mineral deposits fueled growing industry, and railroads, highways, and air routes connected the important cities.

Because of their large populations and the effects of years of industry, cities today are facing many problems. However, they continue to play important roles as capitals of nations and centers of industry and technology.

The nation's capital, Washington, D.C., ⑪ is situated on a triangle of land formed by the Potomac and Anacostia rivers. Washington is part of an "urban corridor," a heavily populated area that extends all the way north to Boston, Massachusetts.

Cairo ⑫ is the capital of Egypt. It is situated where the Nile River broadens into the fertile Nile Delta. Transportation here is limited by the desert, and so all traffic and trade must pass through Cairo on its way north or south. Thus Cairo plays an important role in the economy and military strategy of the Middle East.

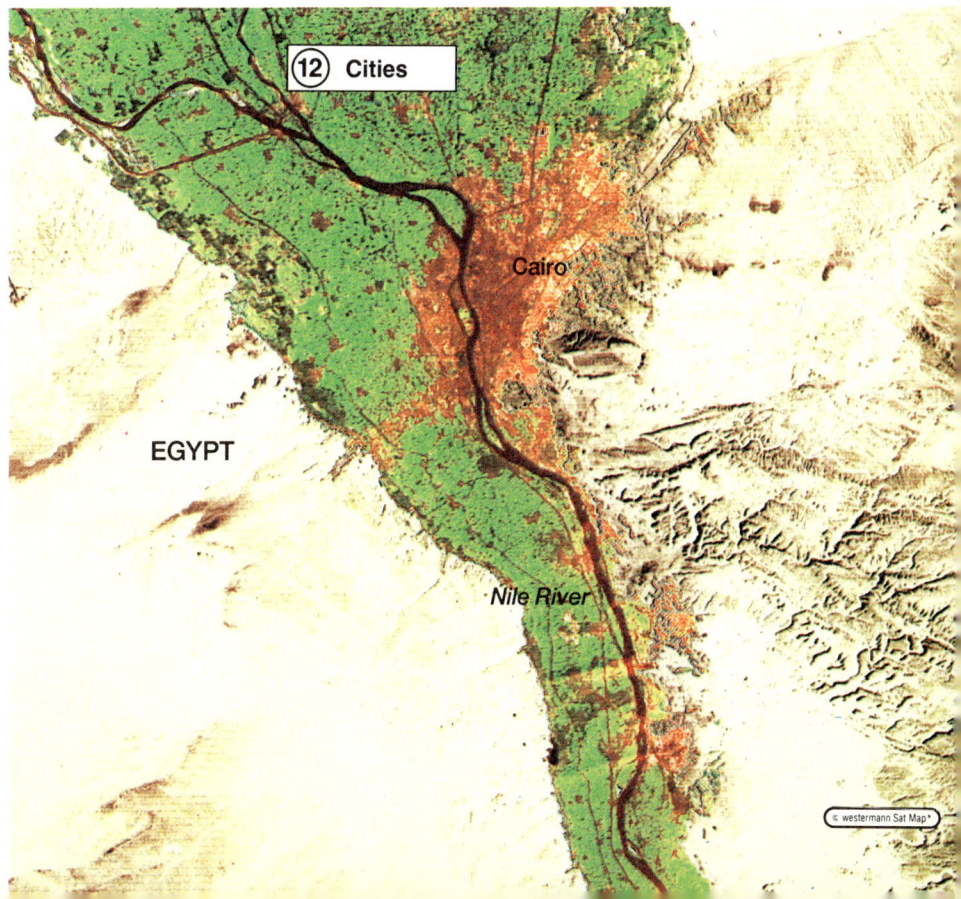

12 Cities

Cairo

EGYPT

Nile River

Using the Atlas

An atlas is a guide to the world that can be used in many ways. You can look up places in the news and learn about the world. If you're interested in history, you can use an atlas to find famous towns and battle sites. You can even use an atlas to find the names of places in movies or to look up the lake you swam in last summer. But to discover the world with your atlas, you must be able to do five things:

1. Measure distances using a map scale
2. Use directions and latitude and longitude
3. Find places on the maps using letter-number keys
4. Use different kinds of maps
5. Use map symbols and legends

Measuring Distances

To understand a map, you must know its scale, or how large an area of the earth it shows. There are different types of map scales, but the bar scale is the easiest to use for determining distance.

For example, to find the distance between Bergen and Oslo in Norway, first you will find out how far Bergen is from Oslo on the map. Then by using a bar scale, you will learn what this means in actual distance on the earth.

1. Find Bergen and Oslo on the map in Figure 1.
2. Lay a slip of paper on the map so that its edge touches the two

cities. Move the paper so that one corner touches Bergen.
3. Mark the paper where it touches Oslo. The distance from the corner of this paper to the mark shows how far Oslo is from Bergen on the map.

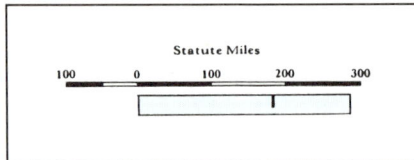

Figure 2

4. The numbers in the map scale in Figure 2 show statute miles, or miles on the earth. Line up the edge of the paper along the map scale, putting the corner at 0.
5. Find the mark on the paper. The mark shows that Bergen is about 200 miles away from Oslo.

Using Directions and Latitude and Longitude

Most of the maps in this atlas are drawn so that north is at the top of the page, south is at the bottom, west is at the left, and east is at the right.

Many of the maps also have lines drawn across them—lines of latitude and longitude. These are lines drawn on a map or globe to make it easier to tell directions and to find places.

Lines of latitude are also called parallels of latitude. As shown in Figure 3, parallels run east and west, and they are numbered with degrees, which measure distance. One degree of latitude is about seventy miles (112.65 kilometers) long.

Latitude is measured as degrees north (N) or degrees south (S) of the equator. The equator was chosen as the dividing point because it marks the middle of the earth. It is at 0° latitude. The place farthest north on earth is the North Pole. It is

located 90° north of the equator, or, simply, at 90° N. The South Pole is the earth's southernmost point, at 90° S.

You can use parallels of latitude to tell how far north or south a place is. For example, the map in Figure 1 shows that Bergen is north of the 60° parallel of latitude and Stockholm is south of it. So Bergen is farther north than Stockholm.

Lines of longitude are also called meridians. Figure 3 shows that meridians run north and south between the two poles. Like parallels, they are numbered with degrees.

But unlike parallels of latitude, meridians have no natural dividing line at which their numbering can begin. In the 1880s, an international conference solved this problem by

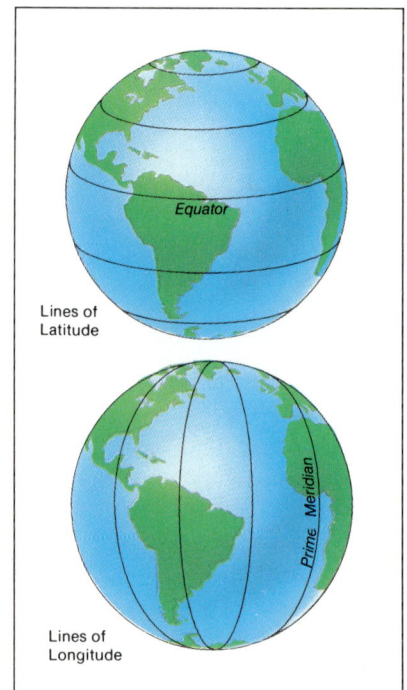

Figure 3

selecting Greenwich, England, near London, to be the prime meridian, or 0° longitude. So, meridians measure how far east (E) or west (W) of Greenwich, England, a place is.

You can use the map in Figure 1 to find out which city is farther east, Bergen or Stockholm. Bergen is about 5° east of the prime meridian, or 5° E. Stockholm is about 20° E. This means that Stockholm is farther east than Bergen.

The east-west parallels and north-south meridians form a grid on a globe or map. You can find any place in the world by using latitude and longitude.

Figure 1

Finding Places

One of the most important things an atlas can do is tell you the location of a place—where it is. You may want to look up the city where a pen pal lives or find a town you're interested in visiting. To help you find places quickly and easily on a map, most atlases include an index of place-names with letter-number keys.

If you were studying South America, and read about Santiago, a city in Chile, here's how you would find it on a map:

1. Look up the city's name, Santiago, in the alphabetical index at the back of the atlas. (See Figure 4.) The number 88 is the page that the map is on. The letter-number key C2 is the guide to finding Santiago on the map on page 88.

2. Turn to the map of southern South America on page 88.

3. Find the letters **A** through **G** along the left-hand side of the map and the numbers **2** through **5** along the top edge of the map. These black letters and numbers are centered between the parallels of latitude and meridians of longitude.

San Juan, P.R. n18 77
San Salvador, Sal. F7 76
Santa Fe, NM C5 74
Santiago, Chile C2 88
Santo Domingo, Dom. Rep. E10 77
São Paulo, Braz. A7 88

Figure 4

---

4. To find Santiago, use the letter-number key C2. Place your left index finger on C and your right index finger on 2. Move your left finger across the map and your right finger down the map, staying within the latitude and longitude grid lines on either side. Your fingers will meet in the box in which Santiago is located. (See Figure 5.)

You can use this method to find any place listed in the index of this atlas.

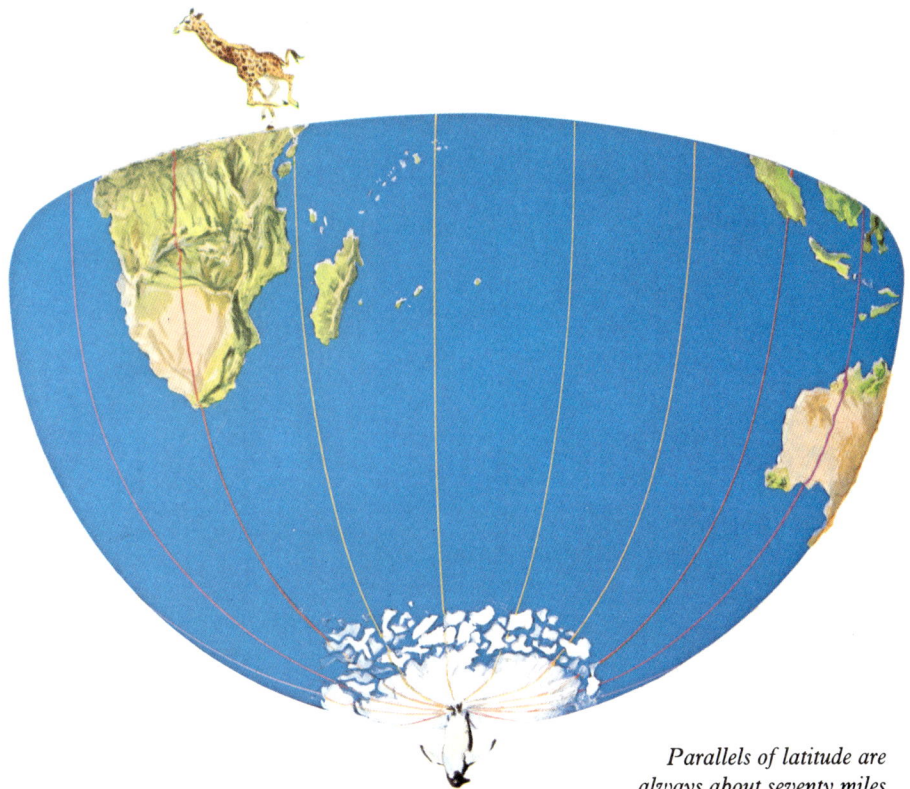

Parallels of latitude are always about seventy miles apart. But the distance between meridians shrinks near the North and South poles. At the equator, a giraffe would have to run seventy miles (112.65 kilometers) to cover one degree of longitude. Near the South Pole, a penguin could merely wiggle a toe over the ice and cross a meridian.

Figure 5

88 **South America, South**/Physical-Political

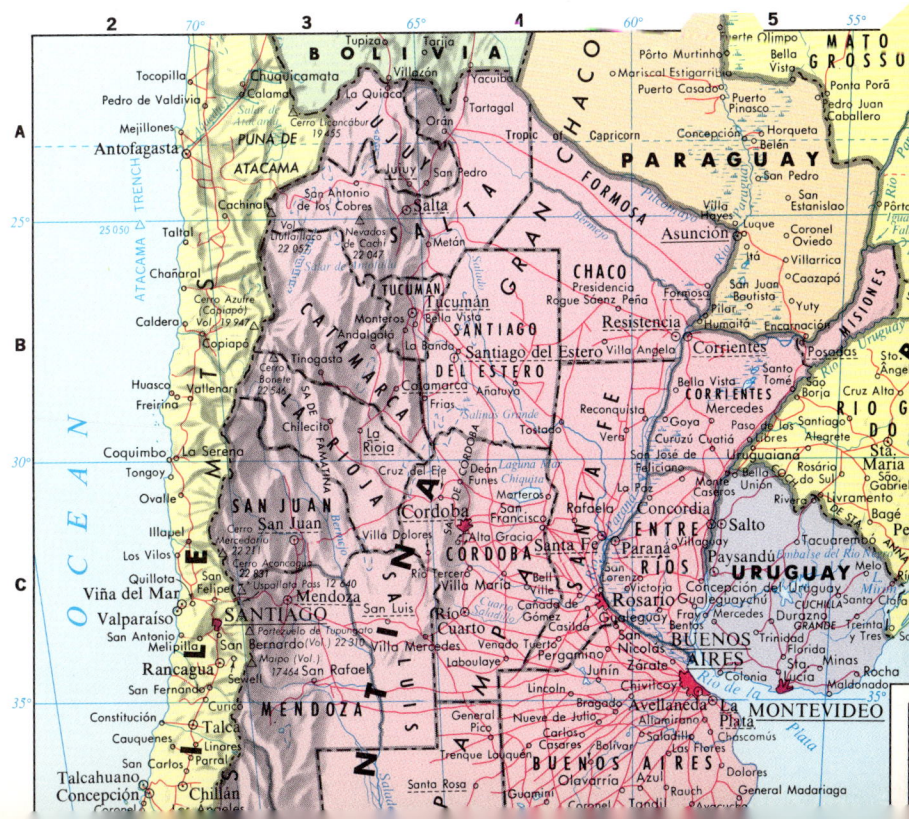

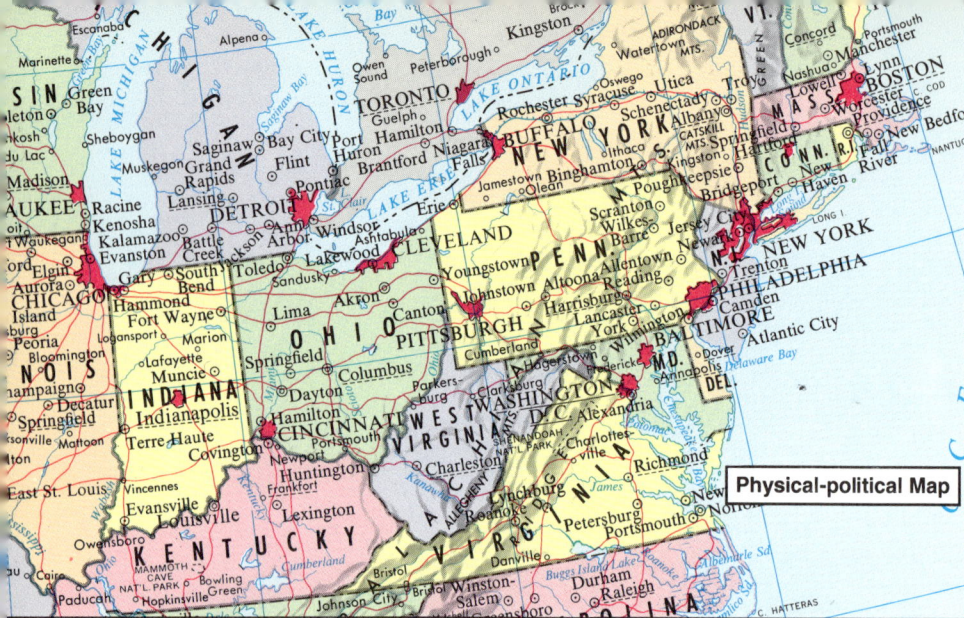

Using Different Kinds of Maps

There are different kinds of maps, and each is especially suited for a certain topic. In this atlas, you'll find physical-political maps, physical maps, political maps, and thematic maps.

When people think of maps, they usually think of physical-political maps. The purpose of a physical-political map is to show the world's physical features and political units. Physical features include oceans, lakes, rivers, mountains, and other natural parts of the earth. Political units are states and countries and all the places they contain. These are human-made features.

Sometimes, the information on a physical-political map is separated to make two maps: a physical map, showing only natural features, and a political map, showing only human-made features.

The physical maps in this atlas are called terrain maps. The terrain maps use shaded relief to show the shape of the earth's surface. Shaded relief is a three-dimensional drawing of mountains and valleys on a map. The political maps in this atlas show countries, major cities, roads, and railroads.

A thematic map tells the story of a special topic, such as rainfall, population, trade, mineral resources, or any special aspect of the physical (natural) or political (human-made) environment. There are two main types of thematic maps in this atlas: environ-

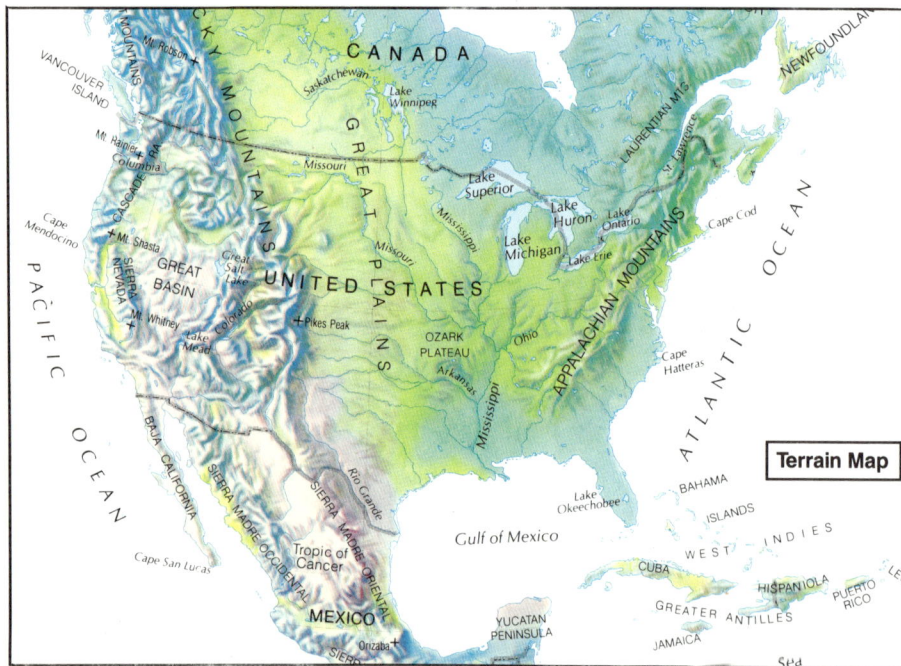

PHYSICAL-POLITICAL MAP (top)
Physical-political maps are sometimes called general reference maps because they give general information about the world's natural and human-made features. You can use physical-political maps to find cities and countries, to measure distances, or to look up mountains, lakes, and other physical features.

TERRAIN MAP (center)
A physical, or terrain, map shows only natural features. On this map of the United States, the shaded relief indicates that the West is marked with high mountains, the central United States is mainly a plain, and the East consists of highlands and low mountains.

THEMATIC MAP (bottom)
Using a thematic map is much like looking at a picture. This thematic map of the United States can tell you what type of wildlife is found in your part of the country.

Physical-political Map

Terrain Map

Thematic Map

ment maps and animal maps. The environment maps show how people use the land. The animal maps show the kinds of wildlife found on each continent.

Using Map Symbols and Legends

A symbol is something that stands for something else. In a way, a whole map is a symbol, because it represents the world or a part of it.

All the world's features—such as cities, rivers, and lakes—are represented with symbols on maps. Map symbols may be points, lines, or areas.

Point symbols are usually dots or stars. For example, the symbol for a city might be a dot, and the symbol for a state capital might be a star.

Line symbols are used for roads, rivers, or railroads. Often, rivers are shown with blue lines, and roads with black.

Area symbols show states, forests, deserts, or anything that covers a large area. On a map of the United States, for example, each state may be shown in a different color so that you can see where one state ends and the next state begins. Large areas of forest might be shown in green, and deserts could be a

sand color. These different colors are area symbols.

A map legend explains the symbols used on the map. It is called a legend because it tells the story of the map. It is sometimes called a map key, because it unlocks the meaning of the map's symbols.

The environment map legend below divides the environment into ten major categories. If the area mapped has a city character with streets, factories, and buildings, it is shown as urban. If most of the area is farmland with crops, it falls into the cropland category. This legend should be used when reading the environment maps in the book.

The physical-political map legend at the right divides the earth's geographic features into three major classes: cultural, land, and water features. Cultural features are human-made and include cities, roads, railroads, and boundaries. Land features are mountain peaks, mountain passes, and spot heights. (Spot heights tell the elevation of certain places on a mountain.) Water features are rivers, lakes, swamps, and any body of water. This legend should be used when working with the physical-political maps in the book.

PHYSICAL-POLITICAL MAP LEGEND

CULTURAL FEATURES
Political Boundaries — International, Intercolonial, Secondary: State, Provincial, etc.

Cities, Towns and Villages (Except for scales of 1:20,000,000 or smaller)
- PARIS — 1,000,000 and over
- Ufa — 500,000 to 1,000,000
- Győr — 50,000 to 500,000
- Agadir — 25,000 to 50,000
- Moreno — 0 to 25,000
- TŌKYŌ — National Capitals
- Boise — Secondary Capitals

Transportation — Railroads, Railroad Ferries, Caravan Routes

Other Cultural Features — Dams, Pipelines, Pyramids, Ruins

LAND FEATURES
- Peaks, Spot Heights
- Passes

WATER FEATURES
Lakes and Reservoirs — Fresh Water, Fresh Water: Intermittent, Salt Water, Salt Water: Intermittent

Other Water Features — Swamps, Glaciers, Rivers, Canals, Aqueducts, Ship Channels, Falls, Rapids, Springs, Water Depths, Sand Bars, Reefs

ENVIRONMENT MAP LEGEND

OASIS Important small areas of cultivation within grassland or wasteland.

Selected CITIES as points of reference.

URBAN — Major areas of contiguous residential, commercial, and industrial development.

FOREST, WOODLAND — Extensive wooded areas with little or no cropland.

CROPLAND — Cultivated land predominates (includes pasture, irrigated land, and land in crop rotation).

SWAMP, MARSHLAND — Extensive wetland areas (includes mangroves).

CROPLAND AND WOODLAND — Cultivated land interrupted by small wooded areas.

TUNDRA — Areas of lichen, shrubs, small trees, and wetland.

CROPLAND AND GRAZING LAND — Cultivated land with grassland and rangeland.

SHRUB, SPARSE GRASS; WASTELAND — Desert shrub and short grass, growing singly or in patches. Wasteland includes sand, salt flats, etc. (Extensive wastelands shown by pattern.)

GRASSLAND, GRAZING LAND — Extensive grassland and rangeland with little or no cropland.

BARREN LAND — Icefields, glaciers, permanent snow, with exposed rock.

Europe/Terrain

Many parts of Europe lie under the shadows of towering mountains. The most splendid of these peaks are the Alps. These shining pyramids of snow and stone are found in Switzerland, southeastern France, Austria, southern Germany, northern Italy, and northern Yugoslavia. The Alps make these countries a sightseer's paradise and a skier's adventureland.

Three major mountain systems flow out of the central mass of the Alps like tails from a kite. One of these tails, the Apennines, reaches south into the boot of Italy. Another, the Dinaric Alps, makes a jagged trail through Yugoslavia and Albania into Greece. The third, the Carpathians, forms a graceful half-moon through Czechoslovakia and Romania.

Also reaching out from the Alps are many hills and plateaus. Nearly all of southern and central France is a wide upland, the Massif Central, that has been cut by rivers into hills. More hills ruffle parts of northern France and eastern Belgium—they are called the Ardennes Mountains, site of many fierce battles throughout history. Similar low hills and plateaus lie across southern Germany, in parts of Czechoslovakia, and in Austria.

Across the English Channel, Great Britain has a bumpy backbone known as the Pennine Chain of mountains. North of them are the famed Scottish Highlands, where long hills covered with heather roll like frozen ocean waves across the countryside.

Northern mainland Europe is

© 1979 Rand McNally & Co.

marked by mountains of another kind. The uplands of Norway and Sweden are bleak and barren, especially as they approach the white magnificence of the Arctic Circle. Huge glaciers once rumbled over the landscape, clawing deep grooves into the mountains. These grooves, flooded by the ocean, have become long waterways called fjords. The fjords attract many tourists because of their awesome beauty.

Far to the east the Soviet Union's Ural Mountains mark the division between Europe and Asia. Such a mountain chain in the middle of a thousand-mile flatland is most unusual. The Urals are very old—formed about 225 million years ago. In that time they have worn down more and more.

Today the tallest of the Urals stands only a little more than six thousand feet (1,828.2 meters) above sea level, quite low in comparison with other major mountains.

Some of the most famous rivers in the world flow from Europe's mountains. Perhaps the best known is the Rhine, which rises in Switzerland and flows north past grape-clothed bluffs in Germany and France where the castles of medieval barons still scowl down on the river. Far longer than the Rhine is the fabled Danube River. It rises in Germany and drifts lazily in a southeasterly direction through seven nations and three capital cities before emptying into the Black Sea.

The north-central part of the continent is made up of the Great Northern European Plain. The huge region's rich farmlands supply food for much of Europe, and its many ores help to make the Ruhr Valley on the Rhine a world center for heavy industry. Food and machinery move out to the rest of Europe on a network of rivers connected by canals. The canals were dug by hand long ago in spillways, the natural trenches that were formed by the melting of the glacier twenty-five thousand years ago.

The Great Northern European Plain stretches from western France to nearly a thousand miles (1,609.3 kilometers) beyond Moscow, where it is broken at last by the rounded Urals. Here bustling Europe ends amid the lonely sweep of the wind through mountain forests.

The Scottish Highlands are so rough and rugged that many people live instead on the lower coastal plains. Here the land is more easily farmed.

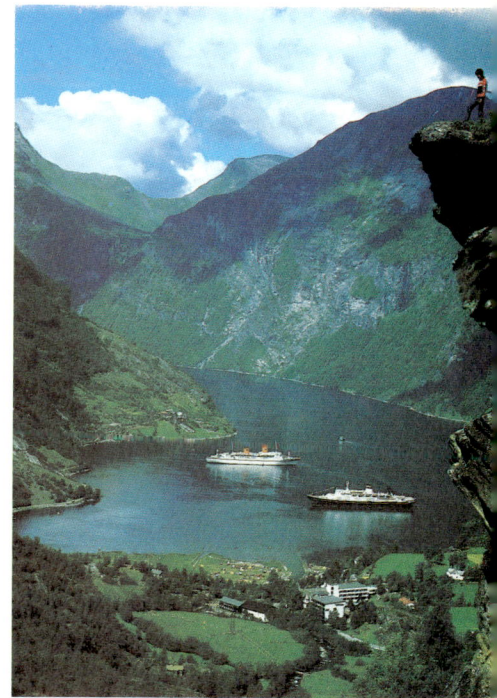

The coasts of Norway and Sweden were formed by glaciers pushing into the sea. When the ice melted, the sea filled the winding fingers, or fjords. Some fjords are nearly 4,000 feet (1,219.2 kilometers) deep.

Mykonos, at left, and the other Greek islands in the Aegean Sea are part of the Pindus Mountains of Greece. Millions of years ago the sea rose until only the tops of the mountains remained above the waters.

Legend

- Urban
- Cropland
- Cropland & Woodland
- Cropland & Grazing Land
- Grassland, Grazing Land
- Forest, Woodland
- Swamp, Marshland
- Tundra
- Shrub, Sparse Grass, Wasteland (pattern)
- Barren Land
- Oasis

ATLANTIC OCEAN

North Sea

Baltic Sea

Gulf of Bothnia

Bay of Biscay

Mediterranean Sea

Tyrrhenian Sea

Adriatic Sea

Aegean Sea

ATLAS MOUNTAINS

PYRENEES

ALPS

CARPATHIANS

Reykjavik

Narvik

Murman

Trondheim

Bergen

Oslo

Helsinki

LENINGRAD

Stockholm

Tallinn

Göteborg

Rīga

Copenhagen

Kaliningrad

Minsk

Glasgow

Belfast

MANCHESTER

Dublin

LONDON

Amsterdam

Hamburg

Elbe

BERLIN

Warsaw

Pripyat

Antwerp

Essen

Leipzig

Oder

Kraków

L'vov

Frankfurt

Prague

Brest

PARIS

Seine

Loire

Strasbourg

Rhine

Munich

Danube

VIENNA

Tisza

BUDAPEST

Dnestr

La Coruña

Bordeaux

Garonne

Zürich

Lyon

Rhône

MILAN

Venice

Zagreb

Sava

Belgrade

Bucharest

Douro

Bilbao

Marseille

Genoa

Danube

Sofia

Lisbon

MADRID

Ebro

BARCELONA

CORSICA

ROME

Tirane

Sevilla

SARDINIA

Naples

ISLAS BALEARES

Tanger

Algiers

Palermo

Athens

Casablanca

Oran

Tunis

SICILY

MALTA

CRETE

Longitude West of Greenwich   0°   Longitude East of Greenwich

Scale   1:16,500,000; one inch to 260 miles. Conic Projection

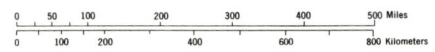

0 50 100 200 300 400 500 Miles

0 100 200 400 600 800 Kilometers

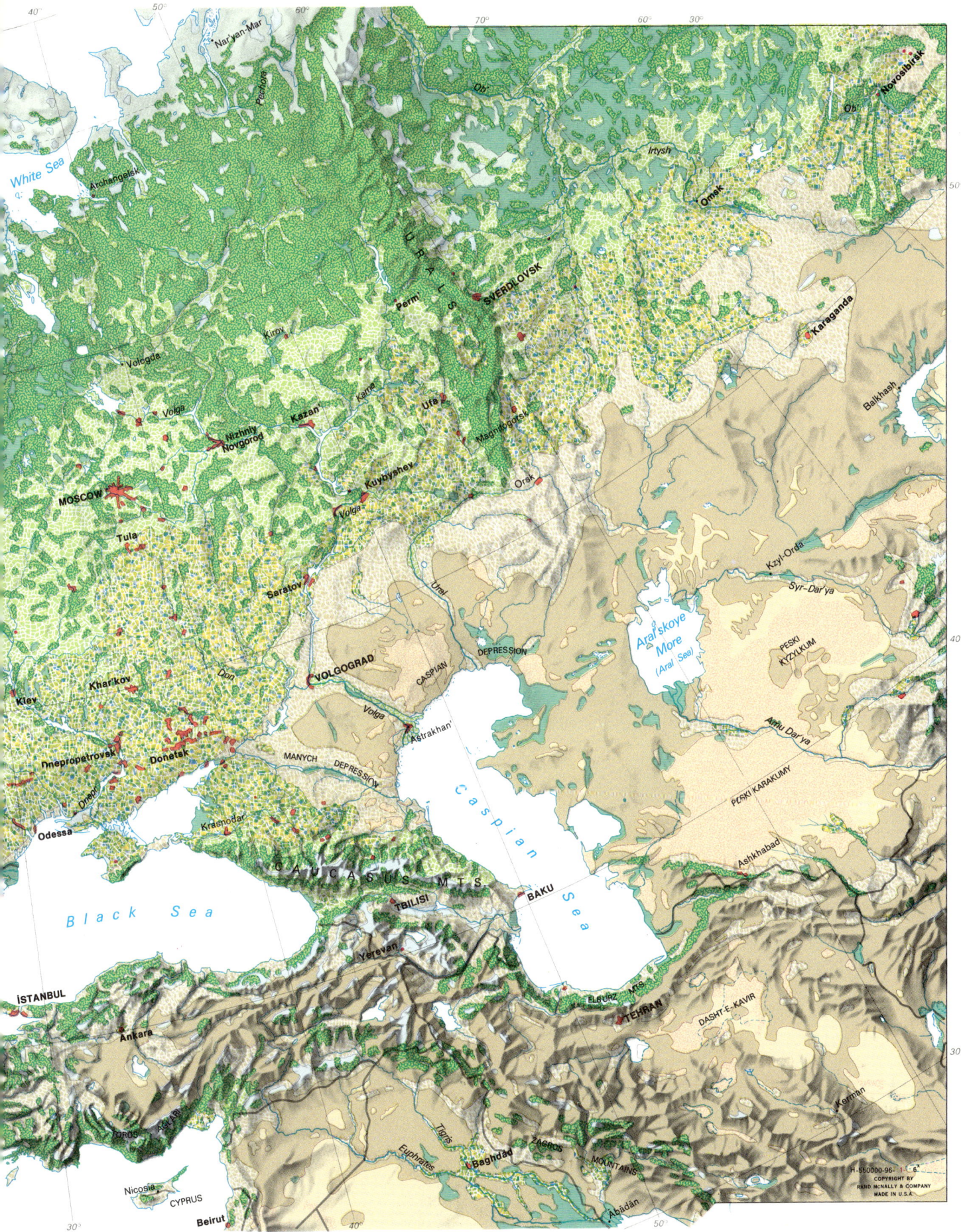

Europe/Animals

Skua

Herring

Barnacle Goose

Reindeer

Grey Seal

Wolverine

Lemming

Hare

Basking Shark

Red Deer

Otter

Black Grouse

Pheasant

Hedgehog

Badger

Atlantic Salmon

Rabbit

Fox

Red-legged Partridge

Chamois

Moorhen

Stork

Marmot

Squirrel

Great Bustard

Barbary Ape

Sole

Ferruginous Duck

Hoopoe

Spanish Mackerel

Raven

Whimbrel

Brown Bear

Pine Marten

Wild Boar

Wolf

Roe Deer

Griffon
Vulture

Lesser
Spotted Eagle

Tur

Octopus

Conger Eel

Most of the vast, animal-filled forests that once covered much of Europe were cut down long ago to make room for farms, cities, and towns. Many of Europe's animals were hunted for centuries, until they were wiped out. But in a few wild places still left—national parks, game preserves, and a few out-of-the-way places—some of the animals that once abounded in Europe can still be found.

A few of the shaggy, tusked boars that were the favorite game animal of medieval nobles still root in the underbrush of small forests in central Europe. Packs of wolves still howl in some places, and in the northern Soviet Union brown bears still lumber about. In the north of Sweden, Norway, Finland, and the western Soviet Union reindeer are herded like cattle by people of the northland, the Lapps.

In the Pyrenees Mountains between France and Spain lives the Pyrenean ibex, a mountain goat with curled horns. Another kind of mountain goat, the chamois, is found in the Alps.

Europe also has numerous small animals. Foxes, badgers, moles, rabbits, and squirrels are found in many places. Little, plump lemmings abound in the mountains of Norway and Sweden. The hedgehog is common in northern Europe and especially well-known in England. It has short, sharp "spikes" all over its back, like the quills of a porcupine only much thicker.

Small, striped wildcats prowl in parts of Yugoslavia and Bulgaria, and a rather large wildcat, the Spanish lynx, lives in Spain. It is three feet (0.91 meter) long with pointed ears and thick whiskers—a fast, fierce hunter.

Sparrows, thrushes, finches, nightingales, and ravens are found throughout central Europe. So are large birds of prey such as falcons and eagles. During the summer the big white stork is a common sight in cities of the Netherlands, Belgium, and Germany, where it nests on the chimneys of houses.

Various kinds of lizards and snakes, tortoises and turtles, frogs, toads, and salamanders are found in woodlands and meadows throughout Europe. Trout, salmon, and other fish swim in clear streams above the polluted areas. Many of the animal species found in Europe are also found on the North American continent.

In a protected forest of Poland about 1,600 wisents, the bisons of prehistoric Europe, live as they did many thousands of years ago—feeding in grassy clearings. Full grown, the animals stand six feet (1.82 meters) high at the shoulder.

Europe/Countries and Cities

In some ways Europe looks more like a jigsaw puzzle than a reasonable grouping of thirty-three nations. The boundaries of those countries—from the huge Soviet Union to tiny Luxembourg—were agreed upon only after much haggling through the centuries. In recent times, World Wars I and II caused boundary changes, and several new nations were formed as well.

The borders of most countries stop at mountains, rivers, or seas. When the first tribes migrated into an area, they usually chose a homeland that had some natural barrier where their warriors could defend them from attack. Today, many countries still are edged by such natural borders.

Cities tell us much about peoples of the past. Rome and Athens were known thousands of years ago, and the Roman Forum and Colosseum and the Acropolis and statues of Athens hint at life in ancient times. Paris dates back more than two thousand years. It was founded around 52 B.C. by Roman

soldiers. Trondheim, in Norway, had its beginning around A.D. 998. Today it is the third largest city in Norway and an important export center. Clues in these and other cities hint at governments, religions, and pastimes of the people who once lived there.

The European continent averages 173 persons per square mile. Some of its countries, especially in the west, are among the most densely packed in the world. The Netherlands has 892 persons per square mile. But it is doing something few other countries are able to do—it is growing by reclaiming land from the sea.

Something a traveler moving through Europe notices is its many languages. Of the several dozen spoken, nearly all fall into three main groups.

The French, Italians, Spanish, Portuguese, and Romanians cannot understand one another. Nevertheless, all of their languages are based on the ancient Latin spoken by the Romans who once conquered those lands. These are the "Romance" languages.

The people of Germany, the Netherlands, England, Denmark, Sweden, and Norway speak six separate languages. Yet these, too, have their roots

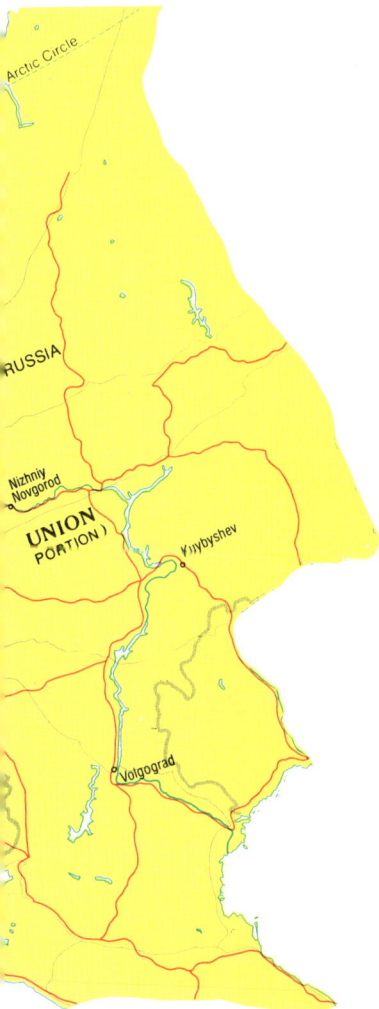

About 2,300 years ago, Rome was the heart of Europe. Still standing are parts of the Roman Forum, which was both a marketplace and a meeting place for Roman citizens. The great pillars of the Forum buildings stood for the strength of the Roman Empire, which ruled over 50 million people on three continents.

in a single language—the German of the tribes which occupied those areas in ages past.

To the east, the peoples of Poland, Czechoslovakia, Yugoslavia, Bulgaria, and Russia all speak languages based on the Slavic language of tribes that once lived there.

You might ask why an Italian doesn't understand a Spaniard, since their languages are alike. Or why the Germanic-speaking Dane doesn't understand the Germanic-speaking Briton. The answer lies in terrain, distance, and culture. Peoples of neighboring lands often were cut off from each other by natural barriers, or were separated by too many miles to meet often and talk. The Pyrenees closed Spain from France. A branch of the Alps shut off France from Italy. The North Sea separated the English from the Danes. And vast differences

in cultures—life-styles—divided the Slavic-speaking Poles and the Russians. Each nation developed—over long ages—different ways of speaking what were once the same languages. In time the German of Germany was slightly different from that of the Netherlands. Across the North Sea the English people developed a distinct language using many German words, but also including words from Latin. And in the north, the Danes, Swedes, and Norwegians all used their own versions of the ancient German.

Today European languages are called Romance, Germanic, and Slavic. Only three major European countries do not fall into these groupings: Finland, Hungary, and Greece.

Each of the thirty-three nations of Europe has its own kind of government and a way of life that is unique to itself.

© 1979 Rand McNally & Co.

— Roads
— Railroads

40,000 SQ MI AREA

0   100   200
Miles

Legend

Cities, Towns, and Villages		
0 to 25,000	○	100,000 to 250,000 ⊙
25,000 to 100,000	●	250,000 to 1,000,000 ◎
		1,000,000 and over ◉

Major urbanized area

0   50   100   200   300   400   500 Miles
0   100   200   400   600   800 Kilometers

ARCTIC OCEAN

ICELAND
Reykjavik
Reykjanes
Saudárkrókur
Eskifjördur
Fontur

Arctic Circle

ATLANTIC OCEAN

NORWAY   SWEDEN   FINLAND   LAPLAND
Hammerfest   Vardø
Murmansk   Monchegorsk   Kirovsk   Kandalaksha
Narvik   Kebnekaise   Pechenga
Lofoten Is.

Trondheim (Nidaros)
Dovre Fjell   Glittertinden
Luleå   Tornio   Oulu
Bergen   Sundsvall   Umeå   Vaasa
Sognefjord
Oslo   Gävle   Turku   Helsinki   Vyborg
Stavanger   Uppsala   Hangö   LENINGRAD
Kristiansand   Norrköping   Tallinn   Narva   Novgorod
Lindesnes   STOCKHOLM   ESTONIAN S.S.R.   Tartu   Pskov
Gotland   Visby   Gulf of Riga   Rīga   Velikiye Luki
Ålborg   Öland   LATVIAN S.S.R.   Jelgava   Vitebsk
DENMARK   Liepāja   Daugavpils
COPENHAGEN (København)   Malmö   Klaipėda   LITHUANIAN S.S.R.   Kaunas   Vilnius   Minsk   Mogilev
Kaliningrad R.S.F.S.R.   Grodno   BELORUSSIA S.S.R.   Baranovichi   Bobruysk
Kiel   Lübeck   Gdańsk   Toruń   Białystok   Brest   Pinsk   Pripyat
HAMBURG   Szczecin   POLAND   Poznań   WARSAW
Bremen   Hannover   BERLIN   Magdeburg   Wrocław   Łódź   Lublin   Rovno   Zhitomir
GERMANY   Leipzig   Dresden   PRAGUE   KATOWICE   Kraków   Przemyśl   L'vov   Berdichev   Vinnitsa
COLOGNE   Bonn   Plzeň   CZECHOSLOVAKIA   Brno   Ostrava   Drogobych   Ivano-Frankovsk
FRANKFURT a.M.   Nürnberg   VIENNA (Wien)   Bratislava   Chernovtsy   UKRAINE
STUTTGART   MUNICH   AUSTRIA   Graz   Miskolc   Debrecen   Oradea   Cluj-Napoca   Kishinev
SWITZERLAND   Zürich   Maribor   Ljubljana   BUDAPEST   Szeged   MOLDAVIA
Bern   Geneva   Mont Blanc   Innsbruck   HUNGARY   Subotica   ROMANIA   Iași   Galați
Lausanne   MILAN   Venice   Trieste   Zagreb   Novi Sad   Braila
TURIN   Genoa   Bologna   YUGOSLAVIA   Belgrade   BUCHAREST   Ploiești   Ruse

UNITED KINGDOM
BRITISH ISLES   SCOTLAND   Aberdeen   Dundee
GLASGOW   Edinburgh   Grampian Mts.   Cheviot Hills
Belfast   NORTHERN IRELAND   Carlisle   NEWCASTLE
IRELAND   Galway (Baile Átha Cliath)   LEEDS   Kingston upon Hull
Dublin   LIVERPOOL   MANCHESTER   Leicester
Cork   Cobh   BIRMINGHAM   AMSTERDAM   NETHERLANDS
Cape Clear   The Hague ('s Gravenhage)
Southampton   LONDON   ROTTERDAM
Portsmouth   Dover   ANTWERP
Isles of Scilly   Lands End   Calais   BELGIUM   BRUSSELS   ESSEN
Cherbourg   Le Havre   LILLE   COLOGNE
Brest   Rouen   LUX.   Mainz
Rennes   PARIS   Reims
St. Nazaire   Orléans
Nantes   Tours   Dijon   Strasbourg
La Rochelle   FRANCE   Lyon   Besançon

El Ferrol   La Coruña   C. de Finisterre
Vigo   Santander   S. Sebastián   Bordeaux
Porto (Oporto)   Oviedo   Bilbao   Bayonne   Toulouse   Nîmes
PORTUGAL   Salamanca   Valladolid   Zaragoza   MARSEILLE   Nice   MONACO
LISBON (Lisboa)   MADRID   SPAIN   ANDORRA   Barcelona   Toulon   CORSICA (Fr.)   Ajaccio
Coimbra   SIERRA DE GUADARRAMA   Tarragona   Tortosa   Livorno   Florence   SAN MARINO   Ancona
Valencia   BALEARES   MENORCA   SARDINIA (It.)   ROME (Roma)
Sevilla   Murcia   Palma   MALLORCA   IBIZA   Cagliari   NAPLES (Napoli)   Vesuvio   Bari   Brindisi
Cádiz   SIERRA NEVADA   Cartagena   Almería   ITALY
Málaga   Gibraltar   Ceuta (Sp.)   Palermo   Messina   SICILY (It.)   Mt. Etna   Catania
Tanger   Tétouan   DEL ALBORAN (Sp.)   Oran   Algiers (El Djazaïr)   Bizerte   Tunis   C. Bon   C. Passero
Rabat   Fès   TUNISIA   MALTA
Casablanca   MOROCCO   ATLAS MOUNTAINS   ALGERIA   Constantine

NORTH SEA   Firth of Forth   Moray Firth   Hebrides
Faeroe Is. (Den.)   Tórshavn
Shetland Is. (Br.)   Lerwick   Orkney Is. (Br.)
English Channel   Bay of Biscay   Gironde   MASSIF CENTRAL   PYRENEES
Gulf of Bothnia   Kattegat   Skagerrak   Gulf of Finland   Baltic Sea   Bornholm (Den.)   RÜGEN
Strait of Gibraltar   MEDITERRANEAN SEA   TYRRHENIAN SEA   IONIAN SEA   Golfo di Taranto

ROMANIA   CARPAȚII MERIDIONALI   TRANSYLVANIA   SUDETES
ALBANIA   Shkodër   Durrës   TIRANE   Bitola   Skopje   Niš
Sarajevo   Split   Zadar   Dubrovnik   Cetinje
BULGARIA   Sofia (Sofiya)   STARA PLANINA (BALKAN MTS.)   Plovdiv   RHODOPE MTS.
GREECE   Thessaloniki   Kérkira   ATHENS (Athínai)   Kórinthos   Kalámai   Lésvos   Izmir
CRETE (Gr.)   Khaniá   Iráklion   AKRA TAINARON

Longitude West of Greenwich   Longitude East of Greenwich

RUSSIAN SOVIET FEDERATIVE SOCIALIST REPUBLIC

S O V I E T   U N I O N

K A Z A K H   S.S.R.

KIRGHIZ STEPPE

U Z B E K   S.S.R.

TURKMEN S.S.R.

T U R K E Y

I R A N (PERSIA)

SYRIA

IRAQ

AFGHANISTAN

CYPRUS   LEBANON

GEORGIAN S.S.R.

AZERBAIJAN S.S.R.

ARMENIAN S.S.R.

TRANSCAUCASIA

CASPIAN SEA

BLACK SEA

WHITE SEA

Sea of Azov (AZOVSKOYE MORE)

ARAL SEA (ARAL'SKOYE MORE)

Moscow (Moskva)
NIZHNIY NOVGOROD
KHAR'KOV
KIEV (Kiyev)
DNEPROPETROVSK
DONETSK
VOLGOGRAD
KUYBYSHEV
SVERDLOVSK
CHELYABINSK
NOVOSIBIRSK
TASHKENT
BAKU
TBILISI

Arkhangel'sk
Petrozavodsk
Vologda
Cherepovets
Syktyvkar
Kirov
Perm'
Izhevsk
Kazan'
Ul'yanovsk
Penza
Saratov
Voronezh
Kursk
Orël
Tula
Ryazan'
Smolensk
Bryansk
Gomel'
Odessa
Simferopol
Sevastopol
Novorossiysk
Sochi
Krasnodar
Stavropol'
Rostov-na-Donu
Astrakhan
Gur'yev
Orenburg
Magnitogorsk
Ufa
Chelny
Omsk
Pavlodar
Karaganda
Balkhash
Samarkand
Bukhara
Ashkhabad
Tehrān
Tabrīz
Mashhad
Ankara (Angora)
Istanbul
Baghdad
Beirut
Nicosia

Scale 1:16,850,000; one inch to 265 miles. Conic Projection

Elevations and depressions are given in feet

Scale 1:21,500,000; one inch to 340 miles.
Lambert's Azimuthal, Equal Area Projection
Elevations and depressions are given in feet

A   17   B   18   19   C

16   15   14   13   12   11   10

40,000 SQ. MI. AREA

0   150   300
Miles

SEVERNAYA ZEMLYA (NORTHERN LAND)

O C E A N

L A P T E V   S E A

E A S T   S I B E R I A N   S E A

VRANGELYA (WRANGEL) I.
M. SHELAGSKIY
CHUKOTSKIY P-OV

CHUKOTSKOYE NAGORYE

KORYAKSKIY KHREBET

Arctic Circle

M. CHELYUSKIN

TAYMYR P-OV   GORY BYRRANGA

Taymyr
Khatangskiy Zaliv
Nordvik
Bol'shoy Begichev
Ust'-Olenek
Tiksi
Bulun

NOVOSIBIRSKIYE O-VA (NEW SIBERIAN ISLANDS)
KOTEL'NYY
FADDEYA
NOVAYA SIBIR
MALYY LYAKHOVSKIY
LYAKHOVSKIYE
DE-LONGA

M. SVYATOY NOS
M. BUOR-KHAYA

Khatanga
Kazach'ye
Zashiversk
Allaykha
Nizhne-Kolymsk
Srednne Kolymsk
Zyryanka
MEDVEZH'I
AYON
M. Ambarchik

M. TAYGONOS
M. OLYUTORSKIY

Abyy
Verkhoyansk
Gora Pobeda 10,171
Oymyakon

Nel'kan

KHREBET   CHERSKOGO

KHREBET GYDAN (KOLYMSKIY)

Zaliv Shelekhova

P-OV KAMCHATKA

Noril'sk
GORY PUTORANA
Turukhansk
Tura
Baykit
Nizhnyaya Tunguska
Podkamennaya Tunguska
Yartsevo
G. Polkan 3543
Yeniseysk

A   S   S   R

Y A K U T

VERKHOYANSKIY KHREBET

Zhigansk
Vilyuysk
Suntar
Mukhtuya
Peleduy
Vilyuy
Vilyuy
Olekminsk

Yakutsk

Aldanskaya
Amga
Tommot
Aldan

DZHUGDZHUR KHREBET

Ayan
Okhotsk
Nel'kan

Chumikan
Udskaya Guba
SHANTAR

Magadan
Gizhiga
Penzhino
Markovo
Anadyrskiy Zaliv

Klyuchevskaya Sop. 15,584
Verkhne-Kamchatsk
Ust'-Kamchatsk
Petropavlovsk-Kamchatskiy
Ust'-Bol'sheretsk

S E A   O F   O K H O T S K

S O C I A L I S T   R E P U B L I C

F E D E R A T I V E

Krasnoyarsk
Bogotol
Balakhta
Kansk
Tayshet
Bratsk
Nizhneudinsk
Tulun
Zhigalovo
Kachug
Kirensk
Ilimsk
Nizhne-Angarsk
Bodaybo
Golets Skalistyy 9186
PATOM PLATEAU
G. Golets Purpula 5977

STANOVOY KHREBET

Tyndinskiy
Skovorodino
Zeya
Belogorsk
Ust'-Tyrma
Bureya
Svobodnyy

Nikolayevsk-na-Amure
Komsomol'sk na-Amure
Sovetskaya Gavan
Amur

M. TERPENIYA
M. ELIZAVETY
Okha
Poronaysk
Udegorsk

SAKHALIN (Sov. Union)

Aleksandrovsk
Khol'msk
Korsakov
Yuzhno-Sakhalinsk

Tatarskiy Proliv

Abakan
Minusinsk
SAYAN
KHREBET
Munku Sardyk 11,457
Cheremkhovo
Angarsk
Irkutsk
Kyren
Gusinoozersk
Gorodok
Ulan-Ude
Petrovsk-Zabaykal'skiy
Yakhtia

BURYAT A.S.S.R.
Baykal (Lake Baykal) Surface elev. 1535 ft. above sea level
Barguzin

BAYKAL'SKIY KHREBET
YABLONOVYY KHREBET
VITIM KHREBET

Chita
Nerchinsk
Nerchinskiy Zavod
Sretensk
Aginskoye
Aksha
Borzya

NERCHINSKIY KHREBET

Blagoveshchensk
Birobidzhan
Khabarovsk
SIKHOTE ALIN
Dal'nerechensk
Spassk-Dal'niy
Ussuriysk
Artem
Portizansk
Nakhodka
Vladivostok
Ol'ga

SIKHOTE KHREBET BUREINSKIY
LESSER KHINGAN RANGE

TANNU-OLA
Kyzyl
Uvs (Us Nuur)
MTS.
Har Us Nuur
Hovd
Hami
Uliastay
HANGAYN NURUU (ARANGAIN MTS.)
Ulan Bator (Ulaanbaatar)
Ondorhaan
Sayr Usa
Ondorhaan
Wenquan
Tao'an
Jorud Qi

Hovsgol Nuur
Selenge
Kerulen
Kerlen

M O N G O L I A

GOBI OR SHAMO (DESERT)
Erast Bogd 13,419

GREATER KHINGAN RANGE

Qiqihar
Hailun
Nenjiang
Goukou
Fuyu
Suihua
Boli

M A N C H U R I A

HARBIN
Mudanjiang
Jilin
Punchon
Dunhua
Nojin
Chongjin

CHANGCHUN
Shuangliao

FUSHUN
SHENYANG

C H I N A

Chifeng
Weichang
Chengde
Zhangjiakou
Fengzhen
BEIJING
TIANJIN
Baoding
Lushun
Dalian

SHANDONG BANDAO
Bo Hai
YELLOW SEA

NORTH KOREA
P'yongyang
Kaesong
SEOUL
SOUTH KOREA
Andong
Taegu
PUSAN
Korea Bay
Korea Str.

Wakkanai
HOKKAIDŌ
Otaru
Sapporo
Eroshi

HONSHŪ
Kanazawa
Tottori
Matsue
KYOTO
Hiroshima
Okayama
KOBE
OSAKA
Kochi

J A P A N
SEA OF JAPAN

10   Longitude East 100° of Greenwich   11

100   200   300   400   500   600 Miles
200   400   600   800   1000 Kilometers

COPYRIGHT BY
RAND McNALLY & COMPANY
MADE IN U.S.A.

12   13   14

Asia/Terrain

Asia covers more area than North America, Europe, and Australia combined. Great numbers of people struggle for a living in Asia—nearly two and a half billion, more people than live in all the rest of the world! Yet because Asia is so big, there are places where an eagle could fly for hours, even days, and never see a human being.

The empty, and nearly empty, parts of Asia take up more space than parts of the continent where people live. For example, the area of the Soviet Union known as Siberia reaches eastward from the Ural Mountains, where Asia begins, for more than three thousand long, lonely miles (4,827.9 kilometers) to the Pacific Ocean. It is a vast region of cold winds and frosty earth.

To the south of Siberia is an equally large, equally harsh region. A desert blots out most life across central Asia. This desert begins in the blowing sand dunes of Saudi Arabia, sweeps across much of Jordan, Iraq, and Iran, and continues through the southern Soviet Union. It blisters Mongolia, where it ends as the forbidding Gobi Desert.

The great Asian desert is bounded on the south by the highest mountain ranges in the world. Highest of all are the Himalayas. Mount Everest, in the Himalayas, reaches five and a half miles (8.85 kilometers) into air so thin that climbers must wear oxygen masks to stay alive.

South of the Himalayas lies a warm, wet triangle of land, the subcontinent of India. Some of the most important areas in India and Bangladesh are around the Ganges and Brahmaputra rivers. This is the agricultural core of the land. Jute, rice, wheat, and sugarcane are grown here.

Summer monsoons—rain-bearing winds—sweep across India from June to September. The monsoons blow from the southwest, across the Indian Ocean, picking up moisture and carrying rain to India and part of Pakistan. The monsoons make the difference between good and bad crops. Since the winds do not reach far into Pakistan, some of the people there must irrigate their land. They rely on water from the Indus River, which rises in Tibet north of the Himalayas and flows through Pakistan.

That part of Asia called the Far East includes three of the most heavily populated countries in the world: China, Japan, and Korea.

For thousands of years, China was cut off from other countries. Frigid Siberia and the bleak Gobi Desert separated China from Europe. The plateau of Tibet, three miles (4.82 kilometers) high, and the Himalayas beyond were a barrier between China and India. With the growth of seamanship in the West, China began to trade with other countries.

China's climate is cool in the north, warm and wet in the south. This makes a difference in the kind of food grown in the areas—wheat in the north, rice in the south.

China has three major rivers. In the north is the Hwang Ho (Yellow) River. The Yangtze is in the south, so is the Hsi. People have settled heavily along these rivers.

Japan was once cut off from its neighbors, too. The Pacific Ocean made trade difficult. China was more than 400 miles (643.72 kilometers) away and Korea was 100 miles (160.93 kilometers) away.

The four main Japanese islands are part of a chain of rather recently formed volcanic mountains. Much of the land is covered with volcanic ash and lava which once spouted from such mighty cones as Mount Fuji. Japan still feels the effects of its volcanic birth. The land somewhere in

Farmers grow rice on the hilly terrain of Nepal by planting their crops in terraced fields. Beyond loom the Himalayas, the highest mountains in the world.

Israel's Negev Desert blooms with the help of water pumped from the Sea of Galilee.

ARCTIC OCEAN

UNITED KINGDOM
NORWAY
SWEDEN
FINLAND
Baltic Sea
POLAND
CZECH
HUNG.
ROMANIA
BUL.
Danube
Black Sea
TURKEY
LEBANON
SYRIA
ISRAEL JORDAN
IRAQ
Euphrates
Tigris
IRAN
KUWAIT
Red Sea
SAUDI ARABIA
ARABIAN PENINSULA
QATAR
UNITED ARAB EMIRATES
OMAN
YEMEN
© 1979 Rand McNally & Co.
Arabian Sea

Mt. Elbrus
CAUCASUS MOUNTAINS
Caspian Sea
UST-URT PLATEAU
Aral Sea
Volga
URAL MOUNTAINS
KIRGHIZ STEPPE
WESTERN SIBERIAN LOWLANDS
Arctic Circle
Yenisey
SOVIET UNION
CENTRAL SIBERIAN UPLANDS
NOVAYA ZEMLYA
SEVERNAYA ZEMLYA
NEW SIBERIAN ISLANDS
VERKHOYANSK MTS.
CHERSKIY MTS.
ANADYR RANGE
Bering Sea
KAMCHATKA PENINSULA
Sea of Okhotsk
SAKHALIN
KURIL ISLANDS
Lena
Lake Baikal
YABLONOVY MTS.
SAYAN MOUNTAINS
ALTAI MOUNTAINS
Lake Balkhash
TIEN SHAN
TAKLA MAKAN
Godwin Austen (K2)
KUNLUN MOUNTAINS
HINDU KUSH
AFGHANISTAN
PLATEAU OF IRAN
PAKISTAN
Indus
GREAT INDIAN DESERT
PLATEAU OF TIBET
HIMALAYAS
NEPAL
Mt. Everest
Ganges
BHUTAN
Brahmaputra
BANGLADESH
INDIA
DECCAN PLATEAU
WESTERN GHATS
EASTERN GHATS
SRI LANKA
Bay of Bengal
BURMA
Irrawaddy
MONGOLIA
GOBI DESERT
GREATER KHINGAN RA.
SIKHOTE-ALIN MTS.
NORTH KOREA
SOUTH KOREA
CHINA
Hwang Ho
Hwang Ho
Yangtze
Hsi
Yellow Sea
HAINAN
Tropic of Cancer
LAOS
THAILAND
CAMBODIA
VIETNAM
MALAY PENINSULA
MALAYSIA
HOKKAIDO
HONSHU
Sea of Japan
JAPAN
KYUSHU
SHIKOKU
East China Sea
TAIWAN
PACIFIC OCEAN
LUZON
PHILIPPINES
MINDANAO
South China Sea
BRUNEI
MALAYSIA
Equator
BORNEO
CELEBES
SUMATRA
INDONESIA
JAVA
INDIAN OCEAN

Asia Facts

Largest continent
First in population: 2,631,600,000
78 cities with over 1 million population
World's highest mountain: Everest, 29,028 feet (8,847.73 meters)
World's largest "lake": Caspian Sea, 152,084 square miles (393,897.56 square kilometers)
World's lowest inland point: Dead Sea, 1,299 feet (395.93 meters) below sea level

Japan shakes with an earthquake on the average of four times a day.

South of China is the area known as Southeast Asia. It includes Indochina, the Malay Peninsula, and the islands of Indonesia. The region is a gigantic rain forest, and the air is steamy. There are a few fertile river valleys— the Mekong, which passes through nearly all of Indochina; the Menam in Thailand; and the Irrawaddy in Burma.

In Indonesia, near the equator, the climate becomes even hotter. These islands are part of a mountain chain which is mostly hidden under the sea. The dark trees, thick undergrowth, and looping vines of dripping rain forests cover all the islands except Java.

Asia is a vast continent. It has some of the world's highest mountains, longest rivers, largest deserts, and coldest and hottest climates.

Legend

- ■ Urban
- Cropland
- Cropland & Woodland
- Cropland & Grazing Land
- Grassland, Grazing Land
- Forest, Woodland
- Swamp, Marshland
- Tundra
- Shrub, Sparse Grass, Wasteland (pattern)
- Barren Land
- • Oasis

ATLANTIC OCEAN

ARCTIC

SPITSBERGEN

NOVAYA ZEMLYA

Kara Sea

Barents Sea

North Sea

Gulf of Bothnia

Murmansk

Arkangelsk

Ob

Kara

Stockholm

Baltic Sea

LENINGRAD

Sukhona

BERLIN

MUNICH

Warsaw

MOSCOW

Kazan

SVERDLOVSK

BUDAPEST

Kiev

Dnepr

Don

Volga

Ural

Orsk

Novosibirsk

Danube

ISTANBUL

Black Sea

VOLGOGRAD

Irtysh

Karaganda

Caucasus Mts.

BAKU

Caspian Sea

Aral Sea

Ozero Balkhash

Syr-Dar'ya

Mediterranean Sea

Beirut

Tashkent

CAIRO

SYRIAN DESERT

Baghdad

Tigris

Ashkhabad

TEHRAN

TIEN SHAN

Red Sea

AN NAFŪD

Euphrates

ZAGROS MTS.

DASHT-E KAVIR

HINDU KUSH

TAKLA MAKAN

Kabul

Scale 1:24,800,000 ; one inch to 390 miles. Lambert Azimuthal Equal-Area Projection

OCEAN

East Siberian Sea

Anadyrskiy Zaliv

Bering Sea

Ambarchik

Laptev Sea

Nordvik

GORY PUTORANA

Olenëk

Lena

KHREBET GYDAN

Magadan

POLUOSTROV KAMCHATKA

Petropavlovsk-Kamchatskiy

Tura

Sea of Okhotsk

Yakutsk

SAKHALIN

Lena

Komsomolsk-na-Amure

Krasnoyarsk

Amur

HOKKAIDŌ

Lake Baikal

GREATER KHINGAN RANGE

Sapporo

Irkutsk

Argun

Harbin

Vladivostok

HONSHŪ

Ulan Bator

Sea of Japan

TOKYO

ALTAI

SHENYANG

MTS.

SEOUL

140°

GOBI (DESERT)

Ūrūmqi

BEIJING

30°

Yellow Sea

KYŪSHŪ

Huang

Zhengzhou

PACIFIC

East China Sea

SHANGHAI

OCEAN

N SHAN

90°   100°   110°   120°   100°

0   100   200   400   600   800 Miles

0   150   300   600   900   1200 Kilometers

Mediterranean Sea

Caspian Sea

Aral Sea

Karaganda

Ozero Balkhash

CAUCASUS MTS.

BAKU

Beirut

CAIRO

SYRIAN DESERT

Baghdad

Tigris

Euphrates

Tashkent

Ashkhabad

TEHRAN

TIEN SHAN

DASHT-E KAVIR

TAKLA MAKAN

ZAGROS MTS.

HINDU KUSH

KUN

AN NAFŪD

Kermán

Kabul

Rawalpindi

Mecca

Riyadh

PLATEAU

Persian Gulf

Red Sea

DELHI

Muscat

KARACHI

AR RUB' AL KHĀLĪ

Nagpur

DANAKIL

BOMBAY

Aden

Gulf of Aden

Arabian Sea

Berbera

WESTERN GHATS

EASTERN GHATS

MADRAS

Calicut

SRI LANK

Colombo

INDIAN OCEAN

🟥 •	Urban
	Cropland
	Cropland & Woodland
	Cropland & Grazing Land
	Grassland, Grazing Land
	Forest, Woodland
	Swamp, Marshland
	Tundra
	Shrub, Sparse Grass; Wasteland (pattern)
	Barren Land
•	Oasis

H-568600-96 -1-9

Scale 1:24,800,000 ; one inch to 390 miles. Lambert Azimuthal Equal-Area Projection

PACIFIC

OCEAN

Sea
of
Japan

HONSHŪ

TOKYO

KYŪSHŪ

SEOUL

Vladivostok

Harbin

SHENYANG

BEIJING

Yellow
Sea

East
China
Sea

SHANGHAI

Zhengzhou

WUHAN

CHONGQING

Huang Ho

GOBI (DESERT)

Ulan Bator

Ürümqi

TIEN SHAN

OF TIBET

HIMALAYAS

Mekong

Brahmaputra

Ganges

CALCUTTA

Mandalay

Salween

Irrawaddy

Rangoon

BANGKOK

Kunming

GUANGZHOU

T'aipei

Tropic of Cancer

T'AIWAN

HAINAN DAO

Hanoi

HO CHI MINH CITY

Philippine
Sea

MANILA

Cebu

MINDANAO

South

China

Sea

Celebes
Sea

Manado

Bay of

Bengal

Andaman

Sea

Kota Kinabalu

Kuching

BORNEO

CELEBES

Ujung Pandang

Medan

SINGAPORE

S U M A T R A

Equator

Java Sea

JAKARTA

JAVA

0   100   200   400   600   800 Miles

0 150 300   600   900   1200 Kilometers

90°

100°

120°

130°

140°

140°

40°

30°

20°

10°

0°

10°

10°

Asia/Animals

Asia, the giant of continents, spreads from far northern lands that are snow-covered nine months a year, to steamy, hot southern jungles. Thus, an enormous number of different kinds of animals are found here.

Most animals of northern Asia are like those in the far north of Europe—reindeer, foxes, hare, and tiny, mouselike lemmings. But in northern China and Korea prowls the thick-furred Siberian tiger, completely at home in cold and snow. The biggest of all cats, it is often as much as thirteen feet (3.96 meters) long.

Cold deserts lie in central Asia, and on them is found the two-humped Bactrian camel. Some of these animals are wild, but many are used as beasts of burden. The Bactrian camel's relative, the one-humped Arabian camel, or dromedary, is found on warmer deserts to the west.

Yaks, huge wild cattle five feet (1.52 meters) high at the shoulder and covered with long, thick fur, live in the high, cold land of Tibet. Many tame yaks are used as beasts of burden by the people of this part of central Asia.

The forests of southern Asia swarm with animals—monkeys, tree-dwelling clouded leopards, small herds of the wild cattle called gaurs, and a dwindling number of tigers. Indian elephants move through the forest in herds of from ten to fifty. Neither as big nor as fierce as African elephants, they are easily tamed, and many have been trained to work for people.

The deadly king cobra, the world's longest poisonous snake, whose bite can kill a human within fifteen minutes, also makes the forest its home. So does the cobra's mortal enemy—the fast, clever, weasellike mongoose which will attack and eat a cobra or any other snake on sight!

In forests on the islands of Borneo and Sumatra lives the red-furred great ape, the orangutan, which may be five feet (1.52 meters) tall. It lives in trees where it swings from branch to branch with its long arms.

And in bamboo forests in a part of Asia where China and Tibet come together lives the famous giant panda. Although it and its relative, the smaller red panda, resemble bears, they are not bears. They belong to a separate family of animals.

Imperial Eagle

Jackal

Dromedary

Jerboa

Ibex

The largest horns grown by any wild animal are those of a sheep called the Pamir argali, or Marco Polo's argali. Marco Polo found this unusual creature during his travels across central Asia. The sheep's horns spiral outward and have been known to reach a record length of seventy-five inches (190.5 centimeters).

Polar Bear

Killer Whale

Arctic Fox

Willow Grouse

Sea Eagle

Wolf

Elk

Snowy Owl

Harbor Seal

Lynx

Przewalski's Horse

Raccoon-like Dog

Japanese Macaque

Saiga

Giant Panda

Bactrian Camel

Mandarin Duck

Japanese Crane

Yak

Snow Leopard

Pheasant

Dolphin

Indian Elephant

Water Buffalo

Cormorant

Flyingfish

Tiger

Peafowl

Gibbon

Macaque

Cobra

Mongoose

Orangutan

Asia/Countries and Cities

Because Asia is so large, its countries have tended to form in clusters. The continent has five big groupings of nations. The first borders the eastern edge of the continent and is called the Far East. China and Japan are the leading countries in the Far East. Indochina and the islands of Indonesia make up the second group. The third group formed on or near the southern triangle of land which contains India. The desert countries occupy the fourth area. Siberia, a part of the Soviet Union, stands alone in the fifth.

China has the most people of any country in the world—over 945 million. One of every five persons on earth is Chinese!

For endless centuries China was the most powerful nation in the Far East. Then the Industrial Revolution occurred in Europe. Goods and arms were manufactured in great numbers. Suddenly Great Britain, France, and other Western nations had military power. China's growing weakness became clear after the British won the so-called Opium War of 1839–1842. Today, under Communist leadership, China is trying to regain its military and industrial strength.

The industrial giant of Asia is tiny Japan. When Commodore Perry opened Japan to foreign trade in 1853, the Japanese began to adopt Western ways of manufacturing. Today they are third only to the United States and the Soviet Union in industrial muscle.

For centuries Korea was caught between the two big Eastern powers. Both China and Japan had ruled the country. After World War II Korea was once more trapped in battle, with the result that the country is now split. The 16 million people of Communist North Korea look to the Soviet Union as their ally. Anti-Communist South Korea, with 36 million people, looks to the Western nations.

The countries of Indochina, the second Asian group, are also somewhat influenced, culturally, by the Chinese. Indeed, the very word *Viet-*

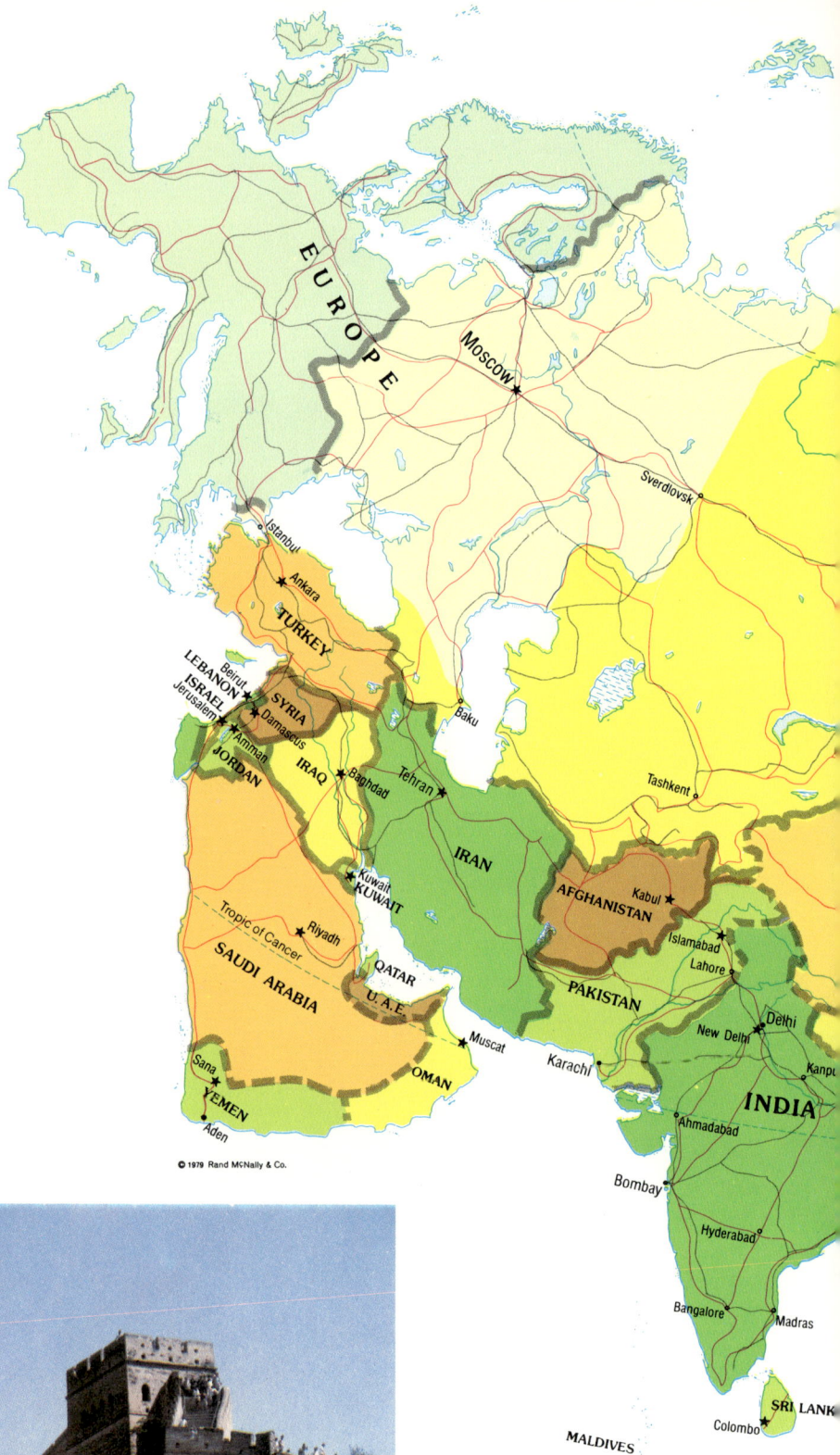

© 1979 Rand McNally & Co.

Built to keep out invading Mongols, the Great Wall of China winds for some 1,500 mountainous miles (2,414 kilometers). It is actually visible from the moon.

nam is Chinese for "far south." Except for the Malay Peninsula at the southern tip, the nations of Indochina formed around river valleys where food grows well. Burma formed around the Irrawaddy River, and Thailand around the Menam. Kampuchea and Vietnam share the lower end of the Mekong River, while Laos grew around a higher part.

Over 153 million people live in Indonesia, making it among the five most populated countries on earth. The Indonesians are scattered over many of the 13,667 islands. They speak a number of languages and have a rather low standard of living. As a result, Indonesia's influence in world affairs is not as great as its population would suggest.

The third grouping of countries is contained on or near the Indian subcontinent. These are India, Pakistan, Bangladesh, and Sri Lanka. All these nations struggle with poverty. India is second only to China as the world's most populated country. Its over 669 million people live in overcrowded cities and villages. In neighboring Bangladesh fewer than ten percent of the people live in cities. The land is fertile, but farming methods are so poor that enough rice cannot be grown to feed the eighty-nine and a half million people of Bangladesh. Hunger visits this part of the world often.

The desert nations occupy the fourth area. People are fewer than in other regions, for there is not enough water for large-scale farming. Turkey has more agricultural land than any other country in the region, but has just 46 million people. Only in Israel, established in 1948 as a Jewish homeland, does the population density reach that of the European countries.

The fifth area of Asia is Siberia, part of the Soviet Union. It has only a few people, who live in widely separated communities. A manufacturing center developed after World War II in the Kuznetsk Basin. A third of the Soviet Union's coal comes from the region —as do farm machinery, chemicals, and building materials.

Civilization is old in Asia. Traditions of the many groups of people who live here had their beginnings in the very dawn of history.

Roads
Railroads

ATLANTIC OCEAN

ARCTIC OCEAN

North Pole

GREENLAND (Den.)

Meridian of Greenwich

Arctic Circle

ICELAND

ZEMLYA FRANTSA-IOSIFA (FRANZ JOSEF LAND)

SVALBARD (SPITSBERGEN) (Nor.)

NOVAYA ZEMLYA

SEVERNAYA ZEMLYA (NORTHERN LAND)

BARENTS SEA

KARA SEA

LAPTEV SEA

SHETLAND ISLANDS

FAEROE IS. (Den.)

NORDKAPP

KOLSKIY P-OV

M. CHELYUSKIN

P-OV TAYMYR

BIRMINGHAM

LONDON

LIVERPOOL

Edinburgh

English Channel

NORTH SEA

BERGEN

OSLO

COPENHAGEN

HAMBURG

STOCKHOLM

Helsinki

Gulf of Bothnia

SCANDINAVIAN PENINSULA

BALTIC SEA

LISBON

MADRID

LYON

PARIS

BERLIN

PRAGUE

VIENNA

WARSAW

KIEV

BUDAPEST

ROME

NAPLES

ATHENS

BUCHAREST

BELGRADE

Brindisi

Bern

Bordeaux

Marseille

CORSICA (Fr.)

SARDINIA

SICILY

MALTA

CRETE

CYPRUS

MEDITERRANEAN SEA

C. DE SÃO VICENTE

C. DE FINISTERRE

Bay of Biscay

PYRENEES

APENNINES

ALPS

CARPATHIANS

BLACK SEA

Tanger

Algiers

Tunis

Tripoli

ATLAS MTS.

LIBYAN DESERT

ALEXANDRIA

CAIRO

Strait of Gibraltar

MOSCOW

LENINGRAD

NIZHNIY NOVGOROD

KUYBYSHEV

Kazan'

Perm'

Arkhangel'sk (Archangel)

SOVIET UNION

SIBERIA

SVERDLOVSK

Tobol'sk

Orenburg

OMSK

Tomsk

Krasnoyarsk

Yeniseysk

NOVOSIBIRSK

Tselinograd

Semipalatinsk

Irkutsk

Tayshet

Bratskoye Vdkhr.

Ozero Baykal

Angara

URALS

Ural

Volga

Don

CASPIAN DEPRESSION

KARGHIZ STEPPE

KIRGHIZ STEPPE

Astrakhan'

CAUCASUS MTS.

Batumi

Tbilisi

BAKU

CASPIAN SEA

PLATO UST-URT

+174

MORE

+1112

Ozero Balkhash

Alma-Ata

Kapchagay

TURKESTAN

TASHKENT

Bukhara

Samarkand

Dushanbe

Kokand

Ashkhabad

Mary

Mashhad

PAMIRS

TIEN SHAN

TARIM BASIN

TAKLA MAKAN (DESERT)

Ürümqi

Hami

ALTAY MTS.

Hovd

Uliastay

Ulan Bator

MONGOLIA

GOBI

Selenge

ANKARA

İSTANBUL

İzmir

Trabzon

TURKEY

TOROS DAĞLARI

LEB.

SYRIA

Aleppo

Damascus

Beirut

ISRAEL

Jerusalem

Amman

JORDAN

IRAQ

Baghdad

Al Başrah

TEHRAN

IRAN

Tabriz

Eşfahān

Shīrāz

Kermān

Bandar-e Büshehr

ELBURZ MTS.

ZAGROS MTS.

SYRIAN DESERT

AN NAFUD

Al Madīnah

Riyadh

Mecca

Jiddah

SAUDI ARABIA

AL HIJAZ

NAJD

AL HASA

AR RUB' AL KHĀLĪ

YEMEN

Şan'ā'

QATAR

UNITED ARAB EMIRATES

OMAN

Muscat

Kuwait

Persian Gulf

Strait of Hormuz

Gulf of Oman

RED SEA

Nile

Lake Nasser

Aswān

Tropic of Cancer

Khartoum

Mitsiwa

Jiddah

ETHIOPIAN PLATEAU

Addis Ababa

Aden (Adan)

Gulf of Aden

Berbera

SOCOTRA (Yemen)

Lake Victoria

Lake Rudolf

AFRICA

AFGHANISTAN

Herāt

Kabul

Quetta

HINDU KUSH

Peshāwar

Islāmābād

Rāwalpindi

Srīnagar

KARAKORAM RA.

PAKISTAN

LAHORE

KARĀCHI

SULAIMĀN RA.

KUNLUN SHAN

ALTUN SHAN

PLATEAU OF TIBET

CHINA

Lanzhou

CHENGDU

CHONGQING

Lhasa

KUNMING

DELHI

New Delhi

Āgra

KANPUR

Allahābād

Vārānasi

Patna

INDIA

GREAT INDIAN DESERT

Ahmadābād

BOMBAY

Nāgpur

HYDERĀBĀD

DECCAN

WESTERN GHĀTS

EASTERN GHĀTS

Narmada

Godāvari

BANGALORE

MADRAS

Calicut

Coimbatore

Madurai

CAPE COMORIN

G. of Khambhāt

G. of Kutch

NEPAL

BHUTAN

Kathmandu

Mt. Everest

HIMALAYAS

BNGL.

Dhaka

CALCUTTA

Brahmaputra

Mandalay

BURMA

Rangoon

Mawlamyine

PAGODA POINT

LAO

Viangcha

THAILAND

BANGKOK (Krung Thep)

Gulf of Thailand

LAKSHADWEEP (India)

SRI LANKA (CEYLON)

Pidurutalagala 8281

Colombo

DONDRA HEAD

G. of Mannar

MALDIVES

ANDAMAN ISLANDS (India)

NICOBAR ISLANDS (India)

Banda Aceh

George Town

MALAYSIA

MALAY PEN.

SUMATRA

BAY OF BENGAL

ARABIAN SEA

INDIAN OCEAN

Equator

40,000 SQ MI AREA

0 300 600 Miles

H-519695-26-016-13-30 XP
COPYRIGHT BY
RAND McNALLY & COMPANY
MADE IN U.S.A.

Longitude East of Greenwich

Scale 1:42,000,000; one inch to 665 miles. Lambert's Azimuthal, Equal Area Projection
Elevations and depressions are given in feet

NORTH AMERICA

CYPRUS

Néa Páfos
Episkopi
Lemesós
AKR. GÁTAS
Ólimbos 6401
Lárnax
Kólpos Lárnakos
AKR. PIDÁLION

Longitude East of Greenwich

Țarābulus (Tripoli)
Ḩalba
Al Qubayr
Al Hirmil
Zgharță
Amyūn 10 131
Al Batrūn
Jubayl (Byblos)
Jūniyah
Ba'labakk

LEBANON

Beirut (Bayrūt)
Zaḩlah
Ad Dāmūr
Az Zabdānī
Şaydā (Sidon)
Jazzīn
Rāshayyā
Al Kiswah

Damascus (Dimashq)
Dūmā

Mari'Uyūn
Qiryat Shemona
Al Quṇayṭirah
Aş Şanamayn
Dar'ā

SYRIA

MEDITERRANEAN
Ṣūr (Tyre)
Tibnin
Nahariyya
Har Meron 3963
Ẕefat
696

SEA
'Akko (Acre)
Teverya
As Suwaydā

Haifa (Ḥefa)
Nazerat
Irbid
Al Mafraq

Ḥadera
'Afula
Bet She'an
Jarash

Netanya
Ṭūlkarm
Shechem (Ruins)
Nābulus
As Salṭ

Herzliyya
Petaḥ Tiqwa
'Athā (Jericho)
Az Zarqā'

Tel Aviv-Yafo
Rishon leẔiyyon
Lod
Rehovot
Jerusalem
Amman

Ashdod
Bayt Laḩm (Bethlehem)
Ma'dabā
Az Zuwayzā

Ashqelon
Qiryat Gat
3323
Dhībān

Gaza (Ghazzah)
Al Khalīl (Hebron)
Al Mazra'ah
Al Karak
Al Mazār

Khān Yūnus
Be'er Sheva'
Sheva'
Arad
Dead Sea
312

Rafaḥ
Dimona
Sedom

Port Said (Būr Sa'īd)
Khalīj aṭ Tīnah
Sabkhat al Bardawīl
Ḥorvot Shivta (Ruins)
Ma'ṭṭaṭ al Qaṭrānah

Al 'Arīsh
Qeẕi'ot
Aṭ Ṭafīlah

Rummānah
Mahattat Jurf ad Darāwīsh

Al Qanṭarah
Al Qusaymah
5383
Jabal al 'Aṭā'iṭah
Ash Shawbak

Daphnae (Ruins)
Ismailia (Al Ismā'īlīyah)
Al Qusaymah
JABAL YU 'ALLIQ 3578
Petrā (Ruins)

Fā'id
Great Bitter Lake
Wādī Mūsā
Ma'ān

NEGEV

Suez (As Suways)
An Nakhl
Ra's an Naqb

MITLA PASS
Aţh Thamad
3513

Ath Thamad

4136
JABAL JALĀLAH AL BAḤRĪYAH
Elat
Al 'Aqabah

Bi'r Za'farānah
JABAL AT TĪH
Mahattat 'Aqabat al Ḥijāzīyah
575
Jabal Ramm
Mahattato ar Ramlah

JABAL AL AJMAH
3789
Al Mudawwarah

4833
JABAL AL JALĀLAT AL QIBLĪYAH
Abū Zanīmah
Ra's al Junaynah
5335
Nuwaybi' al Muẕayyinah

SAUDI ARABIA

SINAI PEN. (SHIBH JAZĪRAT SĪNĀ')
6232
JABAL MAẒHAFAH
Scale 1:4,200,000
0 10 20 30 40 50 Miles
0 20 40 60 80 Kilometers

EGYPT

ISRAEL

JORDAN

Legend

(A) Golan Heights area. Occupied by Israel since 1967. Unilaterally annexed by Israel, 1981.

(B) West Bank area. Unilaterally annexed by Jordan, 1950. Occupied by Israel since 1967. Status to be determined.

(C) Gaza Strip. Occupied by Israel since 1967. Status to be determined.

Left map (East Asia)

Bering Str. (EAST CAPE)
ST. LAWRENCE IS.
Bering Circle
PRIBILOF IS. (U.S.A.)
ALEUTIAN ISLANDS (U.S.A.)
ALEUTIAN TRENCH
West Longitude
East Longitude

CHUKCHI PEN.
WRANGELYA
VOSTOCHNYY
KHOYANSKIY KHREBET
M. DEZHNEVA

SIBERIAN
SEA
Yakutsk
Okhotsk
KORYAKSKIY KHREBET
Petropavlovsk-Kamchatskiy
P-OV KAMCHATKA
M. LOPATKA

KHREBET GYDAN
Amur
STANOVOY KHREBET
SEA OF OKHOTSK
KURIL ISLANDS (Sov. Union)
KURIL TRENCH

Nerchinsk
Blagoveshchensk
Sovetskaya Gavan
Khabarovsk
SAKHALIN (Sov. Union)
Tatar Strait
Sóya Strait

MANCHURIA
GREATER KHINGAN RANGE
SIKHOTE ALIN
Vladivostok
HOKKAIDO
Hakodate

HARBIN
CHANGCHUN
Jilin
SEA OF JAPAN
Sapporo
Sendai
HONSHU

SHENYANG
NORTH KOREA
P'yongyang
TŌKYŌ
YOKOHAMA

BEIJING
Dalian
SEOUL
SOUTH KOREA
KITAKYŪSHŪ
KYŌTO
KOBE
OSAKA

TIANJIN
Jinan
Bo Hai
QINGDAO
KYŪSHŪ
SHIKOKU
Nagasaki

TAIYUAN
NANJING
SHANGHAI

XI'AN
IN LING
WUHAN
EAST CHINA SEA
NANSEI SHOTŌ

Huang
chang
Changsha
Tropic of Cancer
PHILIPPINE SEA

GUANGZHOU
T'AIPEI
TAIWAN (FORMOSA)
Fuzhou
Xiamen
Shantou
Taiwan Strait
PHILIPPINE TRENCH

Wuzhou
HONG KONG
Macao
BABUYAN IS.
Luzon Str.

HAINAN DAO
PHILIPPINES

Hue
Quezon City
MANILA
MINDORO
SAMAR
LEYTE
PHILIPPINE SEA

HO CHI MINH CITY (Saigon)
PANAY
NEGROS
PALAWAN
MINDANAO

MŨI BAI-BUNG
SULU IS.
SULU SEA
Equator

BRUNEI
MALAYSIA
Kota Kinabalu
Sandakan
CELEBES SEA
NEW GUINEA

SINGAPORE
Kuching
BORNEO
CELEBES
INDONESIA

SOUTH CHINA SEA
CHINA
PACIFIC OCEAN

Bottom right map (Malay Peninsula)

Scale 1:4,200,000
0 10 20 30 40 50 Miles
0 20 40 60 80 Kilometers

Kuala Lumpur
Kelang
Kajang
Kuala Klawang
PAHANG

SELANGOR
Gunong Telapa 3915
Burok
Bahau
TIOMAN
Gunong Kajang 3444

Telok Datok
NEGERI SEMBILAN
Rompin
Padang Endau
PEMANGGIL

Sepang
Seremban
Gemas
AUR

Port Dickson
Rantau
Rembau
Tampin
Segamat
Gunong Besar 3403
Mersing
2002
TINGGI

CAPE RACHADO
Alor Gajah
Jasin
Labis
Mt. Ophir 4187
Kota Tinggi

MELAKA
Panchor
MALAYSIA
Paloh

Melaka (Malacca)
JOHOR
3312
Gunong Blumut
MALAY PENINSULA

Bandar Maharani
Keluang
Rengam
Layang Layang
Jason Bay

Jumrah
RUPAT
Teluklecak
TANJONG TOHOR
Ayer Hitam
Batu Pahat
Pontian Kechil
Johor Baharu
TANJONG RAMUNIA

Dumai
Batupanjang
BENGKALIS
Pontian Kechil
TANJONG PIAI
SINGAPORE
Singapore Strait
TANJONG BERAKIT

Bengkalis
Bukitbatu
Ketamputih
SINGAPORE
1181
BINTAN

Pinggir
Kudap
BATAM
KEPULAUAN RIAU

SUMATRA
PADANG
Telesung
341
KARIMUN BESAR
Tanjungbalai
Tanjungpinang

Minas
1837
KUNDUR
RIAU
RANGSANG
Seranggung

Buatan
Siaksriindrapura
TEBINGTINGGI
Baranpuah
30

SOUTH CHINA SEA

STRAIT OF MALACCA

INDONESIA

Cities, Towns, and Villages legend

0 to 25,000 ○
100,000 to 250,000 ◎
1,000,000 and over ◉

25,000 to 100,000 •
250,000 to 1,000,000 ◎
Major urbanized area

Africa/Terrain

One of the world's great natural wonders is Victoria Falls, on the Zambezi River in southern Africa. They are over a mile (1.6 kilometers) long and with a drop of nearly 400 feet (122 meters)—wider and higher than Niagara Falls.

Africa, the second largest continent, is really a gigantic plateau which stands mostly one thousand feet (304.8 meters) above sea level. It is mostly lower in the north and west and higher in the east and south. On all sides the edges of this great tablelike landmass drop off abruptly to the surrounding oceans and seas. A few narrow coastal plains are to be found—such as those along Ghana, Nigeria, and the Ivory Coast.

Four mighty rivers rise in the high interior. The Niger flows out of wild grasslands where lions roam. The Nile, longest of the world's rivers, drifts past temples built by long-dead Egyptian kings. The Congo drains a dark, humid rain forest. The Zambezi cuts across a vast, thorny woodland.

All of Africa's rivers contain impassable rapids and so are only partly open to boat traffic. For this reason, Africa's mineral and vegetable resources cannot readily be shipped to the cities. This is Africa's great misfortune.

Another problem for Africa's economic development is its smooth and regular coastline. For stretches of hundreds of miles there are no shelters for ships. Swampy coasts thick with stands of mangrove trees make access to the land difficult with their thick jumble of roots standing above the shore. Thus Africa has few good harbors around which a Rio de Janeiro or New York could develop.

Africa has some magnificent mountains. The Atlas Range is a major chain that rims the continent's northern edge for 1,500 miles (2,413.95 kilometers) through Morocco, Al-

Africa's Great Rift Valley cuts a north-south trench 4,000 miles (6,437.2 kilometers) long. In places the valley is broken by plateaus and mountains, but it can be traced by the many lakes and seas which fill its long pockets. The cutaway at right shows some of those bodies of water.

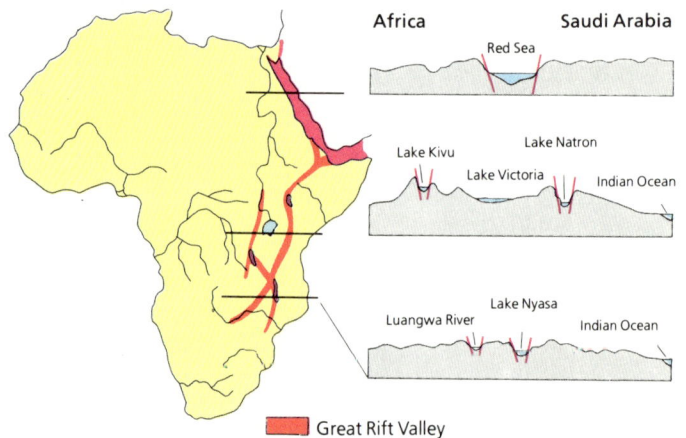

Great Rift Valley

geria, and Tunisia. It was formed at the same time as the European Alps. Both are the result of the collision of Africa with Europe many millions of years ago. After the collision, Africa recoiled, or drifted, back south. The gap between the two continents filled with water to become the Mediterranean Sea.

In East Africa, the peaks of the Ruwenzori Range follow two nearly parallel north-south lines. Among the eastern mountains, snow-crested Mount Kilimanjaro soars to more than nineteen thousand feet (5,791.2 meters)—Africa's highest peak.

Between the high eastern ranges lies the mysterious Great Rift Valley. This is a long rip in the earth's surface where the land dropped down more than a mile (1.6 kilometers). Several beautiful lakes nestle in this rift. Lying on the plateau between the two major branches of the rift is the largest, Lake Victoria, which is almost as big as Scotland.

The Drakensberg Mountains of South Africa are the most unusual range on the continent. As seen from a distance they appear to rise skyward from the earth. Actually, they are not true mountains, just tilted-up portions of the gigantic plateau which makes up Africa.

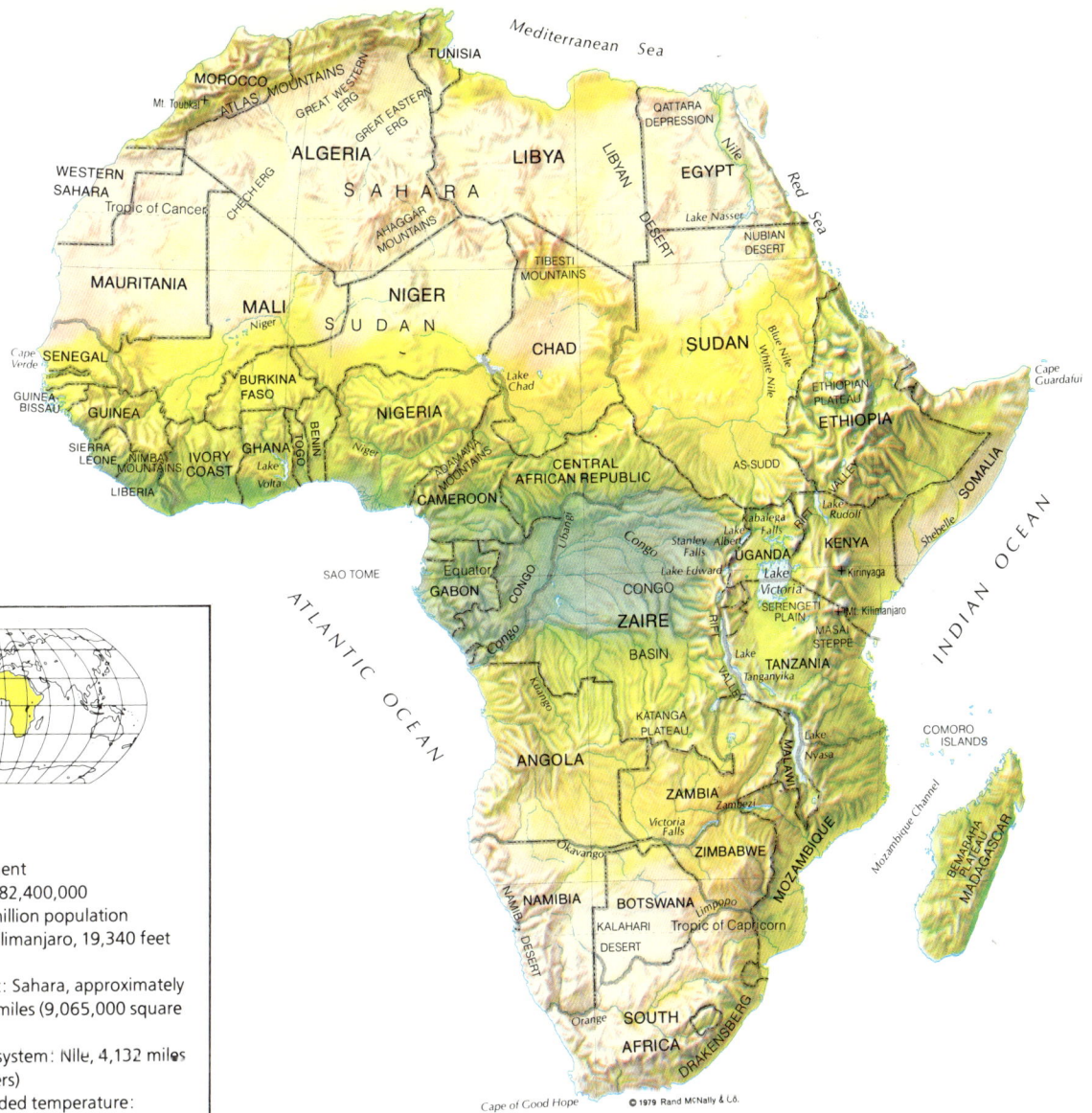

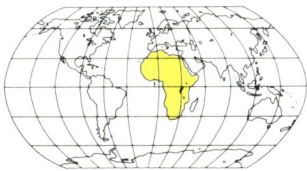

Map Labels

Mediterranean Sea

MOROCCO
ATLAS MOUNTAINS
Mt. Toubkal
GREAT WESTERN ERG
GREAT EASTERN ERG
TUNISIA
QATTARA DEPRESSION
LIBYAN
EGYPT
Nile
Red Sea

WESTERN SAHARA
ALGERIA
LIBYA
SAHARA
Tropic of Cancer
CHECH ERG
AHAGGAR MOUNTAINS
Lake Nasser
NUBIAN DESERT

MAURITANIA
MALI
Niger
NIGER
SUDAN
CHAD
TIBESTI MOUNTAINS
LIBYAN DESERT
SUDAN
Blue Nile
White Nile
ETHIOPIAN PLATEAU
Cape Guardafui

Cape Verde
SENEGAL
BURKINA FASO
Lake Chad
AS-SUDD
ETHIOPIA

GUINEA BISSAU
GUINEA
NIGERIA
Niger
CENTRAL AFRICAN REPUBLIC
RIFT VALLEY
SOMALIA

SIERRA LEONE
NIMBA MOUNTAINS
IVORY COAST
GHANA
TOGO
BENIN
Lake Volta
ADAMAWA MOUNTAINS
CAMEROON
Lake Rudolf
Shebelle

LIBERIA
SAO TOME
Equator
GABON
CONGO
Ubangi
Congo
Stanley Falls
Lake Albert
Lake Edward
UGANDA
Kabalega Falls
Lake Victoria
KENYA
Kirinyaga

ATLANTIC OCEAN
CONGO
ZAIRE
BASIN
SERENGETI PLAIN
Mt. Kilimanjaro
MASAI STEPPE
INDIAN OCEAN

Congo
Kwango
KATANGA PLATEAU
Lake Tanganyika
TANZANIA
Lake Nyasa

ANGOLA
ZAMBIA
Zambezi
MALAWI
COMORO ISLANDS

Victoria Falls
Okavango
ZIMBABWE
MOZAMBIQUE
Mozambique Channel
BEMARAHA PLATEAU
MADAGASCAR

NAMIBIA
BOTSWANA
Limpopo
Tropic of Capricorn

NAMIB DESERT
KALAHARI DESERT

Orange
SOUTH AFRICA
DRAKENSBERG

Cape of Good Hope
© 1979 Rand McNally & Co.

Africa Facts

Second largest continent
Third in population: 482,400,000
11 cities with over 1 million population
Highest mountain: Kilimanjaro, 19,340 feet (5,894.83 meters)
World's largest desert: Sahara, approximately 3,500,000 square miles (9,065,000 square kilometers)
World's longest river system: Nile, 4,132 miles (6,649.62 kilometers)
World's highest recorded temperature: Azizia, Libya, 136.4°F (58°C)
Equator passes through

Great, windswept deserts cover most of Egypt, a northeast African nation that includes the Sinai Peninsula. Yet, people have learned to live in these dry places.

Few people outside Africa realize just how huge the continent is. More than a hundred Great Britains could be deposited within Africa's borders and there would still be more than enough room for five Frances and four West Germanys. The entire United States could be placed in just the Sahara Desert, which extends for 3,200 sandy miles (5,149.76 kilometers) across northern Africa.

Yet despite its great size, Africa is largely undeveloped. To tap the resources locked within the continent remains a great challenge for its people and for the more prosperous nations which wish to invest in Africa's future.

Red Sea

BERLIN

LONDON

PARIS

MADRID

Athens

CRETE

ARABIAN DESERT

Alexandria

CAIRO

Nile

Lake Nasser

NUBIAN DESERT

Nile

Al-Fāshir

LIBYAN DESERT

ROME

SICILY

MALTA

CORSICA

SARDINIA

Banghāzī

Tripoli

Tunis

Algiers

Mediterranean Sea

A

L

I

B

Y

A

N

TIBESTI

ENNEDI

A

H

A

G

G

A

R

GRAND ERG ORIENTAL

GRAND ERG OCCIDENTAL

M O U N T A I N S

A T L A S

PYRENEES

Casablanca

CANARY ISLANDS

El Aaiun

EL DJOUF

S

A

H

A

R

A

Tamenghest

ADRAR
DES IFOGHAS

Lake Chad

N'Djamena

Kano

Niger

Tombouctou

Niger

Bamako

Lake Volta

Lagos

Abidjan

Yaoundé

Gulf of Guinea

Dakar

Freetown

CAPE VERDE
ISLANDS

ATLANTIC OCEAN

ATLANTIC OCEAN

Tropic of Cancer

INDIAN OCEAN

INDIAN OCEAN

Gulf of Aden

Aden

Berbera

DJIBOUTI

Asmera

Addis Ababa

Blue Nile

White Nile

Khartoum

Mountain Nile

Muqdisho

SEYCHELLES

Nairobi

Dar es Salaam

COMORO ISLANDS

Lake Victoria

Lake Tanganyika

MADAGASCAR

Antananarivo

Mozambique Channel

Kisangani

Uele

Bangui

Ubangi

Congo (Zaire)

Kasai

Kinshasa

Lubumbashi

Lusaka

Harare

Luanda

Zambezi

Beira

Limpopo

Johannesburg

Durban

Windhoek

Orange

KALAHARI DESERT

NAMIB DESERT

Orange

Cape Town

Tropic of Capricorn

Equator

■ •	Urban
▦	Cropland
▦	Cropland & Woodland
▦	Cropland & Grazing Land
▦	Grassland, Grazing Land
▦	Forest, Woodland
▦	Swamp, Marshland
▦	Shrub, Sparse Grass, Wasteland (pattern)
□	Barren Land
•	Oasis

H-580000-96
COPYRIGHT BY
RAND McNALLY & COMPANY
MADE IN U.S.A.

0 100 200 400 600 800 Miles
0 150 300 600 900 1200 Kilometers

Africa/Animals

Africa is a continent of great forests, great grassy plains, and great deserts. Each of these different landscapes has its own special animals.

In the north the enormous Sahara Desert spreads across thousands of miles. Not many animals live in that hot wasteland, and those that do are able to survive with little or no water. In places where scrubby plants grow there are a few small herds of addax, a kind of little antelope with tall, twisted horns. An addax never drinks. It gets the moisture it needs from the plants it eats. The jerboa, a mouselike creature with long hind legs and a long, tufted tail, sleeps in a hole in the sand by day and comes out in the cool night to feed on plants and insects. Jerboas and other little animals and birds are hunted by the fennec, a desert fox.

Of course, the best-known animal of the Sahara is the one-humped Arabian camel, also known as the dromedary. But these animals have actually lived in the Sahara for only about two thousand years. They were brought here from the Middle East. All the camels in the Sahara are used as tame beasts of burden.

Across the middle of Africa is a great rain forest. This is the home of the chimpanzee which moves about in small bands living mainly on fruit and tender, young plants. The rain forest is also the home of the big, burly gorilla, actually a shy and gentle creature. Here, too, are found buffalo, leopards, many kinds of monkeys, and the little okapi, a brown-bodied animal with white-striped legs. It resembles a horse, but is related to the giraffe. In swamps and rivers that lie in the forest area crocodiles swim in search of prey, and bulky hippopotamuses munch on water plants.

Vast, grassy plains lie between the Sahara and the rain forest, and south of the forest as well. Herds of zebra, eland, and gnu, or wildebeest, graze on these plains. Giraffes browse among clusters of trees. Rhinoceroses trot to water holes to wallow in the mud after feeding. Herds of African elephants, the largest of all land animals, plod on their way. Here, too, the spotted cheetah, swiftest of all animals, runs down its prey. And here is heard the shattering roar of the powerful African lion, king of all the beasts.

Tarpon

Addax

Fennec

Pangolin

Colobus Monkey

Despite their fearful appearance, gorillas are generally gentle beasts who eat only plants. They will harm people only if bothered or attacked.

Jackal

Dromedary

Crowned Crane

Eared Vulture

Dorcas Gazelle

Barbary Sheep

Striped Hyena

Crocodile

Greater Kudu

Aardvark

Elephant

Giraffe

Baboon

Chimpanzee

Gorilla

Leopard

Black Rhinoceros

Hornbill

Cape Buffalo

Hippopotamus

White Pelican

Eland

Zebra

Lion

Tenrec

Python

Wildebeest

Chameleon

Cheetah

Ring-tailed Lemur

Impala

Angelfish

Ostrich

Sacred Ibis

Africa/Countries and Cities

Africa today has fifty-three countries. Generally, the countries are grouped in five large areas: North Africa, West Africa, central Africa, South Africa, and East Africa. The countries in each area have some things in common.

Civilization has a long history in North Africa. Egypt was the site of one of our very first cultures. Later the ancient city of Carthage, in present-day Tunisia, was the center of a powerful state that for a time rivaled even mighty Rome.

During the seventh century A.D. the religion of Islam—the followers of which are called Muslims—was adopted by most North African nations. Beautiful Muslim mosques were built in what is now Libya, Algeria, Tunisia, and Morocco. Islam is still the religion of North Africa's people.

Contact between the North Africans and the Africans to the south was made difficult by the sandy and rocky wastes of the Sahara. This desert extends south from the Atlas Mountains and the Mediterranean Sea for nearly 1,500 sunbaked miles (2,413.95 kilometers). Caravans did manage to open a few routes across the desert, and there was some trading for goods and slaves.

Country borders mean little to independent nomads like the Masai people, below. They cross the boundary between Kenya and Tanzania often in search of water and grazing land for their cattle.

Roads
Railroads

Algiers · Tunis
Rabat · Casablanca
MOROCCO
TUNISIA
Tripoli
Alexandria
Cairo
ALGERIA
LIBYA
EGYPT
WESTERN SAHARA
Tropic of Cancer
Aswan
Nouakchott
MAURITANIA
MALI
NIGER
Khartoum
SUDAN
CAPE VERDE
Dakar
SENEGAL
Bamako
CHAD
DJIBOUTI
GAMBIA
Niamey
GUINEA-BISSAU
BURKINA FASO
N'Djamena
ETHIOPIA
Conakry
GUINEA
Addis Ababa
Freetown
SIERRA LEONE
IVORY COAST
GHANA
TOGO BENIN
NIGERIA
SOMALIA
LIBERIA
Yamoussoukro
Accra
Lagos
CENTRAL AFRICAN REPUBLIC
Abidjan
CAMEROON
Yaounde
UGANDA
Mogadishu
EQUATORIAL GUINEA
Kampala
KENYA
SAO TOME AND PRINCIPE
Libreville
Equator
Nairobi
GABON
CONGO
RWANDA
Brazzaville
ZAIRE
BURUNDI
Mombasa
CABINDA (ANG)
Kinshasa
TANZANIA
Dar es Salaam
Luanda
COMOROS
ANGOLA
MALAWI
ZAMBIA
Lusaka
Harare
MOZAMBIQUE
NAMIBIA
Windhoek
ZIMBABWE
MADAGASCAR
Antananarivo
Walvis Bay (S. AFRICA)
BOTSWANA
Tropic of Capricorn
Gaborone
Pretoria
Johannesburg
SWAZ.
Maputo
LESOTHO
Durban
SOUTH AFRICA
Cape Town

© 1979 Rand McNally & Co.

Throughout history North Africa has been distinct from the rest of Africa. Most North Africans are white and speak the Semitic language which in several forms is also spoken by the Jewish and Arabian peoples. Almost one-fifth of all the people in Africa live in the countries of North Africa.

West Africa, much of which is a moist, hot lowland area bordering the Atlantic Ocean, was long known as the slave coast. Through the centuries raiders visited these shores, kidnapped the people, carried them away in ships, and sold them as laborers in many parts of the world. Bitter tales of families torn apart, misery, death, and loss of human dignity are still remembered from this terrible period in Africa's history.

Today, more than one-fourth of the people in Africa live in these countries which border the Atlantic. Nigeria, with over 78 million people, is Africa's most populous nation. Ghana, too, is heavily settled along the western coast.

The equator passes through the continent's third area, central Africa. The most important nation here is Zaire, with about 29 million people. The Congo River and the rivers that feed into it are almost completely contained within Zaire, and the country is almost smothered by a rain forest. The climate is steamy, and insects are not only a nuisance but a hazard to good health.

Eastern Africa is like another world, compared to the rest of the continent. Its western border is marked by mountains which soar above the Great Rift Valley. The climate is far drier than in neighboring Zaire.

The people of Tanzania, Kenya, and Uganda live mainly in these uplands, particularly around the deep water of Lake Tanganyika and the huge expanse of Lake Victoria. Farther north, in Ethiopia, most of the population clusters on the Amhara Plateau.

The continent's fifth area, southern Africa, lies mostly outside the hot regions of the equator. The Republic of South Africa boasts some of the most fertile land on the continent and a climate rather like Europe's. For this reason the land appealed to Europeans. The British and the Dutch fought for

Though many Africans still cling to their old ways of life, modern cities have sprung up across the continent. Nairobi, Kenya, is one such teeming center.

Women carry their wares to market as their ancestors did before them. Colorful cotton cloth has been made in the West African country of Nigeria for centuries.

it. Even though the British army won, the Dutch, known as Boers, stayed on in large numbers. It was the Boers who farmed the rich land and founded successful businesses. Out of a population of over 29 million, four and a half million Europeans control the country.

Europeans also settled the area they named Rhodesia. Rhodesia's black peoples, which make up more than 94 percent of the population, recently took control of the government. They renamed the country Zimbabwe. There has been much political strife in this country.

The fifty-three countries which make up Africa are as different from one another as the lofty mountains of the Great Rift are from rain forests found on the equator. The people of Africa have only begun to control their governments in the past thirty or so years. The countries have only begun to grow. We can only guess where that growth will take Africa.

ATLANTIC OCEAN

SPAIN

Cádiz
Str. of Gibraltar
Gibraltar (U.K.)
Ceuta (Sp.)
Tanger (Tangier)
Tetouan
Larache
Melilla (Sp.)
Beni Saf
Ghazaouet
Oujda
Tilimsen
Saïda
El Djelfa

Algiers (El Djazair)
Delles
Bejaïa (Bougie)
El Qoll
Skikda
Annaba
Bône
Bizerte
Carth
Cherchell
Tizi-Ouzou
El Milyya
Guelma
Souk Ahras
Tabarka
Ech Cheliff
Lemdiya
Stif
Constantine
Mestghanem
Oran
Ghilizane
Ain el Beïda
Batna
Tbessa
TUNISIA
Sfax
Sidi bel Abbès
M'Sila
El Kaïrouan
Sousse

Açores (AZORES) (Port.)
GRACIOSA
TERCEIRA
SÃO JORGE
FAIAL
PICO
SÃO MIGUEL
Ponta Delgada
STA. MARIA
Same scale as main map

Funchal
ILHA DE PORTO SANTO
ARQUIPÉLAGO DA MADEIRA (Port.)
ILHA DA MADEIRA

CASABLANCA
El Jadida
Rabat
Salé
Meknès
Fès
Taza
Settat
Oued Zem
Kasba-Tadla
Safi (Asfi)
Demnat
Marrakech
Essaouira
Jebel Toubkal 12665
Boudenib
Figuig
Béchar
Aïn-Sefra
Laghouat
Ghardaïa
El Wad
Touggourt
El Menia
Hassi Messaoud
Wargla
Nälüt
Ghudāmis
AL HAMM AL HAM

MOROCCO
ATLAS MOUNTAINS
ALGERIA

Agadir
Taroudant
Tiznit
ANTI ATLAS
Sidi Ifni
CAP DRÂA
C. YUBY
Igli
Béni Abbas
Timimoun
In Salah
Adrar
PLATEAU DU TADEMAÏT
Bordj Omar Idriss
PLATEAU DU TINGHERT
In Amnas

ISLAS CANARIAS (Sp.)
LANZAROTE
FUERTEVENTURA
LA PALMA
TENERIFE
Sta. Cruz de Tenerife
San Sebastián
GOMERA
GRAN CANARIA
Las Palmas de Gran Canaria
HIERRO
CABO BOJADOR

El Aaiún
WESTERN SAHARA
The Western Sahara is occupied by Morocco

GRAND ERG OCCIDENTAL
GRAND ERG ORIENTAL
ERG IGUIDI
ERG CHECH
Chenachane
TIDIKELT
Ouallene
TASSILI-N-AJJER
Illizi
Sardalas
Ghât
Djanet

Tindouf
EL HANK
EL DJOUF
Taoudenni
TANEZROUFT
AHAGGAR
Tahat 9.541
Tamenghest
Djanet

Dakhla
Tropic of Cancer
SAHARA
Fdérik
Nouadhibou
CAP BLANC
CAP D'ARGUIN
Atar
Chinguetti
OUARANE
EL MREYYÉ
Oued Tamenghest
TUAREG
Mt. Gréboun 6562
Iferouâne
ADRAR DES IFÔGHAS
Monts Tamgak 5906
AÏR
Monts Bagzane 6300

Nouamrhar
CAP TIMIRIS
Akjoujt
Tidjikdja
Mabrouk
Araouane
Kidal
AGADEZ
TÉNÉRÉ

Nouakchott
MAURITANIA
Boutilimit
Aleg
Kiffa
Néma
Oualâta
VALLÉE DU TILEMSI
Tahoua

Saint-Louis
Podor
Dagana
Kaédi
Mbout
Sélibaby
Matam
Linguère
Louga
Nioro du Sahel
Nara
Goumbou
Sokolo
Tombouctou (Timbuktu)
Goundam
Bourem
Gao
Bamba
Niafounké
Debo Swamp
NIGER
Tillabéry
Niamey
Madaoua
Tessaoua
Zinder
Gouré
Ngu

Dakar
CAP VERT
Rufisque
Thiès
Diourbel
SENEGAL
Kaolack
Banjul (Bathurst)
GAMBIA
Tambacounda
Kayes
Bafoulabé
Kita
Bakel
MALI
Ségou
San
Mopti
Bandiagara
Djenné
Ouahigouya
Dori
Niamey
Dosso
BURKINA FASO
Ouagadougou
Fada Ngourma
Suy
Sokoto
Kaura Namoda
Katsina
Gumel
Birnin Kebbi
Gusau
Kano
Hadejia
Geidam
BORN PLAIN
Potiskum
Nguru

Ziguinchor
GUINEA-BISSAU
Bissau
Bolama
ARQUIPÉLAGO DOS BIJAGÓS
Bubaque
Boké
Buba
FOUTA DJALLON
Mt. du Tamgué 5046
GUINEA
Labé
Timbo
Koundara
Mamou
Siguiri
Kankan
Kita
Koulikoro
Bamako
Bougouni
Sikasso
Bobo-Dioulasso
Koudougou
Tenkodogo
Dédougou
Koutiala
Gambaga
Sansanné-Mango
Natitingou
Malanville
Illo
Kandi
BENIN
Kontagora
Zaria
Kaduna
Bauchi
Gombe
Zungeru
Minna
Jos
Keffi
Kontcha
NIGERIA
Yola
ADAMA

Conakry
Forécariah
Makeni
Kabala
Kissidougou
Faranah
Kindia
Boffa
SIERRA LEONE
Freetown
Moyamba
Bonthe
Pendembu
Kolahun
Beyla
Odienné
Korhogo
Kong
KONG
Bouna
Bole
Dabakala
Bondoukou
Yendi
Tamale
Kintampo
Savalou
Abomey
Atakpamé
TOGO
Ilorin
Oyo
Iseyin
Ogbomosho
Oshogbo
Ilesha
Ife
Ibadan
Bida
Oyo
Benin City
Idah
Makurdi
Katsina Ala
Enugu
Onitsha
GOTEL MTS.
Fumban
Dschang
Mamfe

LIBERIA
Monrovia
Robertsport
Bomi Hills
Buchanan
River Cess
Greenville
Harper
CAPE PALMAS
Tabou
Grand Lahou
Grand Bassam
Assini
C. THREE POINTS
Sekondi-Takoradi
Tarkwa
Cape Coast
Saltpond
Keta
Anécho
Lomé
Ouidah
Cotonou
Porto-Novo
Lagos
Ijebu Ode
Sapele
Warri
Forcados
Owerri
Aba
Port Harcourt
Calabar
Brass
Bonny
CAMERO

IVORY COAST
Séguéla
Man
Mont Nimba 5760
Bouaké
Bouaflé
Yamoussoukro
Abidjan
Port-Bouet
GHANA
Kumasi
Koforidua
Accra
Ada

GUINEA
Boffa
Kindia
Mamou
Faranah
Kissidougou
Kabala
Makeni
Kouroussa
Kankan

GULF OF GUINEA
ATLANTIC OCEAN

EQUATORIAL GUINEA
Bata
BIOKO
Malabo
Cameroon Mtn. 13 451
Victoria
RIO MUNI
Oyem
Kribi
Edéa
Eséka
Yaoundé
Douala
Nyong
Bight of Biafra
Ebolowa
Campo
Makoko
Libreville
GABO

ILHA DO PRINCIPE
SÃO TOMÉ AND PRINCIPE
ILHA DE SÃO TOMÉ

CAPE VERDE (inset)
SANTO ANTÃO
SÃO VICENTE
SAL
SÃO NICOLAU
BOA VISTA
SÃO TIAGO
MAIO
Praia
FOGO
Same scale as main map

Bight of Benin

Cities, Towns, and Villages
0 to 25,000
25,000 to 100,000
100,000 to 250,000
250,000 to 1,000,000
1,000,000 and over
Major urbanized area

Longitude West of Greenwich
Longitude East of Greenwich

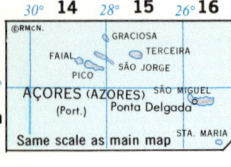

A-589100-26-45-45-29-x
COPYRIGHT BY
RAND McNALLY & COMPANY
MADE IN U.S.A.

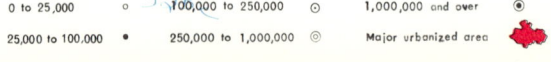

Scale 1:16,850,000; one inch to 265 miles. Sinusoidal Projection
Elevations and depressions are given in feet

7 8 9 10 11 12 13

ITALY
SICILIA (SICILY)
PANTELLERIA (It.)
MALTA
ÎLES KERKENNA

GREECE
Khaniá Iráklion
CRETE (KRITI)
RHODES (RÓDHOS) (GR)

TURKEY
Antalya Adana
Iskenderun Antakya
Halab (Aleppo)
Al-Lādhiqīyah
Hamāh
Hims

NORTH CYPRUS
Nicosia
CYPRUS

SYRIA
Dayr az Zawr
Tudmur (Palmyra)
Damascus (Dimashq)

LEBANON
Beirut

IRAQ
SYRIAN B
DESERT (BĀDIYAT ASH SHĀM)

MEDITERRANEAN SEA

Tripoli (Tarābulus) Al Khums Misrātah
Az Zāwiyah Zlitan Yafran
Zuwārah
Al Marj Zāwiyat al Baydā' Darnah
Tūkrah Tubruq
AL JABAL AL AKHDAR
Banghāzī
BARQAH (CYRENAICA)
Surt Khalīj Surt
An Nawfalīyah Ajdābiyah
Qasr al Burayqah
Qasr al Qaryah Ash Shāriqah
Marādah
Awjilah Wāhat Jālū

ISRAEL
Haifa
Tel Aviv-Yafo
Jerusalem
Gazzah
Dead Sea

JORDAN
'Ammān
Al 'Aqabah
Al Jawf

Sīdī Barrānī Sallūm Marsā Matrūh
ALEXANDRIA (Al Iskandarīyah) Dumyāt Port Said
Al 'Alamayn Damanhūr Al Mansūrah
Tantā Az Zaqāzīq
CAIRO (Al Qāhirah) Suez (As Suways)
Al Fayyūm Banī Suwayf
SINAI PEN.
Jabal Kātrīnā 8668
Gulf of Suez

LIBYA
FAZZĀN (FEZZAN)
IDEHAN
MARZŪQ
Tarbū Mārzuq Wāw al-Kabīr
SARĪR TIBASTI
JABAL AS SAWDĀ
Sawknah Zillah Zaltan

Al Jaghbūb
AL QATTĀRAH
MUNKHAFAD -436
Birket Qarun

EGYPT
LIBYAN DESERT (AS SAHRĀ' AL LĪBĪYAH)
Qasr al Farāfirah Al Bawītī
Al Minyā Asyūt Akhmīm
Sawhāj Qinā
Thebes (Ruins) Al Uqsur (Luxor)
Idfū
Aswān Aswān High Dam
Lake Nasser
RA'S BANĀS
Bi'r Misāhah Ash Shabb
ADMINISTRATIVE BDY.
Halā'ib

Al Kufrah (Oasis)
Rebiana (Oasis) Al Jawf
Buzaymah
Ma'tan Bishārah

ARABIAN DESERT
Būr Safājah Al-Wajh
Al Qusayr

SAUDI ARABIA
AN NAFŪD
Taymā' Hā'il
Buraydah
NAJD
AL HIJĀZ (HEJAZ)
Al Madīnah (Medina)
Yanbu'
Jiddah Mecca (Makkah)
Al Khurmah
Al Qunfudhah
ASĪR
Abhā Qīzān
JĀZĀ'IR FARASĀN

RED SEA

CHAD
Pic Tousside 10 712
TIBESTI
Emi Koussi 11 204
Ouanga Kébir
BORKOU
Kaouar (Oasis)
Bilma Agadem (Oasis)
BODELE
Largeau Fada
ENNEDI
Oum Chalouba
Lake Chad (Lac Tchad)
Mao
Dikwa Kukawa
N'Djamena (Fort-Lamy)
Maiduguri
MANDARA MTS.
Maroua Bousso
Garoua Léré Laï
OUADDAĪ
Yao Abéché
Am Timan
Sarh
Ndélé Bouar
CHAÎNE DES MONGOS
Fort-Crampel
Fort-Sibut
Bambari
Ngaoundéré Koundé
Carnot
CENTRAL AFRICAN REPUBLIC
Bangui
Mbaïki Zongo
Mbaki Liberge Gemena
Mongoumba Businga
Bangassou Rafaï Zémio Yalinga
Mobaye Bondo Bambesa Dungu
Bangassou

SUDAN
'Arbi Kosha
Dalqū
3rd Cataract
Dunqulah Kuraymah Abu Hamad
Al Khandaq Marawi Barbar
4th Cataract
Ad Dabbah Kūrtī
5th Cataract
Al Atrūn
NUBIAN DESERT
Jabal Erba 7274
Bur Sūdān
Sawākin
Tawkar
Taqātu' Hayyā
'Atbarah Ad Dāmir Adarama
Shandi
Kassalā
6th Cataract
Omdurman (Umm Durmān) Al Khartūm Bahrī
Khartoum (Al Khartūm) Al Kāmilīn
Rufā'a Wad Madani
Al Qadārif
Sannār
DĀRFŪR
Al Fāshir
Jabal Marrah 10 131
KURDUFĀN
Ad Duwaym
An Nuhūd Al-Ubayyid
Kūstī Sinjah Qallābāt
Nyala
Al Uqayyah Babanūsah
Sennar Dam
Talawdī
NUBA (AN NUBAH)
Malakāl Kodok
BAHR AL GHAZĀL
Wāw Shambe
Rumbek Bor
Kafia Kingi
Tambura
Mongalla
Jūbā
AS SUDD
Mashra' ar Raqq
Nasir
Kapoeta
White Nile
Blue Nile

ERITREA
Mitsiwa (Massawa)
DAHLAK ARCH.
KAMARAN
Akordat Keren
Asmera
Adi Ugri
Sebderat Barentu
Om Hajer
Adwa

ETHIOPIA
Gonder
Debre Tabor
Amba Farit 13 041
Dangila Talo 14 478
Dese Were Ilu
Debre Markos
Ras Dashen Terara 15 158
Mekele
Sekota
DENAKIL
Tana (L.)
Lake Tana
Nekemte
Addis Ababa (Adis Abeba)
Tulu Welel 10 830
Dembi Dolo
Gore Jima
Gambela
Shewa Gimira
Goba
Sodo Wendo
Moji Bako
Chamo (L.)
Abaya (L.)
SIDAMO
HARERGE
Harer Dire Dawa
AHMAR MTS.
Ginir

YEMEN
Al Hudaydah
Al Mukhā

DJIBOUTI
Djibouti
Tadjoura
Aysha
Seylac

KENYA
Mt. Elgon 14 178
Eldoret Meru
Lake Rudolf 1230
Moyale El Wak

SOMALIA
Doolow

UGANDA
Arua Kitgum Soroti
Masindi
Margherita Peak 16 763
Ruwenzori
Ft. Portal
Kampala Jinja
Entebbe
Lake Victoria
Murchison Falls
L. Albert
Kumu

ZAIRE
Kisangani (Stanleyville)
Boyoma Falls
Equator
Bomongo Basoko
Basankusu Isangi
Bumba Lisala
Aketi Buta
Isiro Gombari
Panga Avakubi
Irumu
Watsa Niangara
Mahagi Port
Dongou Makanza
Impfondo

CONGO
Ouesso
Mbandaka

Mombasa?
40,000 SQ MI AREA
0 100 200 Miles

0 50 100 200 300 400 500 Miles
0 100 200 400 600 800 Kilometers

GABON

CONGO

Libreville
Kango
Ndjolé
Lambaréné
Lastoursville
Franceville
Moanda
Mbigou
Sibiti
Brazzaville
Pointe-Noire
Lândana
Kinshasa (Léopoldville)
CABINDA
Cabinda
Boma Matadi
Soyo
Nóqui
M'banza
Congo
Bembe
N'zeto
Ambriz
Caxito

Equator
Port
Gentil
Sette Cama
Tchibanga
Mayumba

ZAIRE

Mbandaka
Bikoro
Boende
Owando
Irébou
Lukolela
Tumba
Inongo
Lac Mai-Ndombe (Lake Leopold II) +1076
Bolobo
Mushie
Fimi
Lukenie
Ilebo
Bulungu
Lusanga
Kikwit
Tshela
Mbanza-Ngungu
Popokabaka
Cuango
Tshikapa
Kananga (Luluabourg)

Monkoto
Mondombe
Itoko
Kole
Bena Dibele
Lusambo
Kasongo
Kabinda
Kanda Kanda
Ankoro
Kabalo
Kongolo
Kalemie

Ubundu
Kindu
Kabambare
Moba

UGANDA
Entebbe
Kampala
Kisumu
Ripon Falls
Jinja

RWANDA
Kigali
BURUNDI
Bujumbura
Bukavu
Gitega
Uvira
Kigoma
Ujiji

Bukoba
Shirati
Ikoma
Mwanza
Biharamulo
Shinyanga
Tabora

Lake Victoria +3720
Lake Kivu +4790
Lake Tanganyika +2534

TANZAN

Kasanga
Mbala
Karema
Mpulungu

KATANGA
Kamina
Sandoa
Dilolo
Kolwezi
Likasi
Lubumbashi (Elisabethville)
Kambove
Tenke
Kambove
Koni Panda
Sakania
Ndola
Chingola

ANGOLA
Luanda
Golungo Alto
Catete
Dondo
Malanje
Saurimo
Cazombo
Lobito
Benguela
Chinguar
Kuito
Huambo
Munhango
Luena
Cassamba
Caconda
Dongo
Cuchi
Cangumbe
Luanguinga
Dima
Mongu
Mumbwa
Mazabuka
Kafue

ZAMBIA
Lusaka
Livingstone
Cabora Bassa Res.
Zumbo

ZIMBABWE (RHODESIA)

Harare (Salisbury)
Kadoma
Chegutu
Chivhu
Shurugwi
Kwekwe
Gweru
Masvingo
Bulawayo
Zvishavane

MOZAMBIQUE
Beira
Vila de Manica
Tete
Zomba
Blantyre
Chiromo

MALAWI
Lilongwe

OWAMBO
NAMIBIA
DAMARALAND
Windhoek
Swakopmund
Walvis Bay (S. Africa)
Rehoboth

GREAT NAMALAND
Lüderitz
Keetmanshoop
Aroab

BOTSWANA
KALAHARI DESERT
Ghanzi
Serowe
Palapye
Gaborone
Molepolole
Lobatse

TRANSVAAL
BOPHUTHATSWANA
Pretoria
Krugersdorp
JOHANNESBURG
Benoni
Germiston
SWAZI-LAND
Mbabane
Maputo (Lourenço Marques)

ORANGE FREE STATE
Kimberley
Bloemfontein
LESOTHO
Maseru
NATAL
Pietermaritzburg
Durban

SOUTH AFRICA
CAPE
Cape Town
Port Elizabeth
East London
TRANSKEI
CISKEI

The "Homelands" (Bophuthatswana, Ciskei, Transkei, Venda) were unilaterally created by South Africa and are not internationally recognized.

1 Bophuthatswana
2 Ciskei
3 Transkei
4 Venda

CAPE TOWN (inset)

ROBBEN Island
Bloubergstrand
Durbanville
Milnerton
Parow
Bellville
Goodwood
Kuilsrivier
Pinelands
CAPE FLATS
Nuweland
Wynberg
Ottery
Muizenberg
SEAL ISLAND
Simonstad
Kommetjie
CAPE OF GOOD HOPE
KAAPPUNT
Scale 1:1,050,000

Scale 1:16,850,000 ; one inch to 265 miles. Sinusoidal Projection
Elevations and depressions are given in feet

Inset map (Johannesburg–Pretoria area)

Wolhuterskop, Jacksonstuin, Kosmos, Skeerpoort, Hennopsrivier, Foothills, Tarlton, Krugersdorp, Roodepoort, Randfontein, Orlando, Turffontein, Pretoria North, **Pretoria**, Swartspruit, Voortrekkerhoogte, Valhalla, Irene, Lyttelton, Halfway House, Kaalfontein, Modderfontein, Kempton Park, Alexandra, Edenvale, Primrose, Boksburg, Germiston, Brakpan, Springs, **JOHANNESBURG**, Discovery, Florida, Maraisburg, Rosettenville, Pimville, Benoni, Silverton, Rayton, Cullinan, Tierpoort, Bapsfontein, Putfontein

MAGALIESBERG, WITWATERSBERG, WITWATERSRAND

Scale 1:1,050,000

Main map

SOMALIA, Kismaayo, Buur Gaabo, Witu, Lamu, Malindi, Takaungu, Mombasa, Vanga, Tanga, Pangani, Zanzibar, ZANZIBAR, Bagamoyo, Dar es Salaam, Morogoro, Kisaki, Utete, Mahenge, Kilwa Kivinje, Lindi, Masasi, Mikindani, Moçímboa da Praia, Ibo, Pemba, Lúrio, Memba, Nacala, Moçambique, Angoche, ILHA ANGOCHE, Pebane, Quelimane

KENYA, Nairobi, Mt. Kenya, Moshi, Kilimanjaro 19 340

PEMBA ISLAND, MAFIA, CABO DELGADO

COMOROS, Moroni, NJAZIDJA, NZWANI, MWALI, Dzaoudzi, MAYOTTE (Fr.)

ALDABRA IS. (Sey.), COSMOLEDO GROUP (Sey.), ÎLES GLORIEUSES (Fr.), CAP D'AMBRE, Antsiranana, NOSY BE

MADAGASCAR, Antananarivo, Mahajanga, Mandritsara, Maroantsetra, Iharaña, Fenoarivo Atsinanana, Toamasina, Moramanga, Vatomandry, Ambositra, Mahanoro, Manakara, Fianarantsoa, Ivohibé, Farafangana, Manakara, Betroka, Mahaly, Morombe, Morondava, Maintirano, Besalampy, Toliara, Trafonomby 6417, Farodofay

CAP SAINT ANDRÉ, NOSY BARREN, CAP STE. MARIE

ÎLE JUAN DE NOVA (Fr.), BASSAS DA INDIA (Fr.), EUROPA (Fr.)

MOZAMBIQUE CHANNEL, INDIAN OCEAN

ORANGE FREE STATE, Arlington, Paul Roux, Bethlehem, Kestell, Harrismith, Senekal, Fouriesburg, Clarens, ROYAL NATAL NAT'L PK., Bergville, Winterton, Ladysmith, Ficksburg, Clocolan, Butha Buthe, Leribe, Pitseng, Teyateyaneng, Maseru, Mokhotlong, Roma, Mohale's Hoek, Quthing, Matatiele, Cedarville, Kokstad

LESOTHO, MALOTI MTS., Thabana Ntlenyana, DRAKENSBERG

NATAL, Dundee, Glencoe, Dannhauser, Wasbank, Nqutu, Mahlabatini, Pomeroy, Nkandla, Melmoth, Babanango, Colenso, Estcourt, Weenen, Greytown, Mooirivier, New Hanover, Howick, Pietermaritzburg, Camperdown, Richmond, Donnybrook, Ixopo, Pinetown, Durban, Isipingo, Umkomaas, Scottburgh, Park Rynie, Sezela, Umtentweni, Port Shepstone, Uvongo Beach, Margate, Port Edward, Stanger, Verulam, Kranskop, Eshowe, Mapumulo, Mid Illovo, Umzinto

SOUTH AFRICA

TRANSKEI, Herschel, Barkly East, Maclear, Ugie, Qumbu, Tsolo, Mount Frere, Tabankulu, Bizana, Harding, Mount Ayliff, Mount Fletcher, Matatiele, Franklin, Swartberg, Mount Frere, Engcobo, Umtata, Mqanduli, Elliotdale, Ngqeleni, Libode, Lusikisiki, Port St. Johns, RAME HEAD, Idutywa, Willowvale, Butterworth, Kentani, Tsomo, Ngamakwe, Cofimvaba, Tsomo

Jamestown, Rossouw, Dordrecht, Indwe, Cala, Queenstown, Sterkstroom, Molteno, STORMBERG, Lady Frere, Tarkastad, Waverly, Tylden, Cathcart, Whittlesea, Seymour, Stutterheim, Frankfort, Komga, Kei Mouth, Morgan's Bay, King William's Town, Berlin, Breidbach, East London, Kidd's Beach, Gonubie

CAPE, CISKEI, Bisho, Keiskammahoek, Alice, Fort Beaufort, Adelaide, Bedford, Somerset East, Pearston, Cradock, BANKBERG 6606, WINTERBERG 7778, SUURBERGE, Riebeek-Oos, Alicedale, Kirkwood, Addo, Uitenhage, Salem, Grahamstown, Peddie, Hamburg, Bathurst, Port Alfred (Kowie), Alexandria, Kenton, Port Elizabeth, KAAP RECIFE

SAINT CROIX ISLAND, BIRD ISLAND

INDIAN OCEAN

Scale 1:4,200,000

40,000 SQ MI AREA

Cities, Towns, and Villages: 0 to 25,000 · 25,000 to 100,000 · 100,000 to 250,000 · 250,000 to 1,000,000 · 1,000,000 and over · Major urbanized area

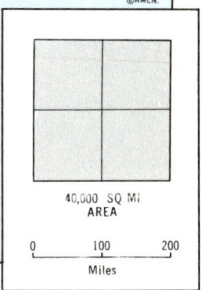

Longitude East of Greenwich

Australia, New Zealand, Oceania/Terrain

The vast expanse of the Pacific is dotted with islands. Some are the tips of volcanoes that push up through the blue waters. Others are atolls, rings of coral surrounding calm lagoons which remain where volcanic peaks have sunk back into the sea. This area includes New Zealand and Australia and is called Oceania.

Australia is the smallest of the continents, yet it has unique features that are world famous—among them the Great Barrier Reef and the "Outback."

The Great Barrier Reef borders the eastern edge of Cape York Peninsula in the north and continues south along the coast for 1,250 miles (2,011.62 kilometers). Coral formations in shades of pink, green, orange, yellow, and purple rise from the ocean floor. Great numbers of different kinds of fish and other sea creatures glide through the tropical waters.

West of the Great Dividing Range, in the central part of the country, is one of the world's lonely desert regions. Australians call it the Outback. Part of it is bush country, where an occasional stunted tree or bush grows.

Australia, New Zealand, Oceania Facts

Australia
Smallest continent
Population: 14,680,000
Highest mountain: Kosciusko, 7,310 feet (2,228.08 meters)

New Zealand
Two main islands, North Island and South Island
Population: 3,125,000

Oceania (not including Australia and New Zealand)
20,000 islands—more or less—scattered throughout the Pacific
Population: 5,095,000

The mountains of New Zealand's North Island give way in the southwest to hills and then to raised beaches washed by the sea.

Two of Fiji's 800 islands in the South Pacific are large, with lovely tree-lined beaches. Most of the others are merely piles of sand on coral reefs.

Ayers Rock towers 1,100 feet (335.28 meters) above the flat Australian desert.

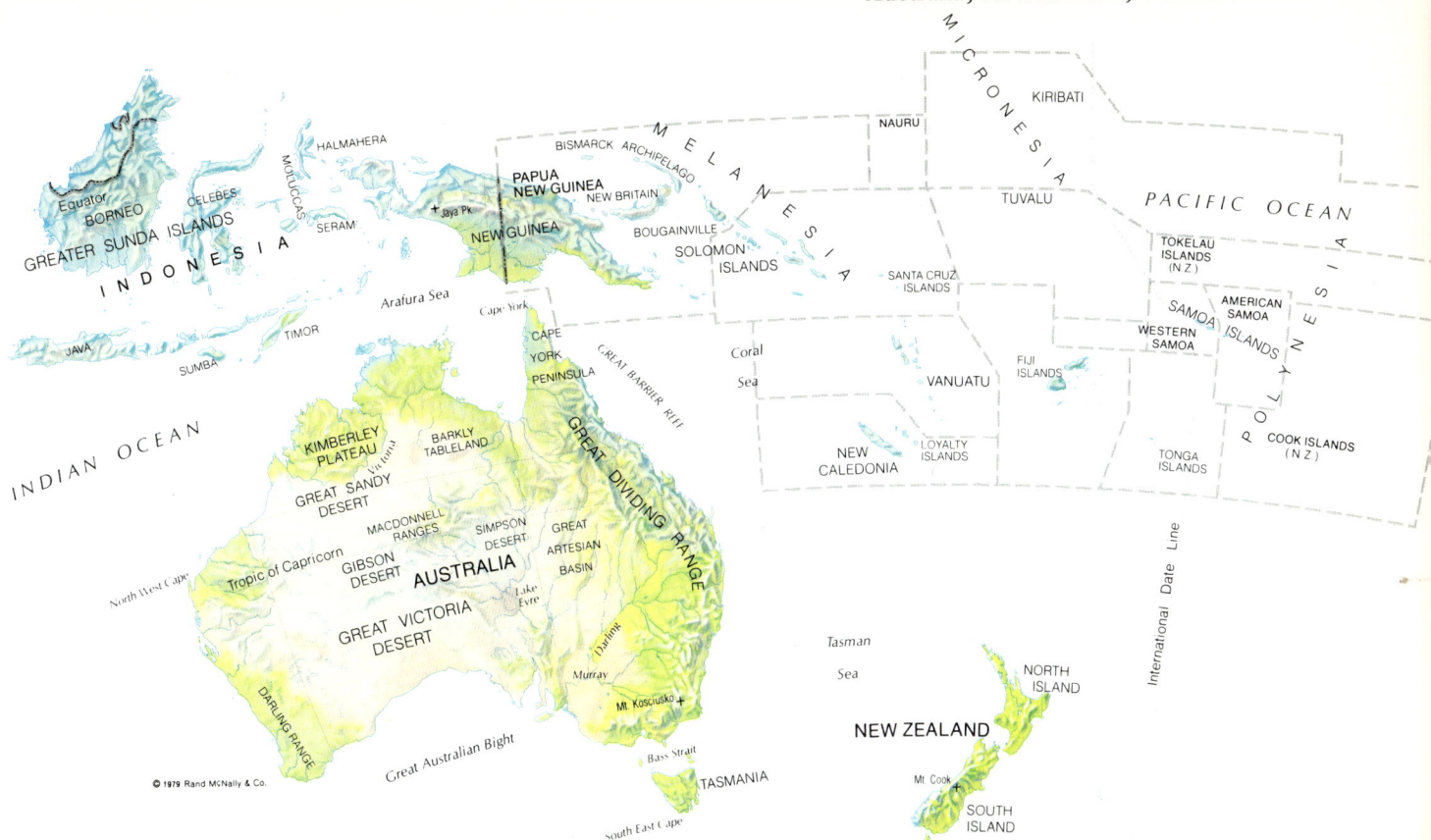

The rest consists of three main deserts—the Great Sandy, the Gibson, and the Great Victoria. Glaring sun fries the sand, rocks, and clay, and only those animals who have adapted over long centuries to desert life are able to survive.

Rain is kept out of the Outback by the Great Dividing Range. Air moving inland from the Tasman Sea is blocked and forced upward. As it rises it cools and drops its moisture along the coast. The continent's main agricultural area is here. Lush wheat fields and big herds of fluffy-backed sheep have made Australia a leading exporter of grain and wool.

The Great Dividing Range, Australia's main mountain chain, hugs the eastern and southeastern coast for about two thousand miles (3,218.6 kilometers). In the south it dips into the sea and pushes upward again 130 miles (209.20 kilometers) from the mainland to form the island state of Tasmania. The hump-shaped mountains of the Great Dividing Range are old, hammered by the wind and rain for hundreds of millions of years. They are not as spectacular as the Alps or Rockies, yet they have their own haunting beauty, especially in the deep canyons of the Blue Mountains near Sydney.

The southwestern coast also has low mountains, the Darling Range, which prevent the movement inland of rain clouds. The coastal area is fertile, and wheat and sheep are raised here.

Very different from the arid Outback and the agricultural regions around the eastern and southwestern edges of the continent is Cape York Peninsula in the north. Heat and rain combine here to make ideal conditions for the growth of tropical jungles.

New Zealand is often linked with Australia. But they are individual countries separated by nearly 1,200 miles (1,931.16 kilometers) of lonely ocean, and their landscapes are completely different.

Two main islands make up New Zealand. They are appropriately called North and South Island. Snowy mountains jab upward from almost all of South Island and from much of North Island. On the southwest coast of South Island the mountains send long shoulders into the sea where they form waterways as beautiful as the fjords of Norway.

The most unusual area of New Zealand is the volcanic region around Lake Taupo on North Island. Here there are boiling springs, geysers with hot water leaping skyward, strange pools of steaming mud, and tiny lakes with beds of brightly colored rocks. Beautiful waterfalls tumble from the encircling volcanic peaks.

South Island, the larger of the two, has magnificent mountain scenery. Glistening glaciers nestle among the heights, and seventeen peaks soar above 10,000 feet (3,048 meters).

The islands of Oceania are thought of in three parts. Most of Polynesia is east of the International Date Line and includes Hawaii, Samoa, Tahiti, and Easter Island. Micronesia in the central Pacific includes the Marshall, Caroline, and Gilbert islands. Melanesia in the southwest includes the Fiji Islands and New Guinea. New Guinea is the second largest island in the world. Only Greenland is bigger.

An expedition headed by Ferdinand Magellan was the first to sail around the world, 1519 to 1522. Crossing the Pacific, Magellan sighted only two islands and finally landed on Guam. There are thousands of islands in Oceania. To have missed all but two was, in a way, a remarkable coincidence!

100° 110° 120° 130° 1 0°

SINGAPORE

BORNEO

CELEBES

SERAM

Jayapu

0°

Palembang

Java Sea

Ujung Pandang

SUMATRA

JAKARTA

Surabaya

Arafura Sea

Banjarmasin

JAVA

SUMBA

TIMOR

Timor

Sea

Darwin

Gulf of

10°

CAPE
YORK
PENINSUL

Daly

INDIAN OCEAN

Carpentaria

KIMBERLEY
PLATEAU

Victoria

Broome

Fitzroy

Mount Isa

GREAT SANDY DESERT

Alice Springs

GREAT
ARTESIAN
BASIN

20°

GIBSON DESERT

SIMPSON
DESERT

Tropic of Capricorn

Carnarvon

GREAT VICTORIA DESERT

Lake
Eyre

Kalgoorlie

NULLARBOR PLAIN

Lake
Gairdner

Broken
Hill

90°

30°

DARLING RA.

Great Australian Bight

Murray

Perth

Adelaide

FLINDERS RANGES

🟥	●	Urban
		Cropland
		Cropland & Woodland
		Cropland & Grazing Land
		Grassland, Grazing Land
		Forest, Woodland
		Swamp, Marshland
		Shrub, Sparse Grass, Wasteland (pattern)
		Barren Land

INDIAN OCEAN

40°

100° 110° 120° 130° 140°

Scale 1:24,800,000 ; one inch to 390 miles. Lambert Azimuthal Equal-Area Projection

NEW
GUINEA

NEW BRITAIN

SOLOMON ISLANDS

rt Moresby

Equator

KIRIBATI

P A C I F I C   O C E A N

0°

Coral   Sea

Cairns

Townsville

VANUATU

SAMOA ISLANDS

Pago Pago

10°

FIJI
ISLANDS

Rockhampton

NEW
CALEDONIA

ÎLES
LOYAUTÉ

Suva

GREAT DIVIDING RANGE

Nouméa

TONGA ISLANDS

20°

Brisbane

SYDNEY

Canberra

Tasman   Sea

P A C I F I C

30°

Auckland

MELBOURNE

NORTH ISLAND

GREAT DIVIDING RANGE

O C E A N

TASMANIA

Hobart

SOUTHERN ALPS

Wellington

Christchurch

SOUTH ISLAND

A-590200-96

COPYRIGHT BY
RAND McNALLY & COMPANY
MADE IN U.S.A.

STEWART
ISLAND

Dunedin

40°

0	100	200		400		600		800 Miles

0	150	300		600		900		1200 Kilometers

Australia, New Zealand, Oceania/Animals

Black Marlin

Triggerfish

Butterfly Fish

Cockatoo

Dingo

Death Adder

Cassowary

Tree Kangaroo

Echidna

Emu

Frilled Lizard

Rabbit

Rock Wallaby

Wombat

Great Gray Kangaroo

Kookaburra

Koala

Red Kangaroo

Platypus

Wandering Albatross

White Shark

Slender-billed Shearwater

Black Swan

Dovey Petrel

Kiwi

Tuatara

Kea

Many of the animals of Australia are very different from those in other places, for Australia was separated from all other parts of the world for about 50 million years and its animals developed in a different way. Most Australian mammals are *marsupials*. Marsupials are animals like the kangaroo whose babies are kept in a pouch on the mother's body until they are old enough to care for themselves. Two of the strangest Australian animals are the echidna, or spiny anteater, and the duck-billed platypus. They are furry and warm-blooded mammals, but their babies hatch out of eggs!

Much of Australia is covered by a desert or by dry plains, but many animals live in these dry lands. Kangaroos, wallabies, wombats, and bandicoots are among the plains marsupials. One plains dweller, the dingo, is not a marsupial. This wild dog was brought here by prehistoric people. Other desert dwellers include lizards, snakes, and a bird known as the emu.

In the eastern part of Australia lives the koala, a tree-dwelling marsupial. The many rabbits in Australia were brought from England long ago.

On some islands near New Zealand live little reptiles called tuataras. They are the descendants of reptiles that lived before the dinosaurs—the only creatures of their kind anywhere in the world!

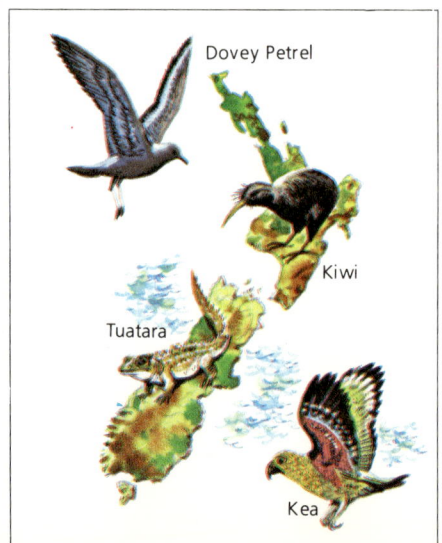

Australia, New Zealand, Oceania/Countries and Cities

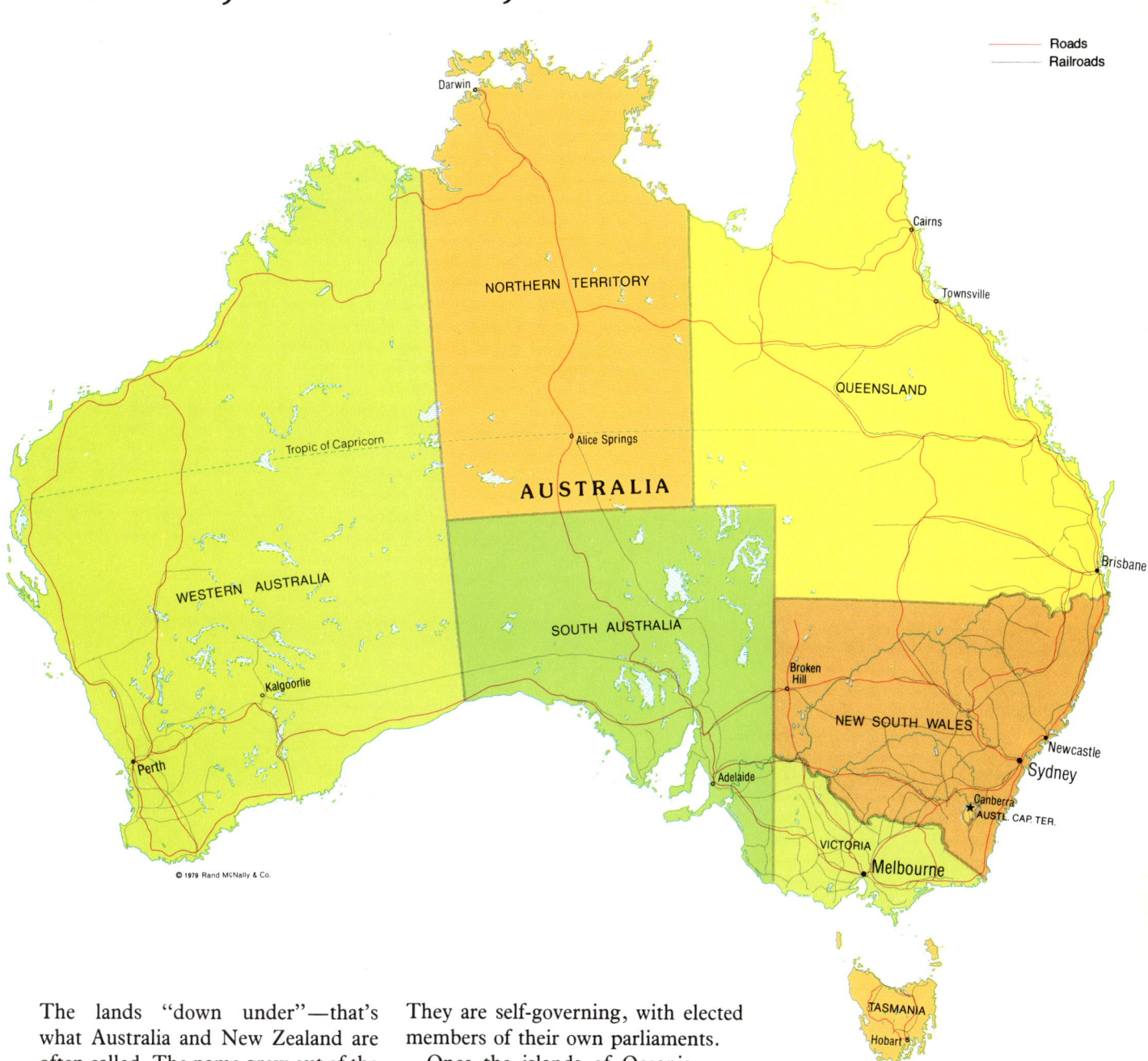

Roads
Railroads

DARWIN

NORTHERN TERRITORY

Cairns

Townsville

QUEENSLAND

Tropic of Capricorn

Alice Springs

AUSTRALIA

WESTERN AUSTRALIA

SOUTH AUSTRALIA

Brisbane

Kalgoorlie

Broken Hill

NEW SOUTH WALES

Newcastle

Sydney

Adelaide

Canberra
AUSTL. CAP. TER.

Perth

VICTORIA

Melbourne

© 1979 Rand McNally & Co.

TASMANIA

Hobart

NEW ZEALAND

Auckland

Wellington

Christchurch

Dunedin

© 1979 Rand McNally & Co.

The lands "down under"—that's what Australia and New Zealand are often called. The name grew out of the idea that these lands were directly opposite, under the feet of, Europeans.

In some ways things in the two countries actually are the opposite of those in the Northern Hemisphere. To go north is to head for the warmth of the equator, and to go south is to travel toward cold weather. Winter occurs in July and summer in January. However, only the physical setting is "opposite." Many customs would be familiar to a traveler from Europe or America, for they were handed down by British settlers.

Both countries are members of the British Commonwealth of Nations.

They are self-governing, with elected members of their own parliaments.

Once the islands of Oceania were colonies of foreign powers. Since 1962 many have become independent. The eastern half of New Guinea is a nation. So are Nauru, Fiji, Tonga, Western Samoa, and the Solomon Islands.

In a way, East and West have met in the Pacific. The islanders—descended from Asian ancestors—explored the sea and created highly developed civilizations on some of the islands. Hundreds of years later, explorers from the West "discovered" the lands, and colonies soon followed. Today, remains of the ancient island customs exist side by side with the European way of life.

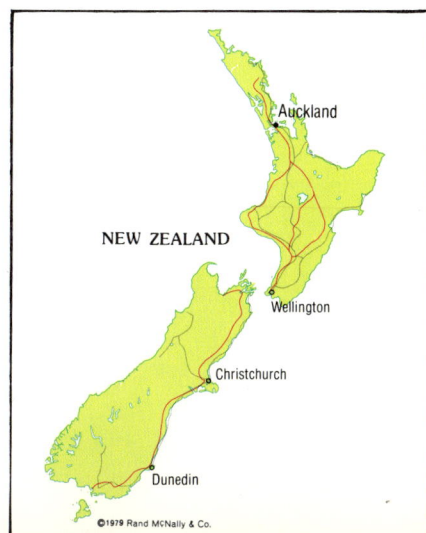

INDONESIA

Pasuruan

G. Mahameru 12 060

Singaraja

Selat

Bali

LOMBOK

SUMBAWA

Sumbawa Besar

Bima

FLORES

Waingapu

SUMBA

SAWU

ALOR

LOMBLEN PANTAR

Dili

TIMOR

Kupang

ROTI

SELARU

TANJUNG VALS

ARAFURA SEA

C. VAN DIEMEN

CROKER

MELVILLE

Van Diemen Gulf

BATHURST

COBURG PEN.

Clarence Str.

Darwin

WESSEL IS.

CAPE ARNHEM

GULF OF

Blue Mud Bay

GROOTE EYLANDT

Limmen Bight

SIR EDWARD PELLEW GROUP

WELLESLEY

CARPENTAR.

SUNDA ISLANDS

SAVU SEA

TIMOR SEA

INDIAN OCEAN

SUNDA TRENCH

CAPE LONDONDERRY

Joseph Bonaparte Gulf

Queens Chan.

ARNHEM LAND

Pine Creek

Katherine

Birdum

Borroloola

Wyndham

BUCCANEER ARCH.

Sundau Str.

Collier Bay

CAPE LEVEQUE

King Sd.

Mt. Hann 2800

KING LEOPOLD RANGES

Derby

DAMPIER LAND

GEKIE RANGE

Fitzroy Crossing

Halls Creek

Roebuck Bay

LaGrange

EIGHTY MILE BEACH

Victoria River Downs

Daly Waters

Newcastle Waters

Woods L.

Tanami

BARKLY TABLELAND

Burketown

NORTHERN

Tennant Creek

Camooweal

Dobby

Mount Isa

Malb

Dajarra

Di

QU

A

NORTHERN TERRITORY

LARREY POINT

RIPON

DAMPIER ARCH.

MONTE BELLO IS.

BARROW

NORTH WEST CAPE

POINT CLOATES

CAPE FARQUHAR

Port Hedland

DeGrey

Roebourne

Marble Bar

Nullagine

GREAT SANDY DESERT

Mackay

Barrow Creek

Mt. Ziel 4955

MACDONNELL RANGES

Arltunga

Alice Springs

JAMES RANGE

Hav

SIMPSON

A

Fortescue

Millstream

Onslow

HAMERSLEY RANGE

Mt. Bruce 4024

Ashburton

Jiggalong

Disappointment

Macdonal

GIBSON DESERT

Amadeus

Darke L.

DESERT

Charlotte Water

Birdsville

Diam

Tropic of Capricorn

CAPE GEORGE

Carnarvon

Gascoyne

Peak Hill

Nabberu

Carnegie

Wells

Gillen

WESTERN

MUSGRAVE RANGES

Mt. Woodroffe 4970

EVERARD RANGES

The Alberga

Oodnadatta

BERNIER DORRE

Shark Bay

DIRK HARTOG

STEEP POINT

Meekatharra

Nannine

Cue

Sandstone

Austin

Mount Magnet

Wiluna

Yeo

Carey

AUSTRALIA

Laverton

GREAT VICTORIA DESERT

Everard

STUART RANGE

William Creek

Eyre 39

SOUTH AUSTRALIA

Marree

Grege

HOUTMAN ROCKS

Geraldton

Ajana

Northampton

Dongarra

Mingenew

Pithara

Milling

Moora

Barlee L.

Moore L.

Menzies

Kalgoorlie

Coolgardie

Boulder

Goddards Soak

Rawlinna

Eucla

NULLARBOR PLAIN

Oldea Station

Hughes

POINT FOWLER

Penong

Ceduna

Oodea

Eyre L.

FLINDERS RANGES

Woomera

Pimba

Kuchlich

FLIN

Port Augusta

DARLING RANGE

Lake Brown

Southern Cross

Lefroy

Cowan

Norseman

Dundas

Eyre

GREAT AUSTRALIAN BIGHT

EYRE PENINSULA

Whyalla

Port Pirie

Peterba

Gladstone

SWANLAND

Perth

Fremantle

Northam

York

Collie

Narrogin

Salmon Gums

Esperance

Port Lincoln

Moonta

Port Waket

Gawler

Adel

Emu

Bri

Geographe Bay

Bunbury

Busselton

CAPE NATURALISTE

Katanning

Hopetoun

Ravensthorpe

ARCHIPELAGO OF THE RECHERCHE

KANGAROO

Narac

CAPE LEEUWIN

Nornalup

Albany

King George Sd.

CAPE JAFFA

Kingston

Mt. Gar

PT. D'ENTRECASTEAUX

WEST CAPE HOWE

INDIAN OCEAN

Longitude East of Greenwich

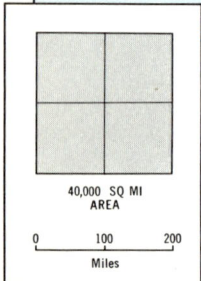

40,000 SQ MI AREA

0   100   200

Miles

Cities and Towns

0 to 50,000

50,000 to 500,000

500,000 to 1,000,000

1,000,000 and over

Longitude East of Greenwich
Scale 1:16,850,000; one inch to 265 miles. Lambert's Azimuthal, Equal Area Projection
Elevations and depressions are given in feet

Main Map

NEW GUINEA — PAPUA NEW GUINEA
Mt. Albert Edward, Buna, TROBRIAND IS., WOODLARK, Mt. Victoria 13,363, Port Moresby, OWEN STANLEY, D'ENTRECASTEAUX ISLANDS
Torres Strait, MULGRAVE, THURSDAY, BANKS, HORN, PRINCE OF WALES, CAPE YORK, SOUTH CAPE, Samarai, LOUISIADE ARCHIPELAGO, TAGULA, ROSSEL

CHOISEUL, VELLA LAVELLA, RENDOVA, NEW GEORGIA, SANTA ISABEL, FLORIDA, MALAITA, RUSSELL IS., TULAGI, Honiara, GUADALCANAL, SOLOMON ISLANDS, SAN CRISTOBAL, RENNELL, SANTA CRUZ ISLANDS

CAPE YORK PENINSULA, Weipa, TORRES IS., BANKS ISLANDS, ESPIRITU SANTO, MAEWO, PENTECOST, MALEKULA, AMBRIM, EPI, VANUATU, AMBAE, EFATE, Vila

CORAL SEA
OSPREY REEF, CAPE MELVILLE, Laura, Cooktown, HOLMES REEFS, WILLIS IS., Palmerville, ATHERTON, Cairns, PLATEAU, Mungana, Mt. Bartle Frere 5287, FLINDERS REEFS, LIHOU REEFS, Forsayth, Ingham, HINCHINBROOK, TREGROSSE IS., Croydon, ormanton, Charters Towers, Townsville, Halifax Bay, GREAT, Bowen, WHITSUNDAY, MARION REEF, Richmond, Hughenden, CUMBERLAND IS., Repulse Bay, Mt. Dalrymple 4190, Mackay, ILES CHESTERFIELD (Fr.), ILES BELEP, EROMANGA, TANA, ANEITYUM, NEW CALEDONIA (Fr.), ILES LOYAUTE (French), OUVEA, LIFOU, MARE, Noumea, ILE DES PINS

PACIFIC OCEAN

QUEENSLAND — GREAT DIVIDING RANGE
ncurry, Kynuna, Winton, Barcaldine, Jericho, Clermont, Emerald, Dingo, Rockhampton, Mount Morgan, CURTIS, Gladstone, BUCKLAND TABLELAND, Blackall, Tambo, Yaraka, NORTHUMBERLAND IS., SWAIN REEFS, Bundaberg, Hervey Bay, SANDY CAPE, FRASER, Maryborough, WRECK REEFS, Capricorn Chan.
Windorah, GREY RANGE, Quilpie, Charleville, Roma, Gympie, Thargomindah, Cunnamulla, St. George, Dirranbandi, DARLING DOWNS, Toowoomba, Ipswich, Brisbane, Southport, N. STRADBROKE I.
Hungerford, Mungindi, Warwick, Mt. Roberts 4493, Tenterfield, Lismore

NEW SOUTH WALES
MAIN BARRIER RANGE, Bourke, Brewarrina, Walgett, Moree, Inverell, Glen Innes, NEW ENGLAND RANGE, Grafton, Wilcannia, Cobar, Coonamble, Narrabri, Armidale, The Round Mountain 5300, oken Hill, Nyngan, Tamworth, Kempsey, WARRUMBUNGLE RA., LIVERPOOL RA., Port Macquarie, MURRAY, Nymagee, Dubbo, Forbes, Orange, Bathurst, Lithgow, Cessnock, Maitland, Newcastle, RIVERINA, Hay, Narrandera, BLUE MTS., SYDNEY, Botany Bay, bingo, Wagga Wagga, Goulburn, Wollongong, aura, Albury, Canberra, AUSTL. CAP. TER., Jervis Bay, Cooma, mark, Denliquin, Mt. Kosciusko 7316, SNOWY MTS., Bega, Bombala

VICTORIA
Echuca, Bendigo, Benalla, GREAT, CAPE HOWE, Ararat, Maryborough, Bairnsdale, Ballarat, Geelong, MELBOURNE, NINETY MILE BEACH, rland, Warrnambool, Wonthaggi, CAPE OTWAY, WILSON'S PROMONTORY, Port Phillip, KING, FLINDERS, FURNEAUX GROUP, CAPE BARREN
MURRAY, TASMAN SEA

TASMANIA
HUNTER IS., Burnie, Ulverstone, Devonport, Launceston, Mt. Ossa 5305, Strahan, New Norfolk, Hobart, BRUNY, SOUTH EAST CAPE

LORD HOWE (NEW S. WALES)

Inset Map — New Zealand

PACIFIC OCEAN
NORTH CAPE, Kaitaia, Russell, GREAT BARRIER, Devonport, Auckland, NORTH ISLAND, Hamilton, Bay of Plenty, EAST CAPE, North Taranaki Bight, New Plymouth, C. EGMONT, Gisborne, NEW ZEALAND, South Taranaki Bight, Wanganui, Napier, Hastings, Palmerston North, CAPE FAREWELL, Karamea Bight, Nelson, Cook Strait, Lower Hutt, Wellington, TASMAN SEA, CAPE FOULWIND, Greymouth, Hokitika, SOUTH ISLAND, SOUTHERN ALPS, Mt. Cook 12,349, Pegasus Bay, Christchurch, Canterbury Bight, Timaru, CASCADE PT., RESOLUTION ISLAND, Dunedin, CAPE SAUNDERS, Foveaux Strait, Invercargill, STEWART ISLAND, SOUTHWEST CAPE, PACIFIC OCEAN
©RMcN.
Same scale as main map

Tropic of Capricorn

0　50　100　200　300　400　500 Miles
0　100　200　400　600　800 Kilometers

North America/Terrain

In many ways the terrain of most of North America is like that of South America. There is a mass of high mountains in the west, a block of lower highlands in the east, and a huge plain in between.

The western mountains are made up of two main chains that stretch from the arctic shores of Alaska to Panama in Central America. Best known are the Rocky Mountains which rise out of the Great Plains like an enormous blue wall. They are breathtaking in Colorado, where more than fifty peaks soar higher than 14,000 feet (4,267.2 meters).

The Rockies reach northward into Canada, where Mount Robson thrusts upward to 12,972 feet (3,953.86 meters). Here the scenery is wilder than it is in the United States. Evergreen forests cover the mountains' lower slopes. Above timberline—where trees are unable to grow—awesome glaciers crunch their way down stony canyons.

Many separate mountain ranges rise west of the Rockies—the Coast Mountains of Canada, and the Cascades, Sierra Nevada, and Coast ranges of the United States. Inactive volcanoes lie, like sleeping giants, among them. Mount Lassen last moved its mighty shoulders in 1914. Mounts Rainier and ancient Mazama whose hollow core holds the mirrorlike waters of Crater Lake have been dormant far longer. Then in March 1980 Mount St. Helens in Washington, dormant since 1857, erupted with a roar, sending plumes of steam more than a mile high and dropping ash 50 miles away—a reminder that sleeping giants can awaken at any time.

Between the Pacific mountain ranges and the Rockies, in the United States, lies the Great Basin. The Sierra Nevada and the Cascades prevent most of the rain clouds that form over the Pacific from reaching the Great Basin. The dry southern end of this

A great plain spreads across Canada's Prairie Provinces—Alberta, Manitoba, and Saskatchewan. Saskatchewan wheat ripens in the sun.

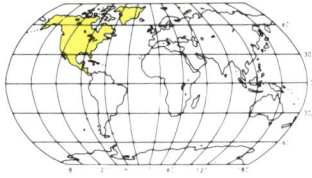

A shallow prehistoric sea once covered what was to become Arizona's Grand Canyon. Over millions of years rock layers built up with the rising and falling waters. It took millions more years for the Colorado River to gouge out the canyon.

Mexico's famous Mounts Popocatepetl and Iztaccihuatl can be seen for miles throughout the surrounding countryside. "Popo" is one of America's highest peaks. It is only 2,433 feet (741.57 meters) less than Alaska's Mount McKinley.

area is called the Mojave Desert. A desertlike region covers much of the American Southwest and reaches deep into the Mexican state of Sonora.

Mexico also has two main mountain ranges. The Sierra Madre Occidental is in the west and the Sierra Madre Oriental is in the east. Plateau country spreads out between them and it is here that most of Mexico's people live.

Two of North America's well-known volcanoes are in Mexico. They sit side by side in the central region—Popocatepetl, or "Popo" as the Mexicans fondly call it, and Iztacci-huatl. Some people see in Popocate-petl a warrior guarding a beautiful sleeping lady, as the second volcano appears to be. The legends are roman-tic, but the volcanoes have a fiery past. Iztaccihuatl last erupted in 1868. Popocatepetl has not erupted since 1702, but from time to time it still gives off a puff of smoke—a reminder of the power that lies deep within its boiling core.

Central America, farther south, is mountain country, except for the narrow plains along its coasts. It fairly bristles with volcanoes. There are more than thirty alone in the tiny country of Guatemala.

The uplands on the eastern side of North America are much lower than those in the West, but they have their own charm. In Canada are the Lauren-tian Mountains. These formed at the edge of a gigantic horseshoe-shaped plateau that surrounded Hudson Bay during the Ice Age.

In the eastern United States the largest upland area is the Appalachian chain which reaches from Maine to Alabama. These are old mountains, worn by time and weather. Among them are the White, Green, Blue Ridge, and Great Smoky Mountains.

One of the world's largest plains, the Great Plains, lies in the center of the continent. The land is wonderfully fertile. In eastern Canada farm-lands surround Toronto for 150 miles (241.39 kilometers). In western Canada, fields of wheat spread to the horizons. In the United States, the Great Plains form the nation's breadbas-ket—its wheat-growing lands.

The waters of the Great Plains are carried away by one of the biggest river systems in the world—the Mississippi-Missouri.

The largest freshwater lake in the world is found on the North American continent. Lake Superior, one of the five Great Lakes, was born during the Ice Age when the glacier scooped out the lake beds.

North America reaches beyond the Arctic Circle in the north. The end of the Boothia Peninsula is the north-ernmost mainland point. At its southern tip, beyond Panama, it dips to within 700 miles (1,126.51 kilometers) of the equator and joins South America.

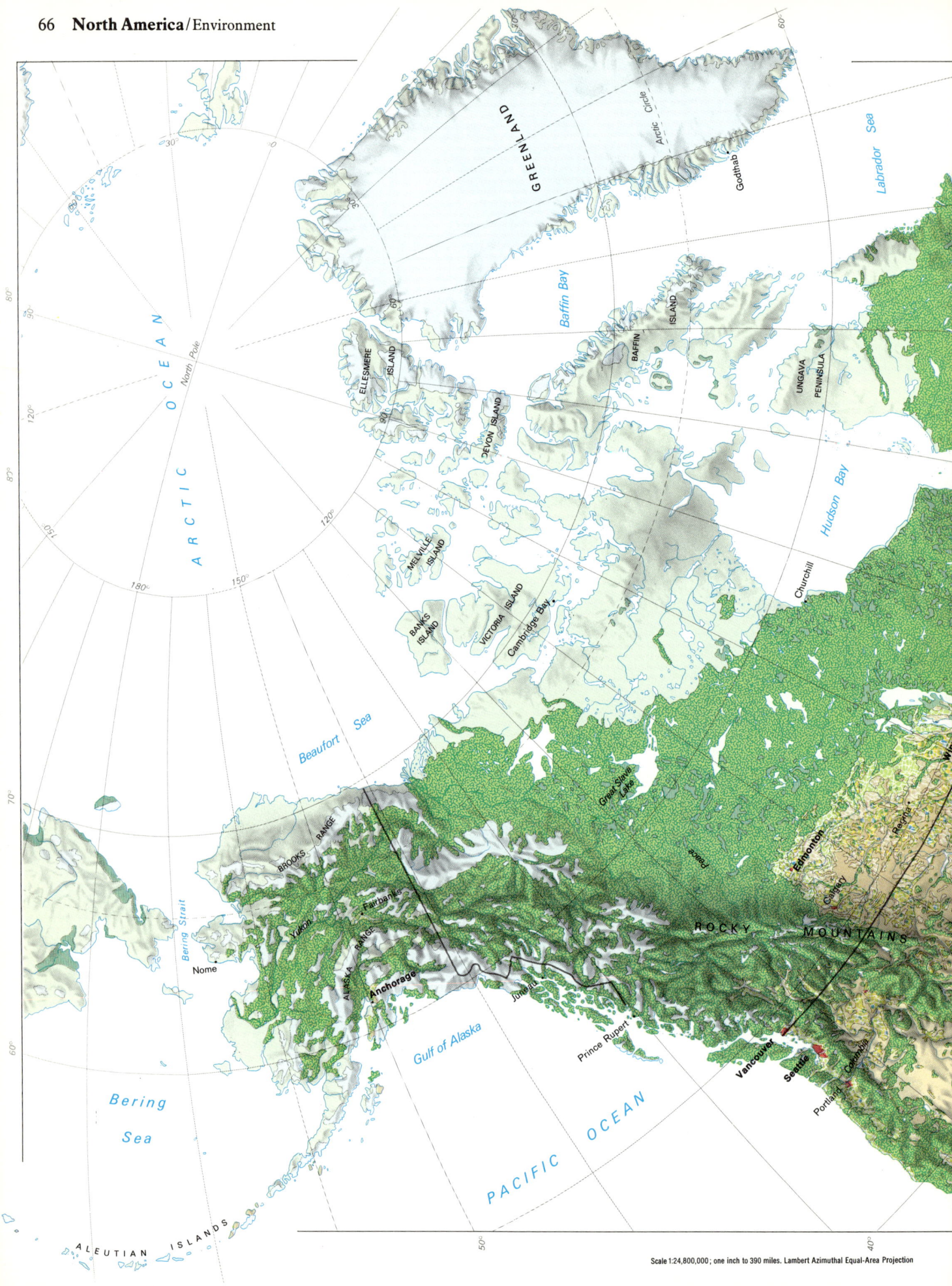

GREENLAND

Godthab

Labrador Sea

Arctic Circle

Baffin Bay

ELLESMERE ISLAND

BAFFIN ISLAND

DEVON ISLAND

UNGAVA PENINSULA

Hudson Bay

MELVILLE ISLAND

BANKS ISLAND

VICTORIA ISLAND

Cambridge Bay

Churchill

A R C T I C   O C E A N

North Pole

Beaufort Sea

Great Slave Lake

BROOKS RANGE

Peace

Fairbanks

Yukon

ALASKA RANGE

Nome

Anchorage

Juneau

R O C K Y   M O U N T A I N S

Edmonton

Calgary

Regina

Winn

Bering Strait

Prince Rupert

Gulf of Alaska

Vancouver

Seattle

Columbia

Portland

Bering Sea

P A C I F I C   O C E A N

ALEUTIAN ISLANDS

Scale 1:24,800,000; one inch to 390 miles. Lambert Azimuthal Equal-Area Projection

St. John's
Halifax

A T L A N T I C

O C E A N

St. Lawrence

MONTREAL

BOSTON
NEW YORK
PHILADELPHIA
WASHINGTON

TORONTO
Lake Ontario
Lake Erie
Pittsburgh

Lake Huron

Lake Superior

Lake Michigan

DETROIT
Cincinnati
Nashville
Ohio
Atlanta

APPALACHIAN MOUNTAINS

CHICAGO

Mississippi

Minneapolis

ST. LOUIS

Kansas City
Missouri
Omaha

Bismarck

Rapid City

Billings

R O C K Y   M O U N T A I N S

Denver

Dallas

Houston

New Orleans

Jacksonville

Gulf of Mexico

Miami
Nassau
BAHAMA ISLANDS
Havana
CUBA
Tropic of Cancer

San Juan
PUERTO RICO
HISPANIOLA
Port au-Prince
JAMAICA   Kingston

Caribbean Sea

Maracaibo
CARACAS
TRINIDAD

Rio Grande

SIERRA   MADRE   ORIENTAL

Monterrey

Chihuahua

SIERRA   MADRE   OCCIDENTAL

Mazatlán

Rio Grande

Guadalajara

MEXICO CITY

SIERRA MADRE DEL SUR

Mérida

San Salvador

Managua

San José

Panamá

P A C I F I C

O C E A N

SAN FRANCISCO

Salt Lake City
Great Basin

SIERRA NEVADA

LOS ANGELES

Phoenix

Colorado

Golfo de California

La Paz

A-520000- 96 ꞏ-1 ꞏ-3 ×
COPYRIGHT BY
RAND McNALLY & COMPANY
MADE IN U.S.A.

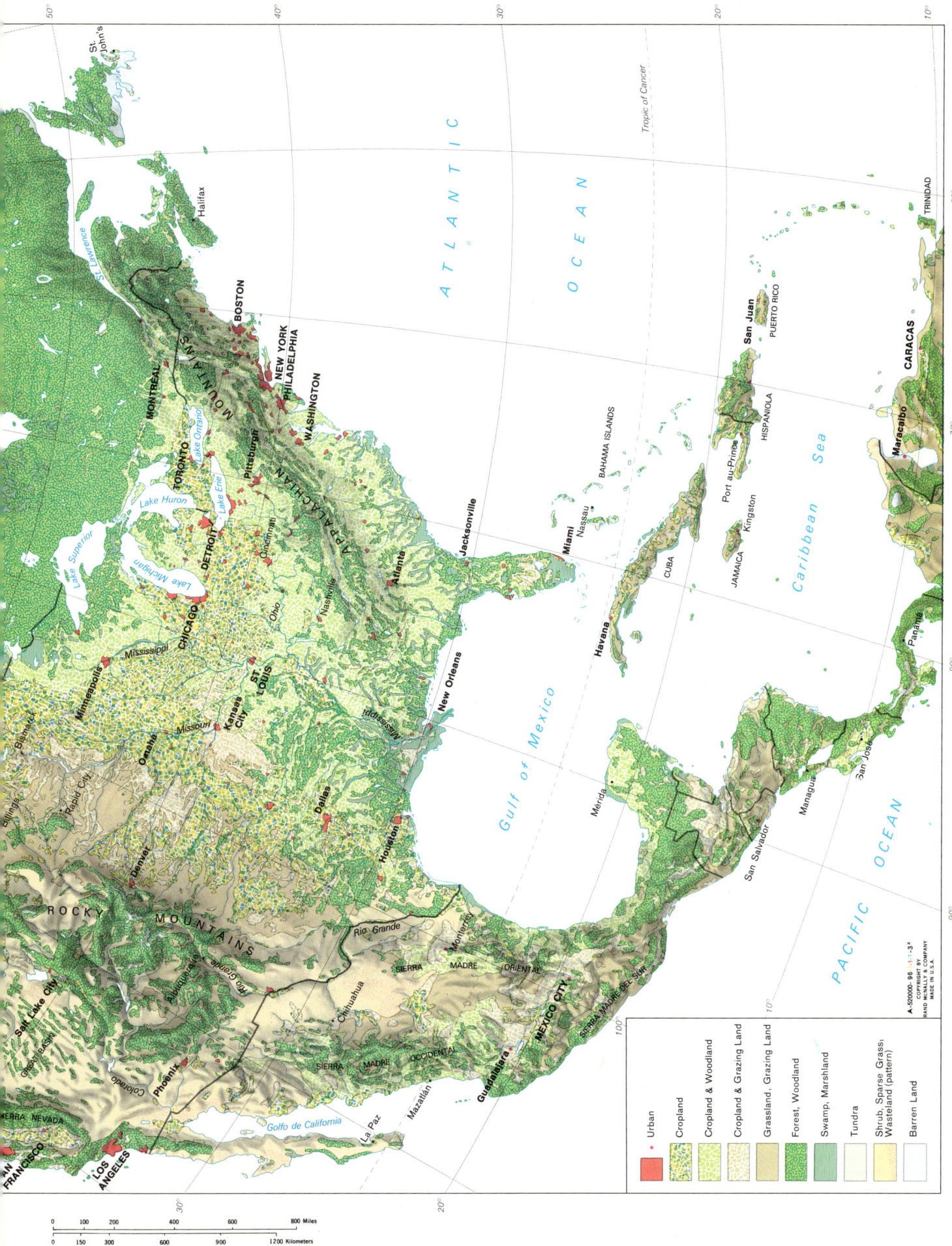

Urban
Cropland
Cropland & Woodland
Cropland & Grazing Land
Grassland, Grazing Land
Forest, Woodland
Swamp, Marshland
Tundra
Shrub, Sparse Grass;
Wasteland (pattern)
Barren Land

0   100   200   400   600   800 Miles
0   150   300   600   900   1200 Kilometers

North America/Animals

North America once teemed with wildlife. But, in just the last hundred years or so, many kinds of creatures have grown fewer, and some are extinct. However, in national parks, and in deserts and other places where there are few people, many kinds of animals can still be found. And some animals have adapted to living near people and busy communities.

The most "typical" North American animal, the big, shaggy buffalo, or American bison, was once nearly wiped out by hunters. But a few were saved, and today herds of thousands still rumble over the rolling plains in a few national parks.

In the northern woods beavers build dams in streams where black bears catch fish. Porcupines amble through the underbrush, and the lynx stalks

its prey. Moose, wapiti, and caribou are found in the north, and far in the north tiny herds of long-haired musk-ox wander.

Packs of wolves still hunt in Canada and the northern United States, but their numbers are growing fewer. However, the smart, bold coyote is growing in numbers, and even prowls the outskirts of towns and cities. Flying squirrels, which only come out at night to glide from tree to tree, and also raccoons and squirrels can be found in almost any wooded area. There are rabbits and chipmunks in every meadow.

Twenty-nine kinds of rattlesnakes live throughout North America. Biggest of them is the eastern diamondback, often seven feet long (2.13 meters). The brightly colored and deadly

coral snake lives in deserts in the southwest, together with the poisonous lizard called the Gila monster, and poisonous scorpions with as many as a dozen eyes!

Alligators lurk in swamps and rivers of the southeast. Here, too, live big, hulking alligator snapping turtles that lure fish into their mouths by wiggling a tongue that looks like a fat worm. Another southern animal, found as far south as Central America, is the shelled armadillo which rolls itself up into an armored ball for protection.

A few hundred grizzly bears still roam in the northwest, and that is also where the bald eagle, national bird of the United States, soars in the sky. But both these creatures are in danger of becoming extinct.

Sea otters live in the sea on the west coast. And in a bay on the west coast, thousands of some of the biggest of all animals gather each year to mate—California gray whales, which may be as much as forty feet (12.19 meters) long.

Animals live, thrive, and become extinct. They are known only from their fossil remains. The passenger pigeon, however, was seen and painted by John James Audubon, the great naturalist, in 1840.

Apatosaurus
135 Million Years Ago

Tyrannosaurus
70 Million Years Ago

Woolly Mammoth
10 Thousand Years Ago

Great Auk
Mid Nineteenth Century

Saber-Toothed Cat
1 Million Years Ago

Passenger Pigeon
Late Nineteenth Century

Grizzly Bear

Walrus

Herring Gull

Polar Bear

Gray Wolf

Red Fox

Rock Ptarmigan

Canada Goose

Mountain Goat

Beaver

Porcupine

Bald Eagle

Mountain Lion

Moose

Robin

Gray Squirrel

Pronghorn

King Salmon

Elk

Raccoon

White-tailed Deer

Willet

Sea Otter

Cottontail

Bison

Gambel's Quail

Diamondback Rattlesnake

Opossum

Turkey

California Sea Lions

Peccary

Alligator

Armadillo

Roseate Spoonbill

Brown Pelican

Squirrel Monkey

Gray Whale

Canada's houses of Parliament, in Ottawa, stand strangely alone amid winter snow and ice. It is here that 386 members of Parliament meet to govern the country's ten provinces and two territories.

Of all the continents, the boundaries between countries are the simplest in North America. Most of the continent is divided among three nations: Canada, the United States, and Mexico.

Borders between countries are never decided upon easily, and such was the case with those in North America. The boundary between Canada and the United States was settled upon in 1783, following the Revolutionary War, and by treaties in 1818, 1842, and 1846. Today, relations between the two countries are close and friendly. The frontier between them is the longest undefended border in the world, 5,525 miles (8,891.38 kilometers).

The boundary between the United States and Mexico was agreed upon only after the bitter Mexican War of 1846 to 1848, and by treaties and purchases of land.

The United States is the giant among the three countries. It has less land than Canada, but has more than nine times as many people. And it has more than three times the population of Mexico. With its vast stores of raw materials and its industrial know-how, enormous quantities of goods—cars, steel, food, and clothing—pour out of the industrial northeast to the country itself and to the rest of the world.

When the Americans revolted against British rule in 1775, the Canadians remained loyal to the crown. Today, they recognize Queen Elizabeth II as official head of state. Nevertheless, Canada is self-ruling. Although a member of the British Commonwealth of Nations, it has its own parliament and prime minister. Canada, too, is rich in natural resources. It is one of the most prosperous countries in the world.

The way of life of people in Canada and the United States is very much alike. Quite different is the way of life in Mexico.

Mexicans can trace their beginnings back to both the highly developed Indian civilizations, such as the Mayas and the Toltecs, and to the Spanish conquerors. Memories of the Indian peoples who ruled the land before the arrival of the Spanish remain alive in such splendid ruins as Teotihuacán, near Mexico City, which contains remarkable pyramids. Links to Spain are present in the country's many churches and palaces, which are like those of sixteenth century Spain. Customs in Mexico, especially in the cities, are in many ways like those of Spain.

Of all the Spanish-speaking countries, Mexico has the most people—more than Argentina, Chile, and Colombia combined—many more than Spain itself. It carries much weight among the Spanish-speaking nations of the world. Important deposits of oil have been found in Mexico in recent years. With oil scarce and expensive, Mexico's future looks highly promising.

Central America covers an area less than a third the size of Mexico. It is made up of six small republics, the Panama Canal Zone (now part of Panama), and newly independent Belize. Here too, the people's roots are Indian and Spanish. For example, the Indian people of Guatemala are descended from the once-mighty Mayan tribes whose ruined cities still rise in eerie splendor out of the jungles of the north. Indian customs are common in Guatemala. On the other hand, the people of Costa Rica have many Spanish as well as Indian ancestors, and customs can still be traced to the way of life in Spain.

Panama is cut through by the American-built canal, a waterway with an impressive series of locks and dams. It joins the Atlantic and Pacific Oceans, separated only by the twenty-seven miles (43.45 kilometers) of the slim isthmus.

Roads
Railroads

GREENLAND
(DENMARK)

AK
Anchorage
YUKON
Arctic Circle
Juneau
N.W. TER.
CANADA
B.C.
ALTA.
SASK.
MAN.
Edmonton
ONT.
NEWF.
QUE.
NEWF.
St. John's
Vancouver
Seattle
WA
MT
ND
MN
Winnipeg
Montreal
ME
N.B.
N.S.
OR
ID
SD
Minneapolis
WI
MI
Ottawa
VT
NH
Toronto
NY
MA
Boston
CT RI
WY
IA
Chicago
Detroit
PA
New York
Cleveland
Philadelphia
NJ
NV
Salt Lake City
NE
IL
IN
OH
MD
DE
Washington
San Francisco
UT
Denver
KS
MO
WV
VA
CA
CO
UNITED STATES
KY
Los Angeles
AZ
NM
OK
AR
TN
NC
SC
Dallas
MS
AL
GA
Atlanta
TX
LA
Houston
New Orleans
FL
Miami
BAHAMAS
Havana
Tropic of Cancer
CUBA
DOM. REP.
San Juan
JAMAICA
HAITI
MEXICO
Kingston
Port-au-Prince
Santo Domingo
Guadalajara
BARBADO
Mexico City
BELIZE
HONDURAS
GUATEMALA
EL SALVADOR
NICARAGUA
COSTA RICA
PANAMA
© 1979 Rand McNally & Co.

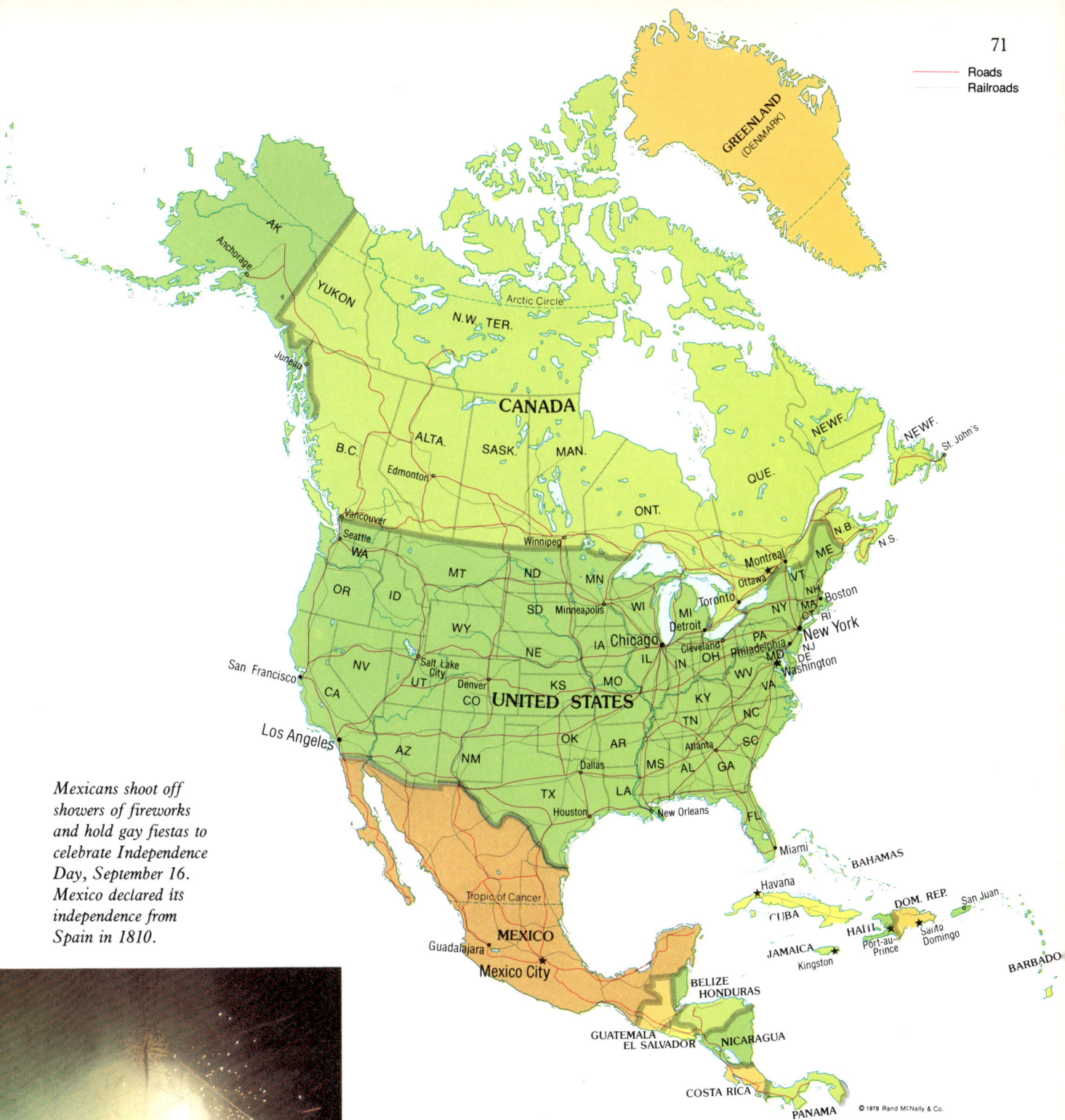

Mexicans shoot off showers of fireworks and hold gay fiestas to celebrate Independence Day, September 16. Mexico declared its independence from Spain in 1810.

Greenland, the largest island in the world, is considered part of North America. So are the islands of the Caribbean, sometimes called the West Indies. These sunny islands have a colorful past, and stories still are told of Spanish galleons loaded with silver and gold, and of French and British pirates.

English is the main language of North America, spoken by most Americans and Canadians. About a quarter of Canada's people speak French. Spanish and Indian tongues are spoken in Mexico. Spanish, English, French, Dutch, and several other languages are spoken in the West Indies.

European explorers who visited North America once called it the New World. It was indeed "new" to them. In some ways it still is new—or at least young. Cities which thrived before the arrival of Columbus have disappeared. Today North American cities are all more or less like those of Europe. All have come into being only since the year 1500.

ALASKA
U.S.A. CANADA
KLONDIKE REGION
OGILVIE MTS.
YUKON
RICHARDSON MTS.
Old Crow
Porcupine
Dawson
Stewart
Mayo
Whitehorse
PELLY MTS.
Frances
Carcross
Skagway
Atlin
Teslin
NAHANNI NAT'L PARK
Watson Lake

MACKENZIE MTS.
MACKENZIE MTS.
DISTRICT OF MACKENZIE
Inuvik
Tuktoyaktuk
Aklavik
Ft. McPherson
Ft. Good Hope
Norman Wells
FRANKLIN MTS.
Arctic Circle
Ft. Norman
Great Bear Lake
Port Radium
Coppermine

MELVILLE HILLS
Amundsen Gulf
CAPE BATHURST
Eskimo Lakes
Anderson

DISTRICT OF
NORTH WEST TERRITORIES
Prince Albert Sound
C. BARING
WOLLASTON PEN.
VICTORIA ISLAND
Dolphin and Union Str.
Coronation Gulf
KENT PEN.
Cambridge Bay
Dease Strait
Queen Maud Gulf
Victoria Strait
KING WILLIAM I.
BOOTHIA PENINSULA
Pelly Bay
SIMPSON PEN.
Chantrey Inlet
Baker Lake
Chesterfield Inlet
Chesterfield
Rankin Inlet

PEACOCK HILLS
Contwoyto
Back
Garry
Pelly
Dubawnt
Nonacho
Pathyed
Aylmer
Clinton-Colden
MacKay
Lac la Martre
Yellowknife
Ft. Providence
Ft. Simpson
HORN PLATEAU
Trout
Great Slave Lake
Ft. Resolution
Hay River
CAMERON HILLS
Ft. Liard
Ft. Nelson

DISTRICT

Nueltin
Seal
Churchill
CHURCHILL
Southern Indian
Reindeer
Wollaston
Cree
Selwyn
Uranium City
Athabasca
Ft. Smith
Ft. Fitzgerald
Ft. Chipewyan
Lake Claire

WOOD BUFFALO NAT'L PARK
CARIBOU MTS.
Ft. Vermilion
BIRCH MTS.
Ft. McMurray
CLEAR HILLS
BUFFALO HEAD HILLS
Peace River
McLennan
High Prairie
Grouard Mission
Lesser Slave Lake
CHEECHAM HILLS
Grande Prairie
SWAN HILLS
ALBERTA
Smith
Athabasca
Barrhead
Whitecourt
Edson
Lac la Biche
St. Paul
Beaver
Edmonton
ELK ISLAND NAT'L PARK
Vegreville
Ft. Saskatchewan
JASPER NAT'L PARK
Wetaskiwin
Camrose
Vermilion
Ponoka
Wainwright
Lloydminster
Lacombe
Red Deer
Innisfail
Stettler
Mountain Park
Rocky Mountain House
Olds
Drumheller
Hanna
Red Deer
Banff
Calgary
Bassano
High River
Brooks
Drumheller
Medicine Hat
Claresholm
Redcliff
Maple Creek
Pincher Creek
Taber
Lethbridge
Magrath
WATERTON GLACIER NAT'L PARK

BRITISH COLUMBIA
ROCKY MOUNTAINS
STIKINE RANGES
Telegraph Creek
Dease Lake
CASSIAR MTS.
Ft. Nelson
Ft. St. James
Hazelton
CARIBOO MTS.
Smithers
Burns Lake
Vanderhoof
Prince George
McBride
Quesnel
Wells
Williams Lake
MONASHEE MTS.
SELKIRK MTS.
GLACIER NAT'L PARK
MT. REVELSTOKE NAT'L PARK
Revelstoke
Golden
Kamloops
Blue River
Clinton
Ashcroft
Merritt
Vernon
Kelowna
Penticton
Cranbrook
Trail
Nelson
Fernie

COAST MTS.
PRINCE OF WALES I.
Ketchikan
Prince Rupert
Dixon Entrance
QUEEN CHARLOTTE ISLANDS
GRAHAM I.
MASSET
Skidegate
MORESBY I.
Hecate Strait
Kitimat
Ocean Falls
Bella Coola
Port Hardy
CALVERT I.
CAPE SCOTT
VANCOUVER ISLAND
Port Alice
Campbell River
Courtenay
Powell River
Port Alberni
NOOTKA
Nanaimo
Duncan
Victoria
CAPE FLATTERY
Str. of Juan de Fuca
Vancouver
Burnaby
New Westminster
Chilliwack
Hope

PACIFIC OCEAN

SASKATCHEWAN
PRINCE ALBERT NAT'L PARK
Meadow Lake
Big River
St. Walburg
Prince Albert
North Battleford
Melfort
Tisdale
Nipawin
Wilkie
Biggar
Saskatoon
Humboldt
Lanigan
Rosetown
Kindersley
Watrous
Last Mountain
Swift Current
Moose Jaw
Regina
Diefenbaker
Qu'Appelle
Indian Head
Gravelbourg
Assiniboia
Weyburn
Estevan
Shaunavon
Coronach
Flin Flon
Canora
Wynyard
Yorkton
Kamsack
Melville
Russell

MANITOBA
Lynn Lake
Granville
Thompson
Sipiwesk
Norway House
Berens River
Amery
Churchill
Lake Winnipeg
Lake Winnipegosis
The Pas
Swan River
Gypsumville
DUCK MTN.
Dauphin
Winnipegosis
RIDING MOUNTAIN NAT'L PARK
Minnedosa
Neepawa
Selkirk
Virden
Brandon
Portage-la-Prairie
Winnipeg
Souris
Carman
Boissevain
Morris
Steinbach
Mordon
Emerson

CANADA
U.S.A.

WASHINGTON
SEATTLE
Tacoma
Olympia
Vancouver
Portland
Salem
Eugene
OREGON
Spokane
Yakima
Moscow
Pullman
Walla Walla
Pendleton
Baker

IDAHO
MONTANA
Great Falls
Helena
Butte
Billings
LITTLE BELT MTS.
BIG BELT MTS.
BITTERROOT RANGE
Missouri
Yellowstone
Granite Peak
WYO.

NORTH DAKOTA
Williston
Minot
Grand Forks
Bismarck
Valley City
Fargo
SOUTH DAKOTA

Cities, Towns, and Villages
0 to 25,000
25,000 to 100,000
100,000 to 250,000
250,000 to 1,000,000
1,000,000 and over
Major urbanized area

Scale 1:12,600,000; one inch to 200 miles. Conic Projection
Elevations and depressions are given in feet

Longitude West of Greenwich

Longitude West of Greenwich

QUEBEC

Gulf of St. Lawrence

CAPE BAULD

Same scale as main map

LONG RANGE MTS.

GROS MORNE NAT'L PARK
Deer Lake
Corner Brook
Stephenville
St. George's

Botwood
Grand Falls
Windsor
Gander
Bonavista
TERRA NOVA NAT'L PARK
Trinity

Twillingate
Notre Dame Bay

Red Indian Lake

Bonavista Bay
Trinity Bay

NEWFOUNDLAND

St. John's

CAPE RAY
Channel-Port-aux-Basques
Fortune Bay
Placentia Bay
Burin

CAPE NORTH
Grand Bank

CAPE BRETON ISLAND

ST. PIERRE AND MIQUELON (Fr.)

ATLANTIC OCEAN

Cabot Strait

MELVILLE PENINSULA

FRANKLIN

BAFFIN ISLAND

Foxe Basin

Arctic Circle

BAFFIN ISLAND NAT'L PARK
Pangnirtung
Cumberland Sound
Nettilling L.
Amadjuak L.
Iqaluit
HALL PEN.
Frobisher Bay
Lake Harbour
EVERETT MTS.
RESOLUTION

SOUTHAMPTON ISLAND
Foxe Channel
Fisher Strait
COATS
MANSEL
NOTTINGHAM I.
SALISBURY
Hudson Strait
C. HOPES ADVANCE
AKPATOK
KILLINIQ I.

Bell Pen.
C. DE NOUVELLE-FRANCE

HUDSON BAY

All islands within bays and straits lie within Northwest Territories.

OF KEEWATIN

Ivujivik
PENINSULE D'UNGAVA
Povungnituk
OTTAWA ISLANDS
Payne L.
Kuujjuaq
Ungava Bay

TORNGAT MTS.
Hebron
Nain

NEWFOUNDLAND

LABRADOR

Hopedale
Makkovik
Rigolet
Cartwright
Hamilton Inlet
MEALY MTS.
Happy Valley-Goose Bay
Michikamau L.
Wabush
Churchill Falls
Lac Little Mecatina

St. Anthony
LONG RANGE MTS.
GROS MORNE NAT'L PARK
Corner Brook
Stephenville
St. George

BELCHER ISLANDS

C. HENRIETTA MARIA
PTE. LOUIS-XIV
Minto L.
Lac Bienville
Grande de la Baleine
Nichicun L.
Caniapiscau L.
MTS. OTISH
Lac Manicouagan
Manicouagan Rés.

Natashquan
Mingan
ÎLE D'ANTICOSTI

James Bay
Chisasibi
Akimiski
La Grande Rés.
Opinaca Rés.
Eastmain
R. aux Outardes
Clarke City
Sept-Îles
Baie-Comeau

Gulf of St. Lawrence
ÎLES DE LA MADELEINE

St. Severn
Ft. Severn
Winisk
Severn
Ft. Albany
Moosonee
Albany
Coral Rapids
Fraserdale

Nottaway
Bersimis
Betsiamites

QUEBEC

St. Lawrence River
Chibougamau
Dolbeau
Mistassini
Roberval
Alma
Kenogami
Chicoutimi
Jonquière
Saguenay
La Malbaie
Baie-St. Paul

MTS. CHIC-CHOCS
Cap-Chat
Matane
Mont-Joli
GASPÉ PEN.
Gaspé
Chandler
New Carlisle
Caraquet

ONTARIO

Lac Seul
Sioux Lookout
Nakina
Armstrong Sta.
Geraldton
Longlac
Hearst
Kapuskasing
Cochrane
Iroquois Falls
Timmins
Kirkland Lake
Chapleau
Cobalt
La Sarre
Amos
Rouyn
Val-d'Or
Malartic
Senneterre
Ville-Marie
Témiscaming
Reservoir Gouin
Parent
La Tuque

Dubreuilhuit
Red Lake
Dryden
Kenora
Lake of the Woods
Rainy River
Fort Frances
Thunder Bay

St. Joseph L.
Nipigon L.
Nipigon
Marathon
Michipicoten
PUKASKWA NAT'L PARK
Wawa

St. Maurice
Shawinigan
Trois-Rivières
Drummondville
Victoriaville
Granby
St. Hyacinthe
Sorel
Joliette
MONTRÉAL
Québec
Lévis
Sherbrooke

DOMAINE
MAINE

NEW BRUNSWICK
Edmundston
Grand Falls
Woodstock
Campbellton
Bathurst
Newcastle
Chatham
Fredericton
Moncton
Sackville
Richibucto
Shediac
FUNDY NAT'L PARK
St. George
St. Stephen
St. Andrews
Saint John

NOVA SCOTIA
Amherst
Springhill
Truro
Windsor
New Glasgow
Stellarton
Antigonish
Kentville
Digby
Bridgewater
Lunenburg
Liverpool
Shelburne
Yarmouth
CAPE SABLE
Dartmouth
Halifax
Sydney
Glace Bay
New Waterford

P.E.I.
PRINCE EDWARD ISLAND NAT'L PARK
Summerside
Charlottetown
CAPE BRETON HIGHLANDS NAT'L PARK

Bay of Fundy
Gulf of St. Lawrence

Lake Nipissing
Sudbury
Espanola
Blind River
Thessalon
Sault Ste. Marie
MANITOULIN
Georgian Bay
Parry Sound
North Bay
Mattawa
Pembroke
Renfrew
Ottawa
Hull
Huntsville
Bancroft
Smiths Falls
Brockville
Kingston
Alexandria Bay
Ogdensburg

Owen Sound
Wiarton
Kincardine
Midland
Orillia
Barrie
Lindsay
Peterborough
Cobourg
Oshawa
Whitby
TORONTO
Kitchener
Hamilton
St. Catharines
Niagara Falls
Buffalo
Rochester
London
Woodstock
St. Thomas
Sarnia
Chatham
Leamington
Windsor
Port Huron

VERMONT
NEW HAMPSHIRE
MASS.
CONN.
R.I.
Concord
Hartford
Providence
BOSTON
CAPE COD
Portland
Albany
NEW YORK
Newark
N.J.
Scranton

Lake Champlain
Montpelier
St. Jean
Valleyfield
Augusta

PENNSYLVANIA
OHIO
Toledo
DETROIT
CHICAGO
MILWAUKEE
Madison
Lansing
Flint
Saginaw
Grand Rapids
Green Bay
MINNEAPOLIS
St. Paul
Superior
Duluth
Marquette
Escanaba

WISCONSIN
MICHIGAN
MINNESOTA
NEW YORK

Lake Superior
Lake Michigan
Lake Huron
Lake Erie
Lake Ontario

ATLANTIC OCEAN

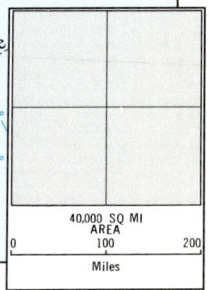

H-520200-26- 9-8-18
COPYRIGHT BY
RAND MCNALLY & COMPANY
MADE IN U.S.A.

40,000 SQ MI
AREA
0   100   200

0   25   50   75   100   200   300   400   500 Miles
0   100   200   400   600   800 Kilometers

BRITISH COLUMBIA
ALBERTA
SASKATCHEWAN
MANIT[OBA]
C A N A D A

WASHINGTON
OREGON
CALIFORNIA
NEVADA
IDAHO
MONTANA
WYOMING
UTAH
ARIZONA
NEW MEXICO
COLORADO
NORTH DAKOTA
SOUTH DAKOTA
NEBRASKA
KANSAS
OKLAH[OMA]
TEXAS

Seattle
Tacoma
Everett
Spokane
Portland
Salem
Eugene
Vancouver
Victoria
Bellingham
Port Angeles
Hoquiam
Aberdeen
Astoria
Olympia
Yakima
Walla Walla
Pendleton
Corvallis
Albany
Bend
Roseburg
Medford
Klamath Falls
Eureka
Santa Rosa
Napa
Vallejo
Berkeley
Oakland
Alameda
San Francisco
San Jose
Santa Cruz
Monterey
Sacramento
Stockton
Fresno
San Luis Obispo
Bakersfield
Santa Barbara
Los Angeles
Santa Monica
Glendale
Pasadena
Long Beach
Santa Ana
Pomona
Riverside
San Bernardino
San Diego
Tijuana
Mexicali
Ensenada

PACIFIC OCEAN

OLYMPIC NAT'L PARK
CRATER LAKE NAT'L PARK
LASSEN VOLCANIC NAT'L PARK
YOSEMITE NAT'L PARK
KINGS CANYON NAT'L PARK
SEQUOIA NAT'L PARK
DEATH VALLEY
MOJAVE DESERT
GREAT BASIN

Mt. Baker 10,778
Mt. Rainier 14,410
Mt. Adams 12,307
Mt. Hood 11,235
Mt. Shasta 14,162
Lassen Peak 10,466
Mt. Whitney 14,494

Reno
Carson City
Winnemucca
Elko
Ely
Tonopah
Las Vegas
Boulder City
Wheeler Peak 13,061

Boise
Nampa
Twin Falls
Pocatello
Idaho Falls
Lewiston
Moscow
Coeur d'Alene
Kalispell
Missoula
Helena
Butte
Anaconda
Bozeman
Livingston
Billings
Great Falls
Lewistown
Havre
Glendive
Miles City
Dickinson
Sheridan

Hyndman Peak 12,078
Borah Peak
Grand Teton 13,766
Yellowstone NAT'L PARK
Grand Teton Nat'l Park
Gannett Peak 13,785
Cloud Peak 13,175
Kings Peak 13,528
UINTA MTS.
WASATCH RANGE
Mt. Elbert 14,431
Mt. Massive 14,418
Longs Peak 14,255
Pikes Pk. 14,110
Blanca Peak 14,317

Salt Lake City
Ogden
Provo
Logan
Great Salt Lake
Great Salt Lake Desert

Rock Springs
Green River
Rawlins
Laramie
Cheyenne
Casper
Flaming Gorge

Denver
Boulder
Fort Collins
Greeley
Sterling
Colorado Springs
Pueblo
Trinidad
Raton
Grand Junction
ROCKY MTN. NAT'L PARK
MESA VERDE NAT'L PARK
SANGRE DE CRISTO RANGE
SAN JUAN MTS.

Delano Peak 12,173
ZION NAT'L PARK
BRYCE CANYON NAT'L PARK
GRAND CANYON NAT'L PARK
GLEN CANYON DAM
HENRY MTS.
Lake Powell

Phoenix
Tucson
Flagstaff
Prescott
Jerome
Globe
Miami
Yuma
Nogales
Bisbee
Douglas
Humphreys Peak 12,633
Baldy Peak 11,590
MOGOLLON PLATEAU
BLACK RANGE

Albuquerque
Santa Fe
Las Vegas
Gallup
Clovis
Roswell
Las Cruces
Deming
Mt. Taylor 11,301
Truchas Pk. 13,110
Sierra Blanca Pk. 12,003
SAN ANDRES MTS.
LLANO ESTACADO

El Paso
Ciudad Juárez
Cananea
Magdalena
Nogales

Williston
Minot
Devils Lake
Grand Forks
Bismarck
Mandan
Jamestown
Valley City
Fargo
Lake Sakakawea

Rapid City
Deadwood
Lead
Pierre
Mitchell
Sioux Falls
Yankton
Huron
Watertown
Aberdeen
Chadron
Valentine
Alliance
WIND CAVE NAT'L PARK
Harney Pk. 7242
BLACK HILLS
Lake Oahe

North Platte
Grand Island
Lincoln
Hastings
Beatrice
Norfolk
Columbus

Manhattan
Salina
Dodge City
Hutchinson
Wichita
Smoky Hill

Oklahoma City
Lawton
Enid
Ardmore
Pampa
Amarillo
Lubbock
Wichita Falls
Fort Worth
Dallas
Abilene
San Angelo
Sweetwater
Brownwood
Waco
Austin
San Antonio
Del Rio
Eagle Pass
Laredo
Brownsville
Harlingen
Corpus Christi

BAJA CALIFORNIA NORTE
SONORA
CHIHUAHUA
COAHUILA
DURANGO
NUEVO LEON
TAMAULIPAS
M E X I C O
Piedras Negras
Nueva Rosita
Nuevo Laredo
Reynosa
Matamoros
Monterrey
Saltillo
Torreón
Gómez Palacio
Big Bend Nat'l Park

Regina
Moose Jaw
Medicine Hat
Lethbridge
Cardston
Brandon
Winnipeg
Winnipegosis
RIDING MTN. PARK

ALASKA
Barrow
Kotzebue
Nome
Bethel
Fairbanks
Anchorage
McGrath
Ruby
Circle
Seward
Cordova
Juneau
Sitka
Ketchikan
Dutch Harbor
BROOKS RANGE
DENALI NAT'L PARK
Mt. McKinley 20,320
KATMAI NAT'L PARK
GLACIER BAY NAT'L PARK
ARCTIC OCEAN
Arctic Circle
SOVIET UNION
CANADA
NORTHWEST TERR.
YUKON
BRITISH COLUMBIA
QUEEN CHARLOTTE IS.
ALEUTIAN IS.
Scale 1:37,900,000
One inch to 600 miles

HAWAII
HAWAIIAN IS.
NIIHAU
KAUAI
OAHU
MOLOKAI
MAUI
LANAI
KAHOOLAWE
HAWAII
Honolulu
Lihue
Kailua
Wailuku
Kahului
Hilo
Mauna Kea 13,796
Mauna Loa 13,680
HAWAII VOLCANOES NAT'L PARK
Scale 1:3,600,000
Longitude West of Greenwich

OAHU
Wahiawa
Waipahu
Kailua
Honolulu
Kahuku
Pearl Harbor
Same scale as main map

A-520500-26
COPYRIGHT BY
RAND M CNALLY & COMPANY
MADE IN U.S.A.

Scale 1:12,600,000; one inch to 200 miles. Polyconic Projection
Elevations and depressions are given in feet

CANADA

ONTARIO

QUEBEC

PRINCE EDWARD ISLAND

NEW BRUNSWICK

NOVA SCOTIA

MINNESOTA
WISCONSIN
MICHIGAN
IOWA
ILLINOIS
INDIANA
OHIO
MISSOURI
KENTUCKY
WEST VIRGINIA
VIRGINIA
TENNESSEE
NORTH CAROLINA
ARKANSAS
SOUTH CAROLINA
MISSISSIPPI
ALABAMA
GEORGIA
LOUISIANA
FLORIDA

MAINE
N.H.
VT.
MASS.
CONN.
R.I.
NEW YORK
PENN.
N.J.
MD.
DEL.

MONTRÉAL
TORONTO
BUFFALO
DETROIT
CLEVELAND
PITTSBURGH
CHICAGO
ST. LOUIS
KANSAS CITY
CINCINNATI
WASHINGTON D.C.
BALTIMORE
PHILADELPHIA
NEW YORK
BOSTON
ATLANTA
MIAMI
HOUSTON

ATLANTIC OCEAN

GULF OF MEXICO

BAHAMAS

Lake Superior
Lake Michigan
Lake Huron
Lake Erie
Lake Ontario

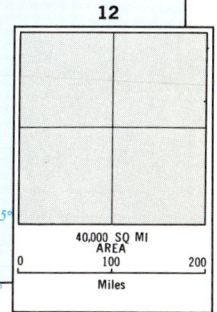

12

40,000 SQ MI
AREA

0   100   200
Miles

Cities
and
Towns

0 to 50,000   500,000 to 1,000,000
50,000 to 500,000   1,000,000 and over

Longitude West of Greenwich

0 25 50 75 100   200   300   400   500 Miles
0   100   200   400   600   800 Kilometers

SAN DIEGO
Tijuana
Ensenada
Mexicali
El Centro
Calexico

CALIFORNIA
ARIZONA
Phoenix
Prescott
Santa Fe
Albuquerque
Socorro
NEW MEXICO

KANSAS
MISSOURI
Springfield
Joplin
ILL.
Evansville
Bowling Green
Hopkinsville
KENT.
Cairo

Yuma
Gila
Tucson
Nogales
Nogales
Bisbee
Douglas
Cananea

NEW MEXICO
Las Cruces
Deming
El Paso
Ciudad Juárez

Oklahoma City
Tulsa
Muskogee
Fort Smith
Wichita Falls
Lawton
OKLAHOMA
ARKANSAS
Hot Springs
Little Rock
Pine Bluff
Nashville
Memphis
Chattanooga
TENNESSEE

BAJA CALIFORNIA NORTE
GUADALUPE (Mex.)
Cerro de la Encantada 10,121
Cerro Pinacate 4560

SONORA
Hermosillo
Guaymas
CHIHUAHUA
Chihuahua
Ciudad Camargo

Childress
Lubbock
Texarkana
San Angelo
Fort Worth
DALLAS
Waco
Corsicana
Shreveport
Vicksburg
Jackson
ALABAMA
Birmingham
Montgomery
Greenville

BAJA CALIFORNIA SUR
STA. CLARA
Santa Rosalía
CEDROS
Vol. Las Tres Vírgenes 6547

Ciudad Obregón
Navojoa
Topolobampo
Hidalgo del Parral
Jiménez
Ciudad del Oro

Del Rio
Piedras Negras
Eagle Pass
COAHUILA
BOLSÓN DE MAPIMÍ
Monclova
Sabinas

Columbus
San Antonio
Austin
Beaumont
HOUSTON
Galveston
LOUISIANA
Baton Rouge
New Orleans
Mobile
Pensacola
CAPE SAN BLAS

C. SAN LAZARO
Bahía Magdalena
STA. MARGARITA
Pico Cupula 3000
La Paz
CERRALVO
C. SAN LUCAS
STA. GENOVEVA 7100

Culiacán
SINALOA
DURANGO
Durango
Gómez Palacio
Lerdo
Torreón
Saltillo
Concepción del Oro

NUEVO LEÓN
Monterrey
Montemorelos
TAMAULIPAS
Linares
Nuevo Laredo
Laredo
Matamoros
Brownsville

GULF OF MEX

Mazatlán
Escuinapa (de Hidalgo)
ZACATECAS
Fresnillo
Zacatecas
Matehuala
SAN LUIS POTOSÍ
Ciudad Victoria

Tropic of Cancer

NAYARIT
Tepic
ISLAS MARIAS
Tuxpan
San Blas
Aguascalientes
Salinas
San Luis Potosí
Ciudad Mante
Valles
Tampico

JALISCO
Guadalajara
GUA.
Querétaro
Celaya
HIDALGO
Pachuca
Papantla de Olarte
Nautla

Progreso
Sisal
Mérida
Temax
Valladolid
YUCATÁN
C. CATOCHE
ISLA DE COZUMEL

Ciudad Guzmán
Colima
Manzanillo
MICHOACÁN
Morelia
MEX.
MEXICO CITY
Toluca
Cuernavaca
Puebla
Jalapa Enríquez
Veracruz
Orizaba

Campeche
QUINTANA ROO
CAMPECHE
Ciudad Chetumal (Payo Obispo)
Bahía de Chetumal

GUERRERO
Acapulco
Chilpancingo
SIERRA MADRE DEL SUR
Oaxaca
OAXACA
Tehuantepec
Salina Cruz
Juchitán
Golfo de Tehuantepec

Ciudad del Carmen
TABASCO
Villahermosa
CHIAPAS
Ciudad de las Casas
Tuxtla Gutiérrez
Comitán

Belize City
BELIZE
Belmopan
TURNEFFE
Gulf of Honduras
ISLAS DE LA BAHIA

GUATEMALA
Quezaltenango
Mazatenango
Guatemala
Antigua
Cobán
Totonicapán

HONDURAS
Pto. Cortés
La Ceiba
Tela
San Pedro
Comayagua
Tegucigalpa

EL SALVADOR
Santa Ana
San Salvador
San Miguel

NICAR.
León
Managua
Granada
San Juan del Sur

Golfo de Fonseca
Matagalpa

CENTRAL

PACIFIC OCEAN

ISLAS REVILLAGIGEDO (Mex.)

ISLA DEL COCO (Costa Rica)

PANAMA inset:

Caribbean Sea
Bahía Limón
Colón
Coco Solito
Rainbow City
Margarita
GATUN LOCKS
Gatun
Lago Gatun
2200
Isaacs Mt. 1847
Salud Mt. 1162
Nuevo San Juan
Chilibre
Chagres
West Hill 527
East Mt. 608
North Gamboa
Balboa Mt. 1149
GAILLARD CUT
Gold Hill 662
Paraíso
PEDRO MIGUEL LOCKS
Pedro Miguel
MIRAFLORES LOCKS
Cocoli
Diablo Hts.
Balboa Heights
Ancon
PANAMÁ
Río Abajo
Cerro Galera 1205
La Chorrera
Bahía de Panamá
TABOGA
TABOGUILLA

Scale 1:1,080,000
0   10 Miles
0 4 8 12 16 Kilometers
©RMcN.

Scale 1:17,200,000; one inch to 270 miles. Polyconic Projection
Elevations and depressions are given in feet

Main Map

KY
W.VIRGINIA
Richmond
Roanoke
VIRGINIA
Norfolk
Chesapeake Bay
oxville
Raleigh
NORTH CAROLINA
Mt. Mitchell 6684
Charlotte
CAPE HATTERAS
ATLANTA
SOUTH
Columbia
CAROLINA
Wilmington
EORGIA
Augusta
CAPE FEAR
Charleston
Savannah
BERMUDA (Br.)
Tallahassee
Jacksonville
St. Augustine
alachee Bay
Ocala
FLORIDA
Tampa
Tampa Bay
W. Palm Beach
Lake Okeechobee
MIAMI
CAPE SABLE
Key West
FLORIDA KEYS
Straits of Florida
GRAND BAHAMA
GREAT ABACO
Nassau
ELEUTHERA
CAT
ANDROS
B A H A M A S
SAN SALVADOR (WATLING)
LONG
ACKLINS
CAT
HAVANA
Guanabacoa
Matanzas
Marianao
Cárdenas
inar del Río
Santa Clara
Cienfuegos
Sancti Spíritus
Ciego de Avila
C U B A
Camagüey
Nuevitas
Trinidad
Holguín
ISLA DE LA JUVENTUD
Manzanillo
Guantánamo
SAN ONIO
GRAND CAYMAN (Br.)
SIERRA MAESTRA
Santiago de Cuba
C. CRUZ
PUNTA MAISÍ
Montego Bay
Mt Denham 2236
port Antonio
Spanish Town
JAMAICA
Kingston
Windward Passage
Cap-Haïtien
ÎLE DE LA GONÂVE
Gonaïves
HAITI
Port-au-Prince
Pico Duarte 3417
Puerto Plata
Santiago de los Caballeros
C. SAMANA
DOMINICAN REPUBLIC
Sánchez
C. ENGAÑO
Santo Domingo
H I S P A N I O L A
CAICOS (BK.)
GT INAGUA
TURKS (BK.)
A N T I L L E S
PUERTO RICO TRENCH
28 374
Mayagüez
San Juan
Ponce
PUERTO RICO (U.S.A.)
Charlotte Amalie
VIRGIN IS.
ST. THOMAS!
SAINT CROIX (U.S.A.)
ANGUILLA (Br.)
BARBUDA
ST. KITTS AND NEVIS
ANTIGUA AND BARBUDA
MONTSERRAT (Br.)
V. Soufrière 4869
Basse Terre
Pointe-à-Pitre
GUADELOUPE (Fr.)
DOMINICA
MARTINIQUE (Fr.)
Fort-de-France
ST. LUCIA
ST. VINCENT AND THE GRENADINES
Kingstown
BARBADOS
Bridgetown
GRENADA
W E S T
NORTH AMERICAN BASIN
A T L A N T I C   O C E A N
G R E A T E R
L E S S E R
W I N D W A R D   I S.
A N T I L L E S
C A R I B B E A N   S E A

AMERICA
Bluefields
RICA
an José
Limón
Cartago
Colón
Portobelo
PANAMA
Golfo de los Mosquitos
Panamá
Antón
David
Santiago
COIBA
PEN. DE AZUERO
Golfo de Panamá
Golfo del Darién
ISTMO
ISLA DE MALPELO (Colombia)
Buenaventura
Cali
Palmira
Cartago
Pereira
Manizales
Armenia
Ibagué
Medellín
Sonsón
Tolima 5215
BOGOTÁ
Girardot
Villavicencio
Tunja
COLOMBIA
Bucaramanga
Barrancabermeja
Pamplona
Cúcuta
San Cristóbal
Ocaña
Mompós
Magangué
Montería
Lorica
Sincelejo
Santa Marta
Barranquilla
Ciénaga
Soledad
Cartagena
PUNTA DE GALLINAS
PENÍNSULA DE GUAJIRA
Maracaibo
Cabimas
Lago de Maracaibo
Trujillo
Valera
Mérida
CORDILLERA DE MÉRIDA
Guanare
Puerto de Nutrias
San Fernando de Apure
ARUBA (Neth.)
CURAÇAO (Neth.)
BONAIRE (Neth.)
PEN. DE PARAGUANÁ
Willemstad
Coro
San Felipe
Puerto Cabello
Maracay
Valencia
Barquisimeto
CARACAS
La Guaira
Puerto la Cruz
Cumaná
Carúpano
ISLA LA TORTUGA
ISLA DE MARGARITA
TRINIDAD AND TOBAGO
TOBAGO
Port of Spain
TRINIDAD
SAN ROMAN
PEN. DE PARAGUANÁ
Golfo de Venezuela
Maturín
El Tigre
Calabozo
V E N E Z U E L A
Cerro Icutú 7800
Ciudad Bolívar
Cerro Bolívar
Ciudad Guayana
Morawhanna
Salto Angel
SERRA PACARAIMA
GUYANA
B R A Z I L
Río Orinoco
Meta
Arauca
Apure
Río Orinoco
Guaviare
Ventuari
Caura
Caroní
Río Orinoco
San Fernando de Atabapo

Inset (upper right) — Puerto Rico

Scale 1:4,300,000
0 10 20 30 40 Miles
0 10 20 30 40 50 60 Kilometers

ATLANTIC OCEAN
Aguadilla
PTA. HIGUERO
Arecibo
San Juan
Bayamón
CABEZAS DE SAN JUAN
ST. THOMAS (U.S.A.)
TORTOLA (Br.)
Utuado
Fajardo
Charlotte Amalie
ST. JOHN (U.S.A.)
Mayagüez
PUERTO RICO (U.S.A.)
Caguas
Cayey
Humacao
Coamo
CULEBRA
Vieques
VIEQUES
CABO ROJO
Ponce
Salinas
Guayama
Christiansted
SAINT CROIX (U.S.A.)
C A R I B B E A N   S E A
Mona Passage
©RMcN.

Inset (middle right) — St. Thomas

Scale 1:5,400,000
LITTLE HANS LOLLIK
OUTER BRASS
HANS LOLLIK
PICARA PT
GRASS CAY
INNER BRASS
STORMY PT
ST. THOMAS
Crown Mt. (U.S.A.) 1558
THATCH CAY
Charlotte Amalie (St. Thomas)
Nadir
WATER
FLAMINGO PT
St. Thomas Harbor
©RMcN.

Scale bars (bottom left)

0 50 100 200 300 400 500 Miles
0 100 200 400 600 800 Kilometers

40 000 SQ MI AREA
0 100 200 Miles

Longitude West of Greenwich

South America/Terrain

Almost in the clouds is Lake Titicaca, on a windswept plateau in the Andes. It is South America's largest lake—3,500 square miles (9,065 square kilometers)—and the highest large lake in the world.

Mountains span the length of South America like a gigantic, rocky backbone. Though scarcely 200 miles (321.86 kilometers) wide in some places, the Andes chain is the longest in the world. It stretches over four thousand miles (6,437.2 kilometers) along the continent's west coast. This range also boasts some of the earth's tallest peaks. Only Asia's Himalaya Mountains are higher than Mount Aconcagua, which frowns down on western Argentina.

Over three-fourths of South America lies in the tropics. The Andes, however, have a climate all their own. Low down, where they break out of the eastern flatlands, the air is hot and tropical plants can grow. Above 7,000 feet (2,133.6 meters) the air becomes cooler. Great forests thrive, giving way at slightly higher altitudes to crop and grazing land. Here the Incas and other Indian peoples built their great civilizations. Beyond, to the frozen snowline, the air grows gradually colder. Above 13,000 feet (3,962.4 meters),

only moss, lichens, and tough, grasslike plants, called sedge, survive.

Where Argentina, Bolivia, and Chile meet, the Andes split into two ranges. They are separated by a windswept plateau about 400 miles (643.72 kilometers) wide. This is the Altiplano, as it is called in Spanish, or "high plateau." It is nearly two and a half miles (4.02 kilometers) above sea level and almost perfectly flat—a strange sight nestled between the towering peaks.

Many rivers and streams tumble from the Andes and other highland areas. The great Amazon River begins in the Andes of Peru and flows 3,900 miles (6,276.27 kilometers) to the Atlantic Ocean. The Amazon contains more water than any river on earth— over 4 million cubic feet (113,200 cubic meters) pour into the Atlantic each second! Small ships can sail more than two thousand miles (3,218.6 kilometers) upstream to the foot of the Andes.

Other major rivers include the

Magdalena in Colombia, the São Francisco in east Brazil, and the Orinoco, life stream of Venezuela. Another, the Paraguay-Paraná, flows southward through Brazil, Paraguay, and Argentina. In South America, only the Amazon is longer and contains more water.

The Amazon carries water away from a huge plain called the Amazon Basin—an area almost as big as forty-eight of the fifty United States! This basin is one of two major flatlands in South America. Its heat and rainy downpours support hundreds of miles of densely packed trees, making the Amazon the world's largest rain forest.

Quite different from the first plain is the second. It stretches across Paraguay and most of Argentina, and is made up of two distinct areas—the Gran Chaco and the Pampa. The Gran Chaco is a dry region with scrubby trees widely spaced. Farther south and closer to the coast, rainfall supports the Pampa, a nearly treeless grassland ideal for cattle and sheep grazing.

The grassy Pampa gives way in the south to a strip of dry, shrubby land known as Patagonia, which covers most of South America's narrow tail. Only the Atacama Desert, between the Chilean Andes and the Pacific Ocean, is more barren.

Aside from the Andes, South America contains two other upland areas. The Brazilian Highlands separate the Amazon Basin from the Gran Chaco and reach nearly two thousand miles (3,218.6 kilometers) inland from the Atlantic. In places they are quite rugged, with spectacular waterfalls that drop over scenic cliffs. Iguassu Falls is one of the most breathtaking. Waters from its 275 falls crash thunderously over a rocky expanse more than one and a half miles (2.41 kilometers) wide.

Despite the many rivers which empty themselves along South America's 5,000-mile (24,140-kilometer) coastline, the continent has few good natural harbors. Even fewer islands hug its shores. The only large ones are Trinidad and Tobago, off Venezuela, and the Galápagos, west of Ecuador. A string of smaller islands follows the coast of Chile south to Tierra del Fuego. Here the continent ends as the Andes sink their slopes into the sea.

Caribbean Sea
VENEZUELA
TRINIDAD
ATLANTIC
Lake Maracaibo
Orinoco
GUYANA
SURINAME
FRENCH GUIANA
OCEAN
LLANOS
Angel Falls
GUIANA HIGHLANDS
PAKARAIMA MTS
COLOMBIA
Equator
Negro
Amazon
Amazon
MARAJO ISLAND
Chimborazo
ECUADOR
Madeira
Cape Sao Roque
PERU
Mt. Huascaran
CORD. OCCIDENTAL
BRAZIL
PACIFIC
Serra dos Parecis
BRAZILIAN
São Francisco
Lake Titicaca
BOLIVIA
MATO GROSSO PLATEAU
HIGHLANDS
SERRA DO ESPINHAÇO
OCEAN
ATACAMA DESERT
GRAN CHACO
PARAGUAY
Tropic of Capricorn
Bandeira Pk.
Mt. Ojos del Salado
Iguassu Falls
Parana
SERRA DO MAR
ANDES
CHILE
Uruguay
Parana
Mt. Aconcagua
ARGENTINA
URUGUAY
Rio de la Plata
PAMPA
ATLANTIC
OCEAN
PATAGONIA
FALKLAND ISLANDS
Strait of Magellan
TIERRA DEL FUEGO
© 1979 Rand McNally & Co.
Cape Horn

South America Facts

Fourth largest continent
Fifth in population: 243,100,000
18 cities with over 1 million population
Highest mountain: Aconcagua, 22,831 feet (6,958.88 meters)
World's highest waterfall: Angel Falls, 3,700 feet (1,127.76 meters)
Equator passes through

All of the world's natural sodium nitrate is blasted from the Atacama Desert, which stretches 600 miles (965.58 kilometers) along the coast of Chile. Nitrate is used to make fertilizer and explosives.

South America's Amazon River contains more water than the Nile, Yangtze, and Mississippi rivers combined—or nearly one-fifth of all the fresh water that runs off the earth's surface. Its outpouring is so great that the water of the open sea is fresh for over 200 miles (321.86 kilometers) beyond the river's mouth.

Tropic of Cancer

A T L A N T I C

O C E A N

Equator

Recife

Fortaleza

Salvador

São Francisco

Belém

Brasília

Cuiabá

M A T O

G R O S S O

Georgetown

Manaus

Amazon

Negro

Port of Spain

TRINIDAD

Orinoco

CARACAS

S E L V A S

Iquitos

Rio Branco

La Paz

Maracaibo

San Juan

PUERTO

RICO

BOGOTÁ

Quito

A N D E S

LIMA

HISPANIOLA

BAHAMAS

Kingston

JAMAICA

Barranquilla

Panama

Caribbean   Sea

Havana

CUBA

Scale 1:24,800,000; one inch to 390 miles. Lambert Azimuthal Equal-Area Projection

ATLANTIC

OCEAN

Bela Horizonte

RIO DE JANEIRO

SÃO PAULO

Paraná

Porto Alegre

Asunción

Montevideo

San Miguel de Tucumán

Córdoba

BUENOS AIRES

Bahia Blanca

P A M P A

GRAN

ANDES

PATAGONIA

SANTIAGO

Puerto Montt

Punta Arenas

TIERRA
DEL FUEGO

SOUTH
GEORGIA

FALKLAND
ISLANDS

Drake Passage

ANTARCTIC PENINSULA

PACIFIC

OCEAN

Tropic of Capricorn

A-540000-96 -1 -3*
COPYRIGHT BY
RAND McNALLY & COMPANY
MADE IN U.S.A.

Urban

Cropland

Cropland & Woodland

Cropland & Grazing Land

Grassland, Grazing Land

Forest, Woodland

Swamp, Marshland

Shrub, Sparse Grass,
Wasteland (pattern)

Barren Land

| 0 | 100 | 200 | 400 | 600 | 800 Miles |

| 0 | 150 | 300 | 600 | 900 | 1200 Kilometers |

South America/Animals

Vast tropical forests spread over much of South America and are the home of a great number of creatures. The big, spotted cats called jaguars prowl among the trees by night, and herds of little piglike peccaries root in the underbrush. One kind of large, hoglike tapir lives here. It is related to both the horse and rhinoceros, and its nose ends in a short trunk.

Many creatures live up in the trees. Little, long-legged sloths, hanging upside down from branches, inch along as they feed on leaves. Monkeys shriek, howl, whistle, and chatter from the treetops—red uakaris, that look like sad old men; long-tailed, black-furred woolly monkeys; large-eyed douroucoulis; and golden marmosets. Brightly colored parrots, macaws, toucans, and other birds flash from tree to tree.

In the rivers swim caimans, the alligators of South America, and many fish including the vicious, flesh-eating piranha, with its razor-sharp teeth. A school of piranhas can devour an animal down to the bare bones in a matter of minutes! Anacondas, giant snakes often more than thirty feet (9.14 meters) long, lurk in some rivers, waiting to seize unwary animals that come to the shores to drink.

On the plains of South America live bushy-furred giant anteaters, which may be more than six feet (1.82 meters) long from tip of nose to end of tail. Here, too, are found long-legged maned wolves, which have been described as looking like a fox walking on stilts.

Many animals live in the long range of mountains along the west coast. This is where the humpless camels of South America are mostly found—llamas, alpacas, guanacos, and vicuñas—small, heavily furred beasts that live in herds. The spectacled bear roams the mountain slopes. It gets its name from the circles of yellowish fur, like eyeglass frames, around its eyes. The chinchilla, a bushy-tailed, mouselike creature with the finest, silkiest fur in the world, lives high up on the snow-capped heights. And gliding through the air between mountain peaks is the great South American condor with a wingspread of nearly ten feet (3.04 meters). It is a kind of vulture that feeds on dead animals.

Nearly a fourth of all the world's animals live in South America. Because forests are rapidly being cleared, and plains used for farming and grazing, many of these animals are in serious danger of becoming extinct.

The mysterious Galápagos Islands lie about 600 miles (965.58 kilometers) off the coast of Ecuador. Here live rare cormorants that cannot fly, great lizardlike iguanas, and giant turtles weighing over 500 pounds (226.8 kilograms).

Sloth

Tapir

Manatee

Scarlet Ibis

Coatimundi

Ocelot

Piranha

Green Turtle

Toucan

Caiman

Spectacled Bear

Anaconda

Vampire Bat

Llama

Spider Monkey

Red Brocket Deer

Howling Monkey

Chinchilla

Capybara

Jaguar

Macaw

Vicuña

Great Anteater

Condor

Guanaco

Maned Wolf

Brazilian Lapwing

Alpaca

Pampas Deer

Blue Marlin

Torrent Duck

Rhea

Elephant Seal

Magellan Goose

Magellan Penguin

Cavy

Black-necked Swan

Sperm Whale

South America/
Countries and Cities

Roads
Railroads

Barranquilla · Caracas · Port of Spain · TRINIDAD AND TOBAGO
Maracaibo
VENEZUELA · Georgetown
GUYANA · Paramaribo
Bogota · SURINAME · Cayenne
COLOMBIA · FR. GUIANA
Equator
Quito · Belem · Fortaleza
ECUADOR
Guayaquil · Manaus
PERU · BRAZIL · Recife
Lima · Brasilia · Salvador
Cuzco · La Paz · BOLIVIA
Sucre · Belo Horizonte
Tropic of Capricorn · PARAGUAY
Antofagasta · Asuncion · Sao Paulo · Rio de Janeiro
Santos
Porto Alegre
CHILE · Cordoba
Valparaiso · Mendoza · Rosario · URUGUAY
Santiago · Buenos Aires · Montevideo
La Plata
Concepcion · ARGENTINA
Bahia Blanca

FALKLAND
ISLANDS
(U.K.)

Punta Arenas

© 1979 Rand McNally & Co.

South America is but one name for a continent which today is divided into twelve independent nations. Along with its Central American and Mexican neighbors, South America is often called Latin America.

Most South Americans speak either Spanish or Portuguese—tongues based on the language of ancient Rome, or *Latium*. Europeans brought these Latin languages with them when they conquered the continent in the mid-1500s. Spanish is the official language of all but three of the continent's twelve nations. Portuguese is spoken in Brazil, South America's largest and most populated country.

Brazil spreads over half the continent and is one of the world's biggest nations. Only the Soviet Union, China, Canada, and the United States are larger in area. Almost 124 million people live in Brazil, more than in all other South American countries combined.

Brazil is a nation on the go. São Paulo, to the south, is the major industrial city of the continent. Factories are going up in ever-increasing numbers, particularly in the coastal region between São Paulo and Rio de Janeiro.

Two small nations north of Brazil also have official languages other than Spanish. The Dutch-speaking people of Suriname and the English-speaking people of Guyana have ancestors who were mainly Hindustanis—people from India—or black Africans. These groups were brought to South America by the Dutch and English during colonial days to work

High in the Andes near Cuzco, Peru, lie the ruins of Machu Picchu—once a walled Incan city. Unknown to the Spanish, it may have been a last hideaway for the doomed Inca people.

on sugar plantations along the marshy coast.

Ninety percent of the people in neighboring French Guiana are black or of mixed African and European ancestry. French is the official language, for French Guiana really belongs to faraway France. In years past, French Guiana was famous for its prison colony on Devils Island, and for the dreaded prison camps at Kourou and Saint-Laurent on the mainland. These camps were closed in 1945.

Spanish-speaking Argentina, to the far south, differs greatly from these three small pockets of northern settlements. After Brazil, Argentina is the largest South American nation in both area and population. The country sprawls over 1,072,162 square miles (413,961.74 square kilometers) and contains around 27 million people. Its lifeblood is the Pampa, a huge plain where rich soil supports fields of grain and grass feeds great herds of cattle.

Argentina has attracted large numbers of Europeans. Its capital, Buenos Aires, has mushroomed until the population of the city and its suburbs tilts toward ten and a half million.

Argentina is especially powerful among the nations of the southern part of the continent. These include Chile, whose over 11 million people live in the narrow strip of land between the Pacific and the Andes, and Uruguay and Paraguay, tiny countries with fewer than three and a half million citizens apiece.

The more northern countries of Peru, Ecuador, and Bolivia have much in common, for their Andean plateaus and valleys once belonged to the golden empire of the Incas. The Incas ruled over a highly civilized realm of about 3 million subjects. Today, Peru alone has over 8 million Indian citizens—more than any other country in the Western Hemisphere. Many Indians still speak Quechua—the language of the ancient Incas.

Cuzco, in modern-day Peru, was the capital of the empire. Still standing is the fortress which crowned the ancient city. Its walls consist of such massive boulders that scientists cannot understand how the Incas were able to build with them.

Farther north along the Pacific coast is Colombia, gateway to the continent. Only through Colombia can land travelers reach Central America. Bogotá, Colombia's capital and largest city, was among the first settled in the New World.

For years neighboring Venezuela was one of South America's poorest nations. But all this changed when, in 1917, vast oil deposits were discovered at Maracaibo. Today, Venezuela has the highest standard of living in South America. And, Venezuela and Ecuador are Latin America's only members of the powerful Organization of Petroleum Exporting Countries (OPEC).

But whatever their power, location, or size, the countries of South America are linked by the strong Latin character of their continent. This tie sets them apart from the people of any other single continent.

Chile possesses a wealth of minerals. It mines about 16 percent of the world's copper and vast amounts of iron ore, nitrates, and coal.

Brazil's capital is the ultra-modern city of Brasília, built in 1960 in the central uplands.

CARIBBEAN SEA

PACIFIC OCEAN

Equator

NICARAGUA
Managua
León
San Juan del Sur
Bluefields
Lago de Nicaragua
San Juan del Norte (Greytown)
Limón
Puntarenas
San José
COSTA RICA
Irazú (Vol.) 11,260
Golfo de Nicoya
Bocas del Toro
David
Golfo Dulce
Golfo de Chiriquí
COIBA
PANAMA
ISTMO
Colón
Panamá
Golfo de Panamá
PENINSULA DE AZUERO

ISLA DEL COCO (Costa Rica)

ISLA DE MALPELO (Colombia)

PINTA
MARCHENA
GENOVESA
SAN SALVADOR
SANTA CRUZ
ISABELA
SAN CRISTOBAL
ARCHIPIELAGO DE COLON (GALÁPAGOS ISLANDS) (Ecuador)

PTA DE GALLINAS
PENINSULA DE GUAJIRA
ARUBA (Neth.)
CURAÇAO (Neth.)
BONAIRE (Neth.)
ISLAS LOS ROQUES
Willemstad
Punto Fijo
PEN. DE PARAGUANÁ
Riohacha
Santa Marta
Puerto Colombia
Barranquilla
Soledad
Cartagena
Sabanalarga
Pico Cristóbal
Ciénaga
Fundación
Villanueva
El Carmen
Calamar
Plato
Sincelejo
Sincé
Lorica
Magangué
El Banco
Ocaña
Ceretó
Montería
Turbo
Golfo del Darien

Maracaibo
Cabimas
San Felipe
Puerto Cabello
Maracay
La Guaira
CARACAS
Los Teques
Cumaná
Puerto la Cruz
Barcelona
Maturín
Barquisimeto
Valencia
Trujillo
MÉRIDA
La Victoria
San Carlos
Ocumare del Tuy
Valle de Barcelona
El Tigre
Ciudad Guayana
Ciudad Bolívar

VENEZUELA

Cúcuta
Pamplona
Bucaramanga
Arauca
San Cristóbal
Puerto de Nutrias
San Fernando de Apure

COLOMBIA

MEDELLIN
Manizales
Pereira
Armenia
Ibagué
BOGOTA
Girardot
Villavicencio
Buenaventura
Bahía de Buenaventura
Cali
Palmira
Buga
Neiva
Popayán
Bolívar
Pitalito
Florencia
Tumaco
Barbacoas
Túquerres
Pasto
Ipiales
Tulcán
Ibarra
Otavalo
Cayambe

ECUADOR
Quito
Latacunga
Cotopaxi 19,347
Archidona
Manta
Portoviejo
Jipijapa
Ambato
Baños
Chimborazo 20,561
Riobamba
Alausí
Babahoyo
Guaranda
Guayaquil
Cuenca
Azogues
Sigsig
Machala
Santa Rosa
Loja
Tumbes
PTA. PARIÑAS
Talara
Paita
Sullana
Chulucanas
Piura
PTA. AGUJA
Castilla

Iquitos
Leticia
Tefé
Coari
São Paulo de Olivença
Içana
Uaupés
Barcelos
Rio Negro

AMAZONAS
SELVAS

PERU
Chiclayo
Chachapoyas
Ferreñafe
Lambayeque
Puerto Eten
Moyobamba
Yurimaguas
Lamas
Tarapoto
Cajamarca
Pacasmayo
Chepén
Huamachuco
Puerto Chicama
Trujillo
Salaverry
Chimbote
Nevs Huascarán 22,205
Huaraz
Tingo María
Huánuco
Cerro de Pasco
Puerto Bermúdez
Huacho
Huaral
GRAN PAJONAL
ISLAS CHINCHAS
Callao
LIMA
La Oroya
Chorrillos
Huancayo
Machu Picchu
Cañete
Huancavelica
Ayacucho
Cuzco
Chincha Alta
Pisco
Abancay
Bahía de Pisco
Ica
Cotabambas
Sicuani
PTA. CARRETAS
Puquio
Ayaviri
Coracora
Juliaca
Nudo Coropuna 21,696
Puno
Arequipa
Camaná
Moquegua
Lago Titicaca
La Paz
Mollendo
Ilo
Tacna
Arica
Oruro
Iquique
BOLIVIA
Cochabamba
Sucre
Potosí
Uyuni
Tropic of Capricorn
Tocopilla
Antofagasta
ARGENTINA
JUJUY

Cerro Cruzeiro do Sul
Pôrto Acre
Rio Branco
Cobija
Riberalta
Guajará Mirim
ACRE
Pôrto Velho
RONDÔNIA (TER.)
MASSIÇO DE PAC
Villa Bella
Guajará
Trinidad
Reyes
Puerto Maldonado

Inset map (Colombia detail):

Pavarandocito
Alto de Tres Morros 11,155
Ituango
Valdivia
Dabeiba
Anorí
Segovia
Yarumal
Remedios
Cañasgordas
Paramillo 12,990
San Andrés
Amalfi
Yolombó
Alto Musinga 12,631
Antioquia
Santa Rosa
Cisneros
ANTIOQUIA
Maro Jarapeto 9,186
Urrao
Sabanas Páramo 13,395
Sopetrán
Barbosa
San Roque
Puerto Berrío
Anzá
Bello
Itagüí
Rionegro
Nare
San Carlos
Bebara
Concordia
Caldas
La Ceja
San Luis
Puerto Niñn
Negua
Andes
Aguadas
Cerro de los Paradas 10,991
Sonsón
Quibdó
Certegui
Riosucio
Salamina
La Dorada
CHOCO
Cerro Caramanta 12,795
Manzanares
Victoria
Honda
Tadó
Istmina
Anserma
Neira
Fresno
Mariquita
Villeta
Cerro Tamaná 13,780
RISARALDA
CALDAS
Santa Rosa de Cabal
Armero
Líbano
Venadillo
Zipaquirá
El Cajón
Manizales
Nevado del Ruiz 17,716
Ambalema
Guasca
Gachetá
Sipí
Cerro Torra 12,721
Cartago
Pereira
Finlandia
Nevado del Tolima 17,110
Facatativá
La Mesa
Fontibón
La Calera
Quibmaya
Ibagué
CUNDINAMARCA
Cajamarca
Rovira
Pico de Chili 12,894
Girardot
Fusagasugá
Quetame
Restrepo
Roldanillo
Armenia
BOGOTA
Fómeque
Zarzal
QUINDIO
Caicedonia
Sevilla
Pico de Mundonuevo 13,123
Espinal
Villavicencio
VALLE DEL CAUCA
TOLIMA
San Antonio
Ortega
Guamo
Acacías
Tulua
Coyaima
Purificación
Prado
San Martín
Buga
Guacarí
Chaparral
Ataco
Natagaima
Dolores
Alpujarra
Colombia
META
Cerito
Cerro el Nevado 14,961
Darién
Restrepo
Coyaima
Aipe
Villavieja
Baraya
San Martín
Cali
Palmira
Florida
Miranda
HUILA
San Juan
Jamundí
Pradera
Boqueroncito
Puerto Tejada
Corinto
Toribío
Nevada de Huila 18,865
Neiva
Palermo
Buenos Aires
Santander
Tello
San Antonio

Scale 1:4,200,000
0 10 20 30 40 Miles
0 10 20 30 40 50 60 Kilometers

©RMCN.

A-549100-26   9-8-16*
COPYRIGHT BY
RAND McNALLY & COMPANY
MADE IN U.S.A.

Cities and Towns
0 to 50,000
50,000 to 500,000
500,000 to 1,000,000
1,000,000 and over

Scale 1:16,850,000 : one inch to 265 miles. Sinusoidal Projection
Elevations and depressions are given in feet

Longitude West of Greenwich

TOBAGO
Port of Spain
TRINIDAD AND TOBAGO
TRINIDAD

Inset map (Caracas region):

CARIBBEAN SEA
Tocuyo de la Costa
Chichiriviche
Cayo Sombrero
Tucacas
Golfo Triste
Puerto Cabello
Maiquetía La Guaira Naiguatá La Sabana
Carayaca
CARACAS
Petare Santa Lucía Guatire
DISTRITO FEDERAL
Los Teques
Higuerote
Río Chico
Boca de Uchire
CABO CODERA
ISLA DE MARGARITA
Boca del Pozo PUNTA ARENAS △ 2303
PUNTA ARENAS Punta de Piedras
NUEVA ESPARTA ISLA CUBAGUA
ISLA LA TORTUGA
PUNTA DE ARAYA
Manicuare
Cumaná
Las Vegas **SUCRE**
Puerto La Cruz Guanta
El Hatillo Barcelona
ISLA LA BORRACHA
Bergantín △ 8000
Santa Inés
Pâto **ANZOÁTEGUI**
Anaco Santa Rosa
Aragua de Barcelona
FALCÓN Morón El Cambur Pico Ceniza △ 7988
Montalbán Guacara Maracay
San Joaquín **MIRANDA**
Valencia Cagua
CARABOBO Lago de Valencia
Güigüe Villa de Cura
Ocumare del Tuy
San Sebastián
San Juan de los Morros
Parapara **GUÁRICO**
Tinaquillo **COJEDES**
Dos Caminos Barbacoas
Camatagua
Libertad de Orituco
Onoto
Aragua de Barcelona
Scale 1:4,200,000
0 10 20 30 40 Miles
0 10 20 30 40 50 60 Kilometers
©RMCN.

Main map labels:

Boca Grande
Morawhanna
Georgetown
Bartica Rosignol New Amsterdam
Wismar Rockstone Skeldon Totness Nieuw Nickerie Paranam Albina Paramaribo
Moengo
St. Laurent
Sinnamary
ILE DU DIABLE (DEVIL'S I.)
GUYANA **SURINAME** **FRENCH GUIANA**
Cayenne
CABO ORANGE
Saint-Georges
Kaieteur Fall
Dr. Ir. W. J. Van Blommestein Meer
GEBERGTE
TUMUC-HUMAC MTS.
ACARAI MTS.
Roraima △ 9094
RORAIMA (TER.)
a Vista do Branco
Amapá
AMAPÁ (TER.)
Macapá
ILHA CAVIANA
Mazagão
Amapá

ATLANTIC OCEAN

Equator

Moura
Manaus (Manáos)
Óbidos Alenquer Faro Parintins Santarém Altamira
Itacoatiara
ILHA TUPINAMBARANAS
Maués Itaituba Brasília Legal (Fordlândia)
Borba
Manicoré
PARÁ
SERRA DOS CARAJÁS
São João do Araguaia
Tucuruí
Gurupá Breves
ILHA DE MARAJÓ
Belém (Pará)
Cametá Abaetetuba
Bragança
Marapanim
Cururupu
São Luís (Maranhão)
Alcântara
Rosário Viana
Itapecurú-Mirim
Monção Brejo
Parnaíba
Tutóia
Camocim Acaraú
FORTALEZA (Ceará)
Maranguape
Sobral Baturité
Ipu Quixadá Aracati
Areia Branca
Russas Mossoró
RIO GRANDE DO NORTE
Ceará-Mirim Nova Cruz **Natal**
MARANHÃO Teresina
Grajaú Barra do Corda
Caxias Codó Campo Maior
Pedreiras Barras Pedro II
Crateús Senador Pompeu Iguatu Içó
Currais Novos
Campina Grande João Pessoa (Paraíba)
Cabedelo
PIAUÍ
Miradoro Floriano Picos Crato
Juàzeiro do Norte Patos **PARAÍBA**
Nazaré da Mata
PERNAMBUCO Caruaru **Olinda**
RECIFE (Pernambuco)
Loreto Oeiras Paulistana Flores Granito Sertânia
Cabrobó Garanhuns Palmares
Pôrto de Pedras
São Raimundo Nonato Petrolina Juàzeiro
Palmeira dos Índios
ALAGOAS Maceió
Parnaguá Remanso Jeremoabo Penedo
Barra Jacobina Itabaiana Coruripe
SERGIPE **Aracaju**
São Cristóvão Estância
Carolina Balsas Santa Filomena
Riachão
Tocantinópolis
BAHIA
Barreiras Morro do Chapéu Serrinha
Feira de Santana Santo Amaro
Cachoeira Nazaré
Alagoinhas Catu
SALVADOR (Bahia)
Pôrto Nacional
Natividade
Correntina Lençóis Mucugê Jequié Valença
Caetité Condeúba Itabuna
Vitória da Conquista Ilhéus
GOIÁS
SERRA DO ESTRONDO
Cavalcante
Pilar de Goiás
Barra
Januária Rio Pardo de Minas
Itabuna Canavieiras
São Francisco Grão Mogol Belmonte
Montes Claros Pôrto Seguro
ARQUIPÉLAGO DOS ABROLHOS
B R A Z I L
Formosa **Brasília**
Luziânia Silvânia
Pirenópolis
Anápolis Goiás
Goiânia
Bela Vista de Goiás
Paracatu Pirapora
Patos de Minas Diamantina
Grão Mogol Teófilo Otoni
Peçanha Caravelas
São Mateus
Ipameri Morrinhos Catalão Araguari
Sete Lagoas
Araxá Pará de Minas Curvelo
MINAS GERAIS
Diamantina Gov. Valadares
Coronel Fabriciano Colatina
Uberlândia Uberaba Formiga
Conselheiro Lafaiete Ponte Nova
BELO HORIZONTE Sta. Bárbara
MATO GROSSO
CHAPADA DE MATO GROSSO
SERRA DO RONCADOR
Diamantino Cuiabá
Rosário Oeste Barão de Melgaço
Cáceres
San José
El Roboré
Puerto Suárez
Corumbá
Bahía Negra
Aguidauana Campo Grande
Fuerte Olimpo
Mariscal Estigarribia
Pôrto Murtinho
Pôrto Pinasco
PARAGUAY
Concepción Belén
Horqueta
San José do Rio Prêto Franca Barretos
Ribeirão Prêto Passos
SÃO PAULO
Araçatuba Araraquara São Carlos
Marília Bauru Piracicaba
Presidente Epitácio Rio Claro
Campinas Jundiaí
Sorocaba Mogi das Cruzes
Santos São Vicente
Londrina Jacarézinho
PARANÁ
Ponta Grossa Castro
Curitiba
Guarapuava
Iguaçu Falls Guaíra
Pôrto Mendes
Três Lagoas
ESPÍRITO SANTO
Aracruz **Vitória**
Guarapari Cachoeiro do Itapemirim
Teresópolis Campos
Petrópolis Nova Friburgo
Juiz de Fora Barbacena
Niterói **RIO DE JANEIRO**
CABO FRIO
Tropic of Capricorn

40,000 SQ MI AREA
0 100 200 Miles

0 50 100 200 300 400 500 Miles
0 100 200 400 600 800 Kilometers

BOLIVIA
PARAGUAY
MATO GROSSO DO SUL
SÃO PAULO
PARANÁ
SANTA CATARINA
RIO GRANDE DO SUL
ARGENTINA
CHILE
URUGUAY

Tocopilla
Chuquicamata
La Quiaca
Villazón
Tupiza
Tarija
Yacuiba
Porto Murtinho
Olimpo
Bella Vista
Pedro de Valdivia
Calama
Cerro Llicancabur 19,455
PUNA DE ATACAMA
Oran
Tartagal
Mariscal Estigarribia
Puerto Casado
Presidente Epitácio
Três Lagoas
Londrina
Araçatuba
Tupã
Lins
Bauru
São Carlos
São José do Rio Prêto
Ribeirão Prêto
Franca
BELO HORIZONTE
MINAS GERAIS
Mejillones
Antofagasta
Cachinal
San Antonio de los Cobres
Salta
Jujuy
San Pedro
Tropic of Capricorn
Concepción
Horqueta
Puerto Pinasco
Pedro Juan Caballero
Ponta Porã
Presidente Prudente
Assis
Piracicaba
Campinas
Sorocaba
SÃO PAULO
Jundiaí
Taubaté
RIO DE JANEIRO
Nova Iguaçu
Petrópolis
Juiz de Fora
25,050 25,052 22,052 22,042
Cerro Licancabur
Taltal
Chañaral
Cerro Azufre (Copiapó) Vol 19,947
Caldera
Copiapó
Vallenar
Nevados de Cachi
Metán
TUCUMÁN
Tucumán
Villa Hayes
ASUNCIÓN
Luque
Coronel Oviedo
Caazapá
São Juan Bautista
Pilar
Formosa
CHACO
Presidencia Roque Sáenz Peña
Resistencia
Humaitá
Encarnación
Posadas
MISIONES
Erechim
Passo Fundo
Caràzinho
Lajes
Florianópolis
Curitiba
Ponta Grossa
Guarapuava
Iguaçu Falls
União da Vitória
Mafra
Joinville
Itajaí
Blumenau
Brusque
Laguna
Tubarão
Porto Mendes
Paranaguá

Huasco
Freirina
Tinogasta
Andalgalá
Belén
La Banda
SANTIAGO DEL ESTERO
Santiago del Estero
Villa Ángela
Corrientes
CORRIENTES
Bella Vista
Sto. Tomé
São Borja
Cruz Alta
Santa Maria
Cachoeira do Sul
Caxias do Sul
São Leopoldo
PORTO ALEGRE
Pelotas
Rio Grande

Coquimbo
La Serena
Tongoy
Ovalle
Illapel
Los Vilos
Viña del Mar
Valparaíso
Catamarca
CATAMARCA
Frias
Chilecito
LA RIOJA
La Rioja
Anatuya
CÓRDOBA
Córdoba
Dean Funes
Cruz del Eje
Reconquista
Vera
Tostado
Goya
Curuzú Cuatiá
Paso de los Libres
Uruguaiana
Alegrete
Rosário do Sul
Livramento
Bagé
Melo
L. dos Patos
L. da Mangueira
Santa Vitória do Palmar

San Juan
SAN JUAN
Cerro Mercedario 22,211
Cerro Aconcagua 22,831
Usapallata Pass 12,540
SANTIAGO
San Bernardo
Cerro Tupungato 22,310 Vol.
Rancagua
Sewell
San Felipe
Mendoza
MENDOZA
Villa Dolores
San Luis
SAN LUIS
Río Cuarto
San Francisco
SANTA FE
Santa Fe
Rafaela
Paraná
ENTRE RÍOS
Concordia
Salto
Paysandú
Concepción del Uruguay
URUGUAY
Tacuarembó
Santa Ana
Rivera
Durazno
San Rafael
Rosario
Pergamino
Junín
Gualeguaychú
Victoria
San Nicolás
Zárate
Campana
Trinidad
Florida
Rocha
Maldonado
San Carlos

Melipilla
San Antonio
San Fernando
Curicó
Talca
Constitución
Cauquenes
San Carlos
Chillán
Talcahuano
Concepción
Coronel
Lota
Los Ángeles
Angol
Victoria
Lautaro
Temuco
Valdivia
Corral
La Unión
Osorno
Laboulaye
General Pico
Nueva de Julio
Bragado
Chivilcoy
General
Lincoln
Venado Tuerto
Casilda
BUENOS AIRES
Avellaneda
La Plata
MONTEVIDEO
Minas
Sta. Lucía
Colonia
Trenque Lauquen
Pehuajó
Bolívar
Las Flores
Dolores
Chascomús
Saladillo
Olavarría
Azul
General Madariaga
RÍO NEGRO
Santa Rosa
LA PAMPA
BUENOS AIRES
Tandil
Rauch
Ayacucho
Guaminí
Coronel Suárez
SA. DEL TANDIL
Coronel Pringles
Tres Arroyos
Necochea
Mar del Plata
Bahía Blanca
Coronel Dorrego
SA. DE LA VENTANA
Balcarce
Juárez
Carmen de Patagones
Viedma
San Antonio Oeste
Golfo San Matías
PENÍNSULA VALDÉS
PTA. DELGADA
Neuquén
NEUQUÉN
Zapala
General Roca
Choele Choel
META DE SOMUNCURÁ
Puerto Madryn
Trelew
Rawson

Osorno
Puerto Varas
Puerto Montt
Ancud
ISLA DE CHILOÉ
Castro
Cerro Tronador 11,700
San Carlos de Bariloche
Esquel
CHUBUT
LOMAS COLORADAS
Gastre
PAMPA DE CASTILLO
Comodoro Rivadavia
Golfo San Jorge
C. BLANCO
Puerto Deseado
CABO DOS BAHÍAS
PUNTA MEDANOSA

ARCHIPIÉLAGO DE LOS CHONOS
PENÍNSULA DE TAITAO
Cerro San Valentín 13,314
GOLFO DE PEÑAS
Puerto Aisén
Buenos Aires
Río Deseado
SANTA CRUZ
GRAN BAJO
San Julián
META DE LAS VIZCACHAS
Puerto Santa Cruz
Río Gallegos

CAMPANA
WELLINGTON
ARCHIPIÉLAGO MADRE DE DIOS
HANOVER
ARCHIPIÉLAGO REINA ADELAIDA
SANTA INÉS
Cerro Chaltén 11,600
Río Turbio
Puerto Natales
Punta Arenas
PEN. DE BRUNSWICK
Estrecho de Magallanes
DESO LACIÓN
Mt. Sarmiento 8100
TIERRA DEL FUEGO
C. DARWIN
Río Grande
ISLA DE LOS ESTADOS
Le Maire
Ushuaia
NAVARINO
HOSTE
CABO DE HORNOS (CAPE HORN)
ISLAS DIEGO RAMÍREZ

Bahía Grande
Bahía Blanca
Bahía Blanca (Golfo)

FALKLAND IS. (ISLAS MALVINAS) (Br.) (Claimed by Argentina)
Stanley

PACIFIC OCEAN
ATLANTIC OCEAN
ATACAMA TRENCH

BANCO BURDWOOD

Longitude West of Greenwich

H-549200-26 11-7-21
COPYRIGHT BY RAND McNALLY & COMPANY
MADE IN U.S.A.

40,000 SQ MI AREA
0 100 200 Miles

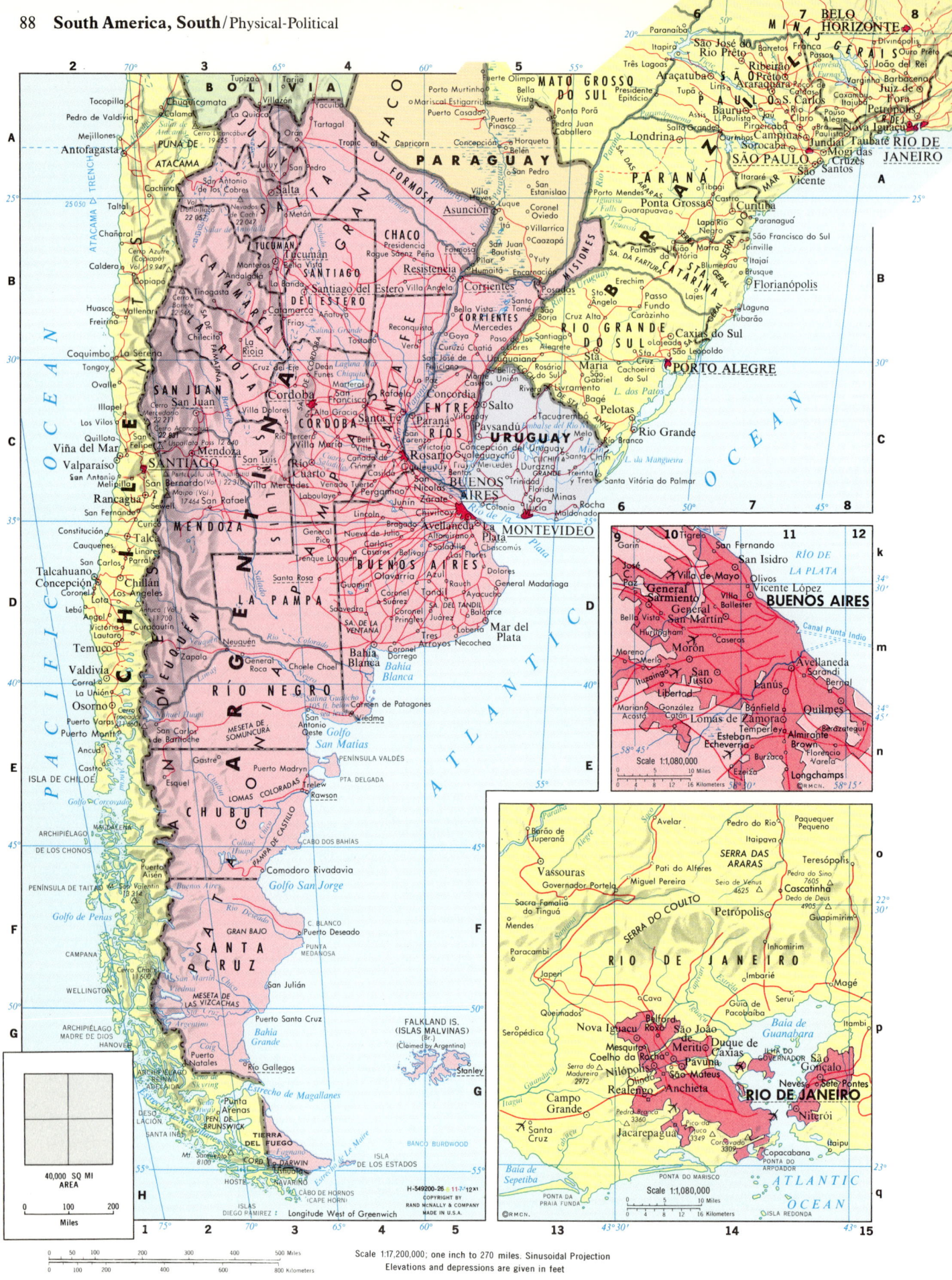

Scale 1:17,200,000; one inch to 270 miles. Sinusoidal Projection
Elevations and depressions are given in feet

0 50 100 200 300 400 500 Miles
0 100 200 400 600 800 Kilometers

BUENOS AIRES
Tigre
Garín
San Fernando
San Isidro
RÍO DE LA PLATA
Villa de Mayo
Olivos
Vicente López
General Sarmiento
Bella Vista
General San-Martín
Villa Ballester
Caseros
Hurlingham
Morón
Moreno
Ituzaingó
San Justo
Avellaneda
Sarandí
Bernal
Libertad
Merlo
Banfield
Lanús
Quilmes
Mariano Acosta
González Catán
Lomas de Zamora
Temperley
Almirante Brown
Berazategui
Esteban Echeverría
Burzaco
Florencio Varela
Ezeiza
Longchamps
Canal Punta Indio
Scale 1:1,080,000
0 4 8 16 Kilometers
0 4 8 16 Miles

RIO DE JANEIRO
Barão de Juperanã
Avelar
Pedro do Rio
Paquequer Pequeno
Itaipava
SERRA DAS ARARAS
Teresópolis
Vassouras
Governador Portela
Miguel Pereira
Pati do Alferes
Seia de Venus 4625
Pedra do Sino 7605
Cascanha
Dedo de Deus 4905
Petrópolis
Guapimirim
Mendes
Paracambi
SERRA DO COULTO
Inhomirim
RIO DE JANEIRO
Imbariê
Magé
Japeri
Queimados
Cava
Guia de Pacobaíba
Seropédica
Nova Iguaçu
Belford Roxo
São João de Meriti
Duque de Caxias
ILHA DO GOVERNADOR
São Gonçalo
Neves
Sete Pontes
Mesquita
Coelho da Rocha
Pavuna
Campo Grande
Nilópolis
Olinda
São Mateus
Anchieta
Realengo
Serra do Madureira 2972
Baía de Guanabara
Itambi
Itapuã
RIO DE JANEIRO
Niterói
Jacarepaguá
Pedra Branca 3360
Pico da Tijuca 3349
Corcovado 3309
Copacabana
PONTA DO ARPOADOR
Santa Cruz
Baía de Sepetiba
PONTA DA PRAIA FUNDA
PONTA DO MARISCO
ISLA REDONDA
ATLANTIC OCEAN
Scale 1:1,080,000
0 4 8 16 Kilometers
0 4 8 16 Miles
©rmcn.

Antarctica

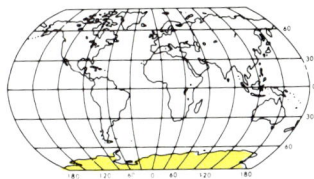

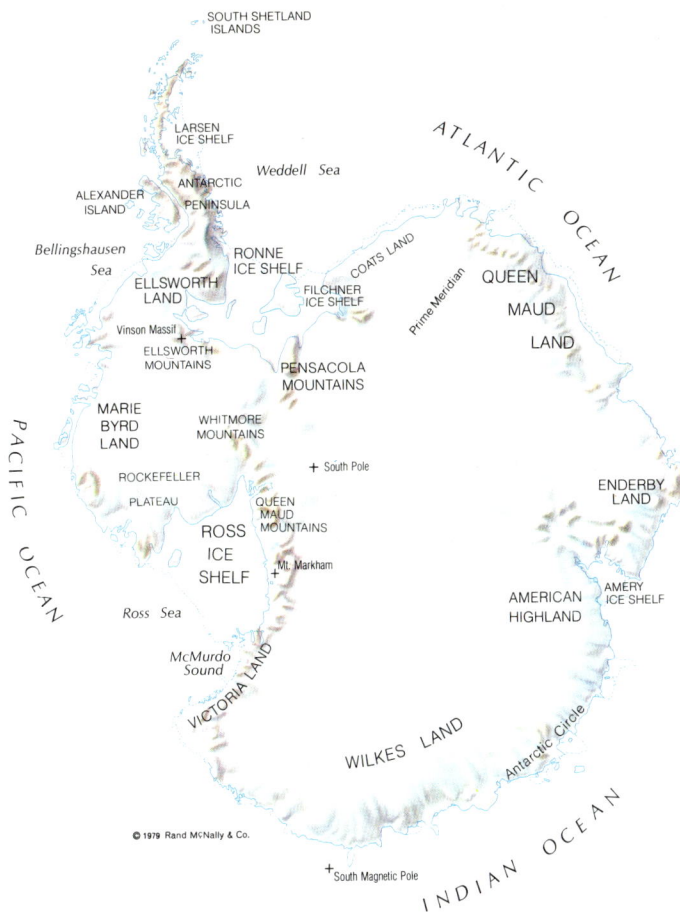

Antarctica Facts

Fifth largest continent
No permanent population
Highest mountain: Vinson Massif, 16,864 feet
(5,140.14 meters)
Location of South Pole
Location of South Magnetic Pole
World's lowest recorded temperature: Vostok,
−126.9°F (−88.3°C)

Antarctica, the coldest continent on earth, rests squarely on the South Pole. It is so cold here that an unprotected visitor would freeze in minutes. In midwinter, June, temperatures inland may drop below −100°F (−73°C).

Because of the tilt of the earth's axis and its path around the sun, Antarctica is without sunlight for months at a time. Even in "summer," the sun's rays strike at such a slanted angle the land receives very little heat.

Many nations have sent teams to Antarctica. Dog sleds are still used, but motorized toboggans are more common.

Most of Antarctica is covered with snow heaped so thick it forms a mile-high plateau at the pole. Bitter winds shriek over the seemingly endless white sheet at speeds averaging forty-four miles (seventy-one kilometers) an hour. In many places the snow has been packed by its own weight and frozen to become a massive ice pack. This ice is so heavy it has pressed parts of the land well below sea level. If the ice cap melted, all that could be seen

above the waters would be the peaks of the mountain chain which twists some 3,000 miles (4,827 kilometers) across the continent.

Many warm-blooded animals thrive in the waters on the fringes of the continent. Among these are seals, birds, and the great blue whales. Antarctica's largest land animal is a wingless insect less than one-tenth inch (2.54 millimeters) long.

Halfway between land and sea animals are Antarctica's penguins. Though penguins are birds, they cannot fly. Their wings are paddles that help them move underwater.

Surprisingly, Antarctica's waters hold more marine life than oceans in warmer parts of the globe. Antarctica's land has yielded small amounts of gold, iron, uranium, and coal. It is also thought to contain oil and natural gas.

Many nations claim parts of Antarctica. But the Antarctic Treaty of 1959 pledges these nations to wait until 1989 to settle their claims. Antarctica's future may well be more exciting than its lonely past.

Glossary and List of Map and Geographical Terms

Air mass: a body of air a hundred to a thousand miles across and reaching several miles upward.

Altitude: the height above sea level of the earth's physical features.

Antarctic and Arctic zones: the bitterly cold areas surrounding the South and North poles.

Astrolabe: an instrument used to observe the stars' positions. Used before the invention of the sextant.

Atmosphere: the entire mass of air surrounding the planet Earth.

Atoll: the ring of coral around an ocean lagoon, all that remains after a volcanic island sinks into the sea.

Axis: an imaginary line between the poles. The earth turns around its axis every twenty-four hours.

Barometer: an instrument that measures the weight of the air.

Barren: any land area that lacks normal vegetation.

Basin: any land area drained by a river and its tributaries.

Beast of burden: an animal used to carry heavy materials or perform other heavy work.

Bush country: a large land area with little vegetation, usually thinly settled.

Butte: an isolated upraised land area with steep sides and a small top.

Canal: any artificial waterway.

Canyon: a deep valley with steep sides.

Cape: a point of land jutting out into water.

Cartographer: a mapmaker.

Chronometer: an instrument used by navigators for measuring time— east-west distances from the prime meridian.

Cirrus: a white wispy cloud formed at very high altitudes.

Coastal: land at the edge of the ocean or sea.

Compass: an instrument for telling direction. A magnetic needle turns freely on a pivot and points to the magnetic north.

Continent: one of the great named divisions of land on earth.

Continental shelf: a shallow undersea area bordering a continent, ending in a steep slope to the deeper ocean.

Contour line: a line on a map joining the land points having the same elevation, or height.

Coral reef: a rocklike deposit of animal skeletons just below the ocean surface.

Cumulus: a huge summer cloud with a flat base and high fluffy top.

Cyclone: a storm or system of winds spinning around a center of low atmospheric pressure.

Desert: dry land which supports only widely scattered plant and animal life.

Doldrums: an area of calm winds and warm updrafts near the equator.

Downdraft: a downward movement of air, as during a thunderstorm.

Earthquake: a shaking of the earth caused by volcanic or plate action.

Earth's crust: the earth's outer layers.

Earth tremor: a quivering on the surface of the earth.

Easterly: wind blowing from the east.

Elevation: the height to which earth features reach above sea level.

Equator: an imaginary line on globes and maps halfway between the poles.

Erosion: the wearing away or destruction of land by wind, water, and ice.

Export: to send a product to another country.

Extinct: no longer existing.

Eye of a storm: nearly calm center of a storm.

Fall line: a line along which rivers plunge from plateaus and hills to the plain below.

Fault: a fracture in the earth's crust.

Feature: an important, usually very noticeable, part of the earth.

Fertile: able to bear fruit or vegetables in great quantities.

Fjord: an ice-carved inlet of the sea between steep cliffs.

Frontal zone: an area of severe weather where two great air masses—one cold and one hot—collide.

Funnel: the funnel-shaped downward section of a storm cloud, particularly in a tornado.

Game preserve: an area where wild animals are protected.

Geologist: a scientist who studies the earth's outer layers.

Geyser: a natural spring that spouts hot water and steam.

Glacier: a large body of ice moving slowly down over an area of land.

Gravitational pull: that force which pulls objects toward itself.

Grid: a set of lines crossing each other on which maps are drawn.

Gulf: part of an ocean or sea reaching into a land area.

Habitat: the place where a plant or animal naturally lives and grows.

Headland: a point of high land jutting out into a body of water.

Hemisphere: half of the earth.

Hill: an upland area of gentle slopes and a broad summit, generally lower than a mountain.

Horse latitudes: about 30° north and 30° south. Areas of descending air and high pressures.

Hurricane: a tropical cyclone with winds of at least seventy-four miles (119.08 kilometers) per hour and heavy rain.

Ice cap: a cover of permanent ice and snow on the earth's surface.

Intermontane: between the mountains.

Island: land, smaller than a continent, surrounded by water.

Isthmus: a narrow strip of land joining two larger land areas.

Jungle: a mass of tropical plant growth.

Lagoon: a shallow pond near a larger body of water.

Landform: a feature of the earth's surface.

Landmark: an outstanding feature of the land used as a guide.

Landmass: a large area of land.

Latitude: the distance between parallels, north or south of the equator.

Lava: melted rock which flows out of the earth's surface.

Legend: key to the symbols and colors used on maps.

Longitude: the east-west distance between meridians.

Marine: having to do with the sea.

Marsupials: mammals whose young develop within pouches on the females' abdomens, such as kangaroos and opossums.

Mattang: stick chart used by Micronesian islanders 2,000 years ago to show ocean wave patterns.

Meridians: imaginary lines joining the North and South poles. The distance between meridians is called longitude.

Mesa: an isolated tableland with steeply sloping sides and a large flat land area on top.

Meteorologist: a scientist who studies the earth's atmosphere and forecasts the weather.

Microscopic: invisible to the naked eye unless magnified through a microscope.

Migrate: to move from one region or climate to another in order to survive.

Molten rock: rock turned into liquid by intense heat.

Monsoon: a seasonal wind in southern Asia.

Mountain: a landmass, with steep slopes and a sharp peak.

Natural barrier: any geographical feature which separates two areas.

Navigation: the science of moving around on—or above—the earth.

Nimbus: a dark rain cloud reaching as far as one can see.

Ocean: the whole body of saltwater covering nearly three-fourths of the earth's surface.

Oceanographer: a scientist who studies the sea and everything in it.

Outback: bush country and deserts, found in Australia.

Ozone: a special form of oxygen. High in the atmosphere, a layer of ozone surrounds the earth, screening out the sun's harmful rays. Closer to the earth's surface, ozone sometimes forms as the result of pollution. Even in small amounts, ozone is irritating to breathe.

Pampas: a grass-covered plain found in South America.

Parallels: imaginary lines circling the earth in an east-west direction. Like railroad tracks, they never meet. The distance between parallels is called latitude.

Peninsula: an area of land almost surrounded by water.

Physical: that which can be seen and measured and, perhaps, weighed. Things that have height and width and depth. A physical map shows the earth's major features—mountains, hills, plains, oceans, rivers, lakes.

Piedmont: the area lying or formed at the base of mountains. May consist of plateaus or low hills.

Plain: an area of level-to-rolling, almost treeless land.

Plankton: microscopic animal and plant life found in the sea.

Plateau: large level land area raised sharply above the surrounding land.

Plates: sections underlying the surface of the earth. Their movement may cause faults or other changes in the surface.

Polar: having to do with the North or South poles or the areas around them.

Portolan charts: detailed maps used for navigation by European sailors in the 1500s.

Prehistoric: the time before history was written down.

Prime meridian: the meridian chosen to be 0° or prime meridian. It passes through Greenwich, England.

Quake: to quiver or shake. A shortened term for earthquake. A tremor.

Rain forest: a densely grown tropical woodland with almost daily rainfall.

Range: a series of mountains in a group.

Rapid: part of a river where the current is fast and the surface is broken by large rocks.

Ridge: a long narrow upper crest. Can be of very high formations on mountains, hills, waves, even parts of the ocean floor.

Rift: a deep crack in the earth's crust.

Scale: a mathematical key which tells how much the earth or an area of the earth was reduced to fit on a map.

Sea: a saltwater body smaller than an ocean.

Sea level: the average level of the ocean between high tide and low tide. Land areas are measured above or below sea level.

Sedge: tufted marsh plants.

Seismologist: a scientist who studies earthquakes.

Silt: water-carried earth material, finer than sand.

Smog: a combination of fog and smoke.

Solar energy: power from the sun.

Solar system: the sun and the planets and other space objects which revolve around it.

Space orbit: a circular path outside the solar system.

Spillway: a passage for extra water to run over or around something that stands in its way.

Steppe: a vast level or rolling tract of treeless land.

Stratus: a wide flat cloud at a low altitude.

Subcontinent: a large peninsulalike area of land. For example, India.

Tectonic: having to do with changes in the shape of the earth's surface and the forces that produce those changes.

Terrain: the landscape.

Tornado: a destructive whirling cyclone over a land area.

Trade winds: the winds that blow out of the horse latitudes toward the doldrums. In the Northern Hemisphere they are the northeast trade winds; in the Southern Hemisphere they are the southeast trade winds.

Trench: a long, narrow, steep-sided ditch in the ocean floor.

Tropics: the area on both sides of the equator where temperatures are always high and rainfall is plentiful.

Tundra: a treeless plain in arctic regions. Areas below the surface are permanently frozen.

Updraft: an upward movement of air.

Upland: high land—mountains, hills, plateaus, mesas, buttes.

Valley: a low area between ranges of hills or mountains.

Volcanic cone: the top of a volcano.

Volcano: an opening in the earth's surface from which molten rock and steam erupt.

Volcanologist: a scientist who studies volcanoes.

Westerly: wind blowing from the west.

Map Names and Abbreviations

This table lists the names and the abbreviations used for features on the physical-political maps. Each entry includes the feature name, the language from which it comes, and, in the case of foreign names, its English translation. Abbreviations are shown for those names that are abbreviated on the maps.

Ákra (Greek): cape, *Akr.*
Cabo (Spanish, Portuguese): cape, *C.*
Cap (French): cape, *C.*
Cape (English): *C.*
Cerro (Spanish): mountain, hill
Cordillera (Spanish): mountain chain, *Cord.*
Erg (Arabic): strait
Estrecho (Spanish): strait
Fort (English): *Ft.*
Golfo (Spanish, Italian): gulf, bay, *G.*
Gora (Russian): mountain, *G.*
Gulf (English): *G.*
Hai (Chinese): sea
Île (French): island
Ilha (Portuguese): island
Isla (Spanish): island, *I.*
Jabal (Arabic): mountain
Khrebet (Russian): mountain range
Lake (English): *L.*
Lago (Spanish, Portuguese): lake, *L.*
More (Russian): sea
Mountain(s) (English): *Mt. (Mts.)*
Mys (Russian): cape, *M.*
National (English): *Nat'l*
Occidental (Spanish): western

Oriental (Spanish): eastern
Óros (Greek): mountain
Ozero (Russian): lake, *Oz.*
Peninsula (English): *Pen.*
Peski (Russian): desert
People's Democratic Republic (English): *P.D.R.*
Plato (Russian): plateau
Point (English): *Pt.*
Pointe (French): point, *Pte.*
Poluostrov (Russian): peninsula, *P-Ov.*
Proliv (Russian): strait
Punta (Spanish): point
Reservoir (English): *Res.*
Río (Spanish): river, *R.*
River (English): *R.*
Salto (Spanish, Portuguese): waterfall
Serra (Portuguese): mountain chain, *Sa.*
Shan (Chinese): mountain, hill
Sierra (Spanish): mountain range, *Sa.*
Sound (English): *Sd.*
Soviet Socialist Republic (English): *S.S.R.*
Vodokhranilishche (Russian): reservoir, *Vdkhr.*
Volcano (English): *Vol.*

World Facts and Comparisons

General Information

Equatorial diameter of the earth, 7,926.38 miles.
Polar diameter of the earth, 7,899.80 miles.
Mean diameter of the earth, 7,917.52 miles.
Equatorial circumference of the earth, 24,901.46 miles.
Polar circumference of the earth, 24,855.34 miles.
Mean distance from the earth to the sun, 93,020,000 miles.
Mean distance from the earth to the moon, 238,857 miles.
Total area of the earth, 197,000,000 square miles.

Highest elevation on the earth's surface, Mt. Everest, Asia, 29,028 feet.
Lowest elevation on the earth's land surface, shores of the Dead Sea, Asia, 1,312 feet below sea level.
Greatest known depth of the ocean, southwest of Guam, Pacific Ocean, 35,810 feet.
Total land area of the earth (incl. inland water and Antarctica), 57,900,000 square miles.

Area of Africa, 11,700,000 square miles.
Area of Antarctica, 5,400,000 square miles.
Area of Asia, 17,400,000 square miles.
Area of Europe, 3,800,000 square miles.
Area of North America, 9,400,000 square miles.
Area of Oceania (incl. Australia) 3,300,000 square miles.
Area of South America, 6,900,000 square miles.
Population of the earth (est.1/1/90), 5,236,000,000.

Principal Islands and Their Areas

ISLAND	Area (Sq. Mi.)
Baffin I., Can.	195,928
Banks I., Can.	27,038
Borneo (Kalimantan), Asia	287,300
Bougainville, Papua New Guinea	3,600
Cape Breton I., Can.	3,981
Celebes (Sulawesi), Indon.	73,057
Ceram (Seram), Indon.	45,801
Corsica, France	3,352
Crete, Greece	3,189
Cuba, N.A.	42,800
Cyprus, Asia	3,572
Devon I., Can.	21,331
Ellesmere I., Can.	75,767
Flores, Indon.	5,502
Great Britain, U.K.	88,795
Greenland, N.A.	840,000
Guadalcanal, Solomon Is.	2,060
Hainan Dao, China	13,100
Hawaii, U.S.	4,034
Hispaniola, N.A.	29,300
Hokkaidō, Japan	32,245
Honshū, Japan	89,176
Iceland, Europe	39,800
Ireland, Europe	32,600
Jamaica, N.A.	4,200
Java (Jawa), Indon.	51,038
Kodiak I., U.S.	3,670
Kyūshū, Japan	17,129
Leyte, Philippines	2,785
Long Island, U.S.	1,377
Luzon, Philippines	40,420
Madagascar, Africa	227,000
Melville I., Can.	16,274
Mindanao, Philippines	36,537
Mindoro, Philippines	3,759
Negros, Philippines	4,907
New Britain, Papua New Guinea	14,093
New Caledonia, Oceania	6,252
Newfoundland, Can.	42,031
New Guinea, Asia-Oceania	309,000
New Ireland, Papua New Guinea	3,500
North East Land, Norway	6,350
North I., New Zealand	44,274
Novaya Zemlya, Sov. Un.	31,900
Palawan, Philippines	4,550
Panay, Philippines	4,446
Prince of Wales I., Can.	12,872
Puerto Rico, N.A.	3,500
Sakhalin, Sov. Un.	29,500
Samar, Philippines	5,100
Sardinia, Italy	9,301
Shikoku, Japan	7,258
Sicily, Italy	9,926
Somerset I., Can.	9,570
Southampton I., Can.	15,913
South I., New Zealand	57,870
Spitsbergen, Norway	15,260
Sri Lanka, Asia	24,900
Sumatra (Sumatera), Indon.	182,860
Taiwan, Asia	13,900
Tasmania, Austl.	26,200
Tierra del Fuego, S.A.	18,600
Timor, Indon.	5,743
Vancouver I., Can.	12,079
Victoria I., Can.	83,897
Vrangelya (Wrangel), Sov. Un.	2,800

Principal Lakes, Oceans, Seas, and Their Areas

LAKE Country	Area (Sq. Mi.)
Arabian Sea,	1,492,000
Aral'skoye More, (Aral Sea) Sov. Un.	24,700
Arctic Ocean,	5,400,000
Athabasca, L., Can.	3,064
Atlantic Ocean,	31,800,000
Balkhash, Ozero, (L.) Sov. Un.	7,100
Baltic Sea, Eur.	163,000
Baykal, Ozero, (L. Baikal) Sov. Un.	12,200
Bering Sea, Asia-N.A.	876,000
Black Sea, Eur.-Asia	178,000
Caribbean Sea, N.A.-S.A.	1,063,000
Caspian Sea, Iran-Sov. Un.	143,240
Chad, L., Cameroon-Chad-Nig.	6,300
Erie, L., Can.-U.S.	9,910
Eyre, L., Austl.	3,700
Gairdner, L., Austl.	1,700
Great Bear Lake, Can.	12,095
Great Salt Lake, U.S.	1,680
Great Slave Lake, Can.	11,030
Hudson Bay, Can.	475,000
Huron, L., Can.-U.S.	23,000
Indian Ocean,	28,900,000
Japan, Sea of, Asia	389,000
Koko Nor, (Qinghai Hu) China	1,650
Ladozhskoye Ozero, (L. Ladoga) Sov. Un.	683
Manitoba, L., Can.	1,785
Mediterranean Sea, Eur.-Afr.-Asia	967,000
Mexico, Gulf of, N.A.	596,000
Michigan, L., U.S.	22,300
Nicaragua, Lago de, Nic.	3,150
North Sea, Eur.	222,000
Nyasa, L., Malawi-Mozambique-Tanz.	11,150
Onezhskoye Ozero, (L. Onega) Sov. Un.	3,753
Ontario, L., Can.-U.S.	7,540
Pacific Ocean,	63,800,000
Red Sea, Afr.-Asia	169,000
Rudolf, L., Ethiopia-Kenya	2,473
Superior, L., Can.-U.S.	31,700
Tanganyika, L., Afr.	12,350
Titicaca, Lago, Bol.-Peru	3,200
Torrens, L., Austl.	2,300
Vänern, (L.) Swe.	2,156
Van Gölü, (L.) Tur.	1,420
Victoria, L., Ken.-Tan.-Ug.	26,820
Winnipeg, L., Can.	9,416
Winnipegosis, L., Can.	2,075
Yellow Sea, China-Korea	480,000

Principal Mountains and Their Heights

MOUNTAIN Country	Elev. (Ft.)
Aconcagua, Cerro, Argentina	22,831
Annapurna, Nepal	26,504
Antofalla, Volcán, Argentina	20,013
Api, Nepal	23,399
Apo, Mt., Philippines	9,692
Ararat, Turkey	16,804
Ayers Rock, Australia	2,844
Barú, Volcán, Panama	11,410
Belukha, Gol'tsy, Soviet Union	14,783
Bia, Phu, Laos	9,252
Blanc, Mont, France-Italy	15,771
Blanca Pk., Colorado, U.S.	14,317
Bolívar (La Columna), Venezuela	16,411
Borah Pk., Idaho, U.S.	12,662
Cameroon Mtn., Cameroon	13,451
Carrauntoohil, Ireland	3,414
Chimborazo, Ecuador	20,561
Chirripó, Cerro, Costa Rica	12,530
Citlaltépetl, Mexico	18,701
Colima, Nevado de, Mexico	13,993
Cook, Mt., New Zealand	12,349
Cotopaxi, Ecuador	19,347
Cristóbal Colón, Pico, Colombia	19,029
Damāvand, Qolleh-ye, Iran	18,386
Dhaulāgiri, Nepal	26,810
Duarte, Pico, Dominican Rep.	10,417
Dychtau, gora, Soviet Union	17,073
Egmont, Mt., New Zealand	8,260
Elbert, Mt., Colorado, U.S.	14,431
El'brus, Gora, Soviet Union	18,510
Elgon, Mt., Kenya-Uganda	14,178
eNjesuthi, South Africa	11,306
Erciyeş Dağı, Turkey	12,848
Etna, Mt., Italy	10,902
Everest, Mt., China-Nepal	29,028
Fairweather, Mt., Alaska-Canada	15,300
Finsteraarhorn, Switzerland	14,022
Foraker, Mt., Alaska, U.S.	17,400
Fuji-san, Japan	12,388
Gannett Pk., Wyoming, U.S.	13,785
Gasherbrum, China-Pakistan	26,470
Gerlachovský Stít, Czechoslovakia	8,710
Giluwe, Mt., Papua New Guinea	14,331
Glittertinden, Norway	8,110
Gongga Shan, China	24,790
Grand Teton Mtn., Wyoming, U.S.	13,766
Grossglockner, Austria	12,461
Gunnbjørn Fjeld, Greenland	12,139
Hadūr Shu'ayb, Yemen	12,336
Haleakala Crater, Hawaii, U.S.	10,025
Haltiatunturi, Finland-Norway	4,357
Hekla, Iceland	4,892
Hkakabo Razi, Burma	19,296
Hood, Mt., Oregon, U.S.	11,239
Huascarán, Nevado, Peru	22,205
Huila, Nevado de, Colombia	18,865
Hvannadalshnúkur, Iceland	6,952
Illampu, Nevado, Bolivia	20,873
Illimani, Nevado, Bolivia	21,151
Iztaccíhuatl, Mexico	17,343
Jaya, Puncak, Indonesia	16,503
Jungfrau, Switzerland	13,642
K2 (Godwin Austen), China-Pakistan	28,250
Kāmet, China-India	25,447
Kānchenjunga, India-Nepal	28,208
Karisimbi, Volcan, Rwanda-Zaire	14,787
Kātrīnā, Jabal, Egypt	8,668
Kebnekaise, Sweden	6,962
Kenya, Mt., Kenya	17,058
Kerinci, Gunung, Indonesia	12,467
Kilimanjaro, Tanzania	19,340
Kinabalu, Gunong, Malaysia	13,455
Klyuchevskaya, Soviet Union	15,584
Kommunizma, Pik, Soviet Union	24,590
Korab, Albania-Yugoslavia	9,026
Kosciusko, Mt., Australia	7,316
Koussi, Emi, Chad	11,204
Kula Kangri, Bhutan	24,784
Lassen Pk., California, U.S.	10,457
Llullaillaco, Volcán, Argentina-Chile	22,057
Logan, Mt., Canada	19,524
Longs Pk., Colorado, U.S.	14,255
Makālu, China-Nepal	27,825
Margherita Pk., Zaire-Uganda	16,763
Markham, Mt., Antarctica	14,272
Maromokotro, Madagascar	9,436
Matterhorn, Italy-Switzerland	14,692
Mauna Kea, Hawaii, U.S.	13,796
Mauna Loa, Hawaii, U.S.	13,680
McKinley, Mt., Alaska, U.S.	20,320
Meru, Mt., Tanzania	14,978
Misti, Volcán, Peru	19,098
Mitchell, Mt., North Carolina, U.S.	6,684
Moldoveanu, Romania	8,343
Mulhacén, Spain (continental)	11,424
Musala, Bulgaria	9,596
Muztag, China	25,338
Muztagata, China	24,757
Namjagbarwa Feng, China	25,446
Nanda Devi, India	25,645
Nānga Parbat, Pakistan	26,650
Narodnaya, Gora, Soviet Union	6,214
Neblina, Pico da, Brazil-Venezuela	9,888
Nevis, Ben, United Kingdom	4,406
Ojos del Salado, Nevado, Argentina-Chile	22,615
Ólimbos, Cyprus	6,401
Ólimbos, Greece	9,570
Orohena, Mont, French Polynesia	7,352
Paektu san, North Korea-China	9,003
Paricutín, Mexico	9,213
Parnassós, Greece	8,061
Pelée, Montagne, Martinique	4,000
Pico, Cape Verde	9,281
Pidurutalagala, Sri Lanka	8,281
Pikes Pk., Colorado, U.S.	14,110
Pissis, Monte, Argentina	22,241
Pobedy, pik, China-Soviet Union	24,406
Popocatépetl, Volcán, Mexico	17,887
Pulog, Mt., Philippines	9,606
Rainier, Mt., Washington, U.S.	14,410
Ras Dashen Terara, Ethiopia	15,158
Rinjani, Gunung, Indonesia	12,224
Rosa, Monte, Italy-Switzerland	15,203
Ruapehu, New Zealand	9,175
St. Elias, Mt., Alaska, U.S.-Canada	18,008
Sajama, Nevado, Bolivia	21,463
Sawdā', Qurnat as, Lebanon	10,114
Scafell Pikes, England, U.K.	3,210
Semeru, Gunung, Indonesia	12,060
Shām, Jabal ash, Oman	9,902
Shasta, Mt., California, U.S.	14,162
Snowdon, Wales, U.K.	3,560
Tahat, Algeria	9,541
Tajumulco (Vol.), Guatemala	13,816
Tirich Mīr, Pakistan	25,230
Tomanivi (Victoria), Fiji	4,341
Toubkal, Jebel, Morocco	13,665
Triglav, Yugoslavia	9,393
Trikora, Puncak, Indonesia	15,584
Tupungato, Portezuelo de, Argentina-Chile	22,310
Turquino, Pico de, Cuba	6,496
Vesuvio (Vesuvius), Italy	4,190
Victoria, Mt., Papua New Guinea	13,238
Vinson Massif, Antarctica	16,864
Waddington, Mt., Canada	13,260
Washington, Mt., New Hampshire, U.S.	6,288
Weisshorn, Switzerland	14,783
Whitney, Mt., California, U.S.	14,491
Wilhelm, Mt., Papua New Guinea	14,793
Wrangell, Mt., Alaska, U.S.	14,163
Xixabangma Feng (Gosainthan), China	26,286
Zugspitze, Austria-Germany	9,721

Principal Rivers and Their Lengths

RIVER Continent	Length (Mi.)
Albany, N.A.	610
Aldan, Asia	1,412
Amazonas-Ucayali, S.A.	4,000
Amu Darya, Asia	1,578
Amur, Asia	2,744
Amur-Argun, Asia	2,761
Araguaia, S.A.	1,400
Arkansas, N.A.	1,459
Athabasca, N.A.	765
Brahmaputra, Asia	1,770
Branco, S.A.	580
Brazos, N.A.	900
Canadian, N.A.	906
Churchill, N.A.	1,000
Colorado, N.A. (U.S.-Mex.)	1,450
Columbia, N.A.	1,200
Congo (Zaïre), Africa	2,900
Cumberland, N.A.	720
Danube, Europe	1,776
Darling, Australia	864
Dnepr, (Dnieper) Europe	1,400
Dnestr, (Dniestr) Europe	840
Don, Europe	1,162
Elbe, Europe	720
Euphrates, Asia	1,510
Fraser, N.A.	851
Ganges, Asia	1,560
Gila, N.A.	630
Godāvari, Asia	930
Green, N.A.	730
Huang, (Yellow) Asia	3,395
Indus, Asia	1,800
Irrawaddy, Asia	1,300
Juruá, S.A.	1,250
Kama, Europe	1,122
Kasai, Africa	1,338
Kolyma, Asia	1,323
Lena, Asia	2,700
Limpopo, Africa	1,100
Loire, Europe	625
Mackenzie, N.A.	2,635
Madeira, S.A.	2,013
Magdalena, S.A.	950
Marañón, S.A.	1,000
Mekong, Asia	2,600
Meuse, Europe	575
Mississippi, N.A.	2,348
Mississippi-Missouri, N.A.	3,740
Missouri, N.A.	2,315
Murray, Australia	1,566
Negro, S.A.	1,300
Neman, Europe	582
Niger, Africa	2,600
Nile, Africa	4,145
North Platte, N.A.	618
Ob'-Irtysh, Asia	3,362
Oder, Europe	565
Ohio, N.A.	981
Oka, Europe	900
Orange, Africa	1,300
Orinoco, S.A.	1,600
Ottawa, N.A.	790
Paraguay, S.A.	1,610
Paraná, S.A.	2,800
Parnaíba, S.A.	850
Peace, N.A.	1,195
Pechora, Europe	1,124
Pecos, N.A.	735
Pilcomayo, S.A.	1,550
Plata-Paraná, S.A.	3,030
Purús, S.A.	1,860
Red, N.A.	1,270
Rhine, Europe	820
Rhône, Europe	500
Rio Grande, N.A.	1,885
Roosevelt, S.A.	950
St. Lawrence, N.A.	800
Salado, S.A.	900
Salween, (Nu) Asia	1,750
São Francisco, S.A.	1,988
Saskatchewan-Bow, N.A.	1,205
Sava, Europe	585
Snake, N.A.	1,038
Sungari, (Songhua) Asia	1,140
Syr Dar'ya, Asia	1,370
Tagus, Europe	625
Tarim, Asia	1,328
Tennessee, N.A.	652
Tigris, Asia	1,180
Tisa, Europe	607
Tobol, Asia	989
Tocantins, S.A.	1,640
Ucayali, S.A.	1,220
Ural, Asia	1,509
Uruguay, S.A.	1,025
Verkhnyaya Tunguska, (Angara) Asia	1,105
Vilyuy, Asia	1,647
Volga, Europe	2,194
White, N.A. (Ar.-Mo.)	720
Wisła (Vistula), Europe	630
Xiang, Asia	930
Xingu, S.A.	1,230
Yangtze, (Chang) Asia	3,900
Yellowstone, N.A.	671
Yenisey, Asia	2,543
Yukon, N.A.	1,770
Zambezi, Africa	1,700

Principal Cities of the World

Abidjan, Ivory Coast	1,500,000
Accra, Ghana (1,250,000)	859,640
Addis Ababa, Ethiopia (1,500,000)	1,412,575
Adelaide, Australia (977,721)	14,157
Ahmadābād, India (2,400,000)	2,059,725
Aleppo (Halab), Syria (1,115,000)	1,060,002
Alexandria (Al Iskandarīyah), Egypt (3,350,000)	2,821,000
Algiers (El Djazaïr), Algeria (2,300,000)	1,721,607
Alma-Ata, Soviet Union (1,170,000)	1,108,000
Ammān, Jordan (1,250,000)	833,500
Amsterdam, Netherlands (1,860,000)	679,140
Ankara (Angora), Turkey (2,400,000)	2,235,035
Anshan, China	1,300,000
Antwerp (Antwerpen), Belgium (1,100,000)	490,524
Asunción, Paraguay (700,000)	455,517
Athens (Athínai), Greece (3,027,331)	885,737
Atlanta, Georgia, U.S. (1,962,500)	425,022
Auckland, New Zealand (850,000)	149,046
Baghdād, Iraq (4,000,000)	2,200,000
Baku, Soviet Union (2,005,000)	1,115,000
Baltimore, Maryland, U.S. (1,960,400)	786,741
Bandung, Indonesia (1,800,000)	1,461,407
Bangalore, India (2,950,000)	2,476,355
Bangkok (Krung Thep), Thailand (6,450,000)	5,446,708
Barcelona, Spain (4,040,000)	1,694,064
Beijing (Peking), China (6,450,000)	5,970,000
Beirut, Lebanon (1,675,000)	509,000
Belém, Brazil (1,200,000)	1,116,578
Belfast, N. Ireland, U.K. (685,000)	318,600
Belgrade (Beograd), Yugoslavia (1,400,000)	936,200
Belo Horizonte, Brazil (2,950,000)	2,114,429
Berlin, Ger. (3,825,000)	3,115,473
Bilbao, Spain (985,000)	378,221
Birmingham, England, U.K. (2,675,000)	1,013,995
Bogotá, Colombia (4,550,000)	4,260,000
Bombay, India (9,950,000)	8,243,405
Bonn, Ger. (570,000)	291,439
Boston, Massachusetts, U.S. (3,971,700)	562,994
Brasília, Brazil	1,567,709
Bremen, Ger. (800,000)	521,976
Brisbane, Australia (1,149,401)	705,755
Brussels (Bruxelles), Belgium (2,395,000)	137,738
Bucharest (Bucureşti), Romania (2,250,000)	1,989,823
Budapest, Hungary (2,565,000)	2,104,700
Buenos Aires, Argentina (10,750,000)	2,922,829
Buffalo, New York, U.S. (1,483,000)	357,870
Cairo (Al Qāhirah), Egypt (9,300,000)	6,205,000
Calcutta, India (11,100,000)	3,305,006
Cali, Colombia (1,400,000)	1,350,565
Canberra, Australia (271,362)	247,194
Cape Town, South Africa (1,790,000)	776,617
Caracas, Venezuela (3,600,000)	3,041,000
Cardiff, Wales, U.K. (625,000)	262,313
Casablanca, Morocco (2,475,000)	2,139,204
Changchun, China (1,910,000†)	1,740,000
Chelyabinsk, Soviet Union (1,300,000)	1,119,000
Chengdu, China (2,640,000†)	1,810,000
Chicago, Illinois, U.S. (7,717,100)	3,005,072
Chittagong, Bangladesh (1,391,877)	980,000
Chongqing (Chungking), China (2,830,000†)	2,450,000
Cincinnati, Ohio, U.S. (1,480,100)	385,457
Cleveland, Ohio, U.S. (2,218,400)	573,822
Cologne (Köln), Ger. (1,760,000)	914,336
Colombo, Sri Lanka (2,050,000)	623,000
Columbus, Ohio, U.S. (963,600)	565,032
Copenhagen (København), Denmark (1,685,000)	473,000
Curitiba, Brazil (1,700,000)	1,279,205
Dakar, Senegal	1,428,084
Dalian (Lüda), China	1,680,000
Dallas, Texas, U.S. (2,727,300)	904,078
Damascus (Dimashq), Syria (1,850,000)	1,259,000
Dar es Salaam, Tanzania	757,346
Delhi, India (7,200,000)	4,884,234
Denver, Colorado, U.S. (1,405,300)	492,365
Detroit, Michigan, U.S. (4,691,900)	1,202,463
Dhaka (Dacca), Bangladesh (3,430,312)	2,365,695
Dnepropetrovsk, Soviet Union (1,600,000)	1,182,000
Donetsk, Soviet Union (2,220,000)	1,090,000
Dresden, Ger. (670,000)	519,810
Dublin (Baile Átha Cliath), Ireland (1,140,000)	502,749
Durban, South Africa (1,550,000)	634,301
Düsseldorf, Ger. (1,190,000)	560,572
Edinburgh, Scotland, U.K. (630,000)	408,822
Essen, Ger. (4,950,000)	615,421
Florence (Firenze), Italy (650,000)	453,293
Fortaleza, Brazil (1,825,000)	1,582,414
Frankfurt am Main, Ger. (1,855,000)	592,411
Fukuoka, Japan (1,750,000)	1,160,440
Fushun, China	1,270,000
Gdańsk (Danzig), Poland (909,000)	468,400
Geneva (Genève), Switzerland (460,000)	160,645
Genoa (Genova), Italy (830,000)	760,300
Glasgow, Scotland, U.K. (1,800,000)	754,586
Gor'kiy, Soviet Union (2,005,000)	1,425,000
Guadalajara, Mexico (2,325,000)	1,626,152
Guangzhou (Canton), China (3,360,000†)	3,050,000
Guatemala, Guatemala (1,100,000)	754,243
Guayaquil, Ecuador (1,255,000)	1,204,532
Hamburg, Ger. (2,225,000)	1,571,267
Hannover, Ger. (1,000,000)	505,718
Hanoi, Vietnam (1,500,000)	897,500
Harare, Zimbabwe (890,000)	656,011
Harbin, China	2,670,000
Hartford, Connecticut, U.S. (1,013,600)	136,392
Havana (La Habana), Cuba (1,975,000)	1,914,466
Helsinki, Finland (900,000)	484,263
Hiroshima, Japan (1,575,000)	1,044,118
Ho Chi Minh City (Saigon), Vietnam (3,100,000)	2,700,849
Hong Kong, Hong Kong (4,515,000)	1,183,621
Honolulu, Hawaii, U.S. (762,600)	365,048
Houston, Texas, U.S. (2,755,100)	1,595,138
Hyderābād, India (2,750,000)	2,187,262
Ibadan, Nigeria	1,144,000
Indianapolis, Indiana, U.S. (1,072,500)	700,807
Irkutsk, Soviet Union	609,000
İstanbul, Turkey (5,750,000)	5,475,982
İzmir, Turkey (1,550,000)	1,489,772
Jakarta, Indonesia (8,600,000)	6,503,449
Jerusalem, Israel (490,000)	468,900
Jiddah, Saudi Arabia	1,300,000
Jinan, China	1,460,000
Johannesburg, South Africa (3,650,000)	632,369
Kābul, Afghanistan	972,836
Kānpur, India (1,875,000)	1,481,789
Kansas City, Missouri, U.S. (1,272,400)	448,033
Kaohsiung, Taiwan (1,785,000)	1,302,849
Karāchi, Pakistan (5,300,000)	4,901,627
Kathmandu, Nepal (320,000)	235,160
Katowice, Poland (2,778,000)	367,300
Kawasaki, Japan (*Tōkyō)	1,088,624
Kazan', Soviet Union (1,120,000)	1,068,000
Khar'kov, Soviet Union (1,905,000)	1,587,000
Khartoum (Al Kharṭūm), Sudan (1,450,000)	476,218
Kiev, Soviet Union (2,850,000)	2,544,000
Kingston, Jamaica (770,000)	586,930
Kinshasa, Zaire	3,000,000
Kitakyūshū, Japan (1,525,000)	1,056,402
Kōbe, Japan (*Ōsaka)	1,410,834
Kowloon, Hong Kong (*Hong Kong)	799,123
Kuala Lumpur, Malaysia (1,475,000)	919,610
Kunming, China (1,520,000†)	1,280,000
Kuwait (Al Kuwayt), Kuwait (1,375,000)	44,335
Kuybyshev, Soviet Union (1,510,000)	1,280,000
Kyōto, Japan (*Ōsaka)	1,479,218
Lagos, Nigeria (3,800,000)	1,213,000
Lahore, Pakistan (3,025,000)	2,707,215
Lanzhou, China (1,390,000†)	1,270,000
La Paz, Bolivia	992,592
Leeds, England, U.K. (1,540,000)	445,242
Leipzig, Ger. (700,000)	550,641
Leningrad, Soviet Union (5,750,000)	4,393,000
Liège, Belgium (755,000)	207,496
Lille, France (1,020,000)	168,424
Lima, Peru (4,608,010)	371,122
Lisbon (Lisboa), Portugal (2,250,000)	807,167
Liverpool, England, U.K. (1,525,000)	538,809
Łódź, Poland (1,061,000)	847,400
London, England, U.K. (11,100,000)	6,851,400
Los Angeles, California, U.S. (9,763,600)	2,968,579
Louisville, Kentucky, U.S. (891,400)	298,694
Luanda, Angola	1,200,000
Lucknow, India (1,060,000)	895,721
Lyon, France (1,275,000)	413,095
Madras, India (4,475,000)	3,276,622
Madrid, Spain (4,650,000)	3,123,713
Managua, Nicaragua	644,588
Manchester, England, U.K. (2,775,000)	437,612
Manila, Philippines (6,800,000)	1,630,485
Mannheim, Ger. (1,400,000)	294,648
Maracaibo, Venezuela	929,000
Marseille, France (1,225,000)	874,436
Mecca (Makkah), Saudi Arabia	550,000
Medan, Indonesia	1,208,678
Medellín, Colombia	2,095,000
Melbourne, Australia (2,832,893)	60,828
Memphis, Tennessee, U.S. (852,900)	646,174
Mexico City, Mexico (14,100,000)	8,831,079
Miami, Florida, U.S. (2,827,300)	346,865
Milan (Milano), Italy (3,775,000)	1,634,638
Milwaukee, Wisconsin, U.S. (1,374,700)	636,297
Minneapolis, Minnesota, U.S. (2,012,400)	370,951
Minsk, Soviet Union (1,600,000)	1,543,000
Monterrey, Mexico (2,015,000)	1,090,009
Montevideo, Uruguay (1,550,000)	1,246,500
Montréal, Canada (2,921,357)	1,015,420
Moscow (Moskva), Soviet Union (12,900,000)	8,614,000
Munich (München), Ger. (1,955,000)	1,274,716
Nagoya, Japan (4,800,000)	2,116,381
Nāgpur, India (1,302,066)	1,219,461
Nairobi, Kenya	1,103,600
Nanjing, China	2,290,000
Naples (Napoli), Italy (2,765,000)	1,210,503
Netzahualcóyotl, Mexico (*Mexico City)	1,341,230
Newcastle upon Tyne, England, U.K. (1,300,000)	199,064
New Delhi, India (*Delhi)	273,036
New Kowloon, Hong Kong (*Hong Kong)	1,651,064
New Orleans, Louisiana, U.S. (1,185,000)	557,927
New York, New York, U.S. (16,000,000)	7,071,639
Novosibirsk, Soviet Union (1,580,000)	1,423,000
Nürnberg, Ger. (1,030,000)	467,392
Odessa, Soviet Union (1,210,000)	1,141,000
Oklahoma City, Oklahoma, U.S. (742,000)	403,484
Omsk, Soviet Union (1,160,000)	1,134,000
Ōsaka, Japan (16,450,000)	263,624
Oslo, Norway (720,000)	448,747
Ottawa, Canada (819,263)	300,763
Panamá, Panama (625,000)	413,992
Paris, France (9,775,000)	2,127,100
Perm', Soviet Union (1,145,000)	1,075,000
Perth, Australia (994,472)	79,409
Philadelphia, Pennsylvania, U.S. (5,208,600)	1,688,210
Phnum Pénh, Cambodia	700,000
Phoenix, Arizona, U.S. (1,482,400)	790,044
Pittsburgh, Pennsylvania, U.S. (2,218,800)	423,959
Port-au-Prince, Haiti (760,000)	684,284
Portland, Oregon, U.S. (1,227,200)	368,139
Porto (Oporto), Portugal (1,225,000)	327,368
Porto Alegre, Brazil (2,600,000)	1,272,121
Prague (Praha), Czechoslovakia (1,310,000)	1,193,513
Pretoria, South Africa (960,000)	443,059
Providence, Rhode Island, U.S. (921,800)	156,804
Pune, India (1,775,000)	1,203,351
Pusan, South Korea (3,550,000)	3,514,798
P'yŏngyang, North Korea (1,600,000)	1,283,000
Qingdao, China	1,270,000
Qiqihar, China (1,300,000†)	1,150,000
Québec, Canada (603,267)	164,5
Quezon City, Philippines (*Manila)	1,165,8
Quito, Ecuador (1,050,000)	890,35
Rabat, Morocco (980,000)	518,616
Rangoon (Yangon), Burma (2,800,000)	2,458,712
Rāwalpindi, Pakistan (1,040,000)	457,091
Recife, Brazil (2,625,000)	1,287,623
Rīga, Soviet Union (990,000)	900,000
Rio de Janerio, Brazil (10,150,000)	5,603,388
Riyadh, Saudi Arabia	1,250,000
Rome (Roma), Italy (3,115,000)	2,830,569
Rosario, Argentina (1,045,000)	938,120
Rostov-na-Donu, Soviet Union (1,145,000)	1,004,000
Rotterdam, Netherlands (1,110,000)	571,372
St. Louis, Missouri, U.S. (2,203,000)	452,801
St. Paul, Minnesota, U.S. (*Minneapolis)	270,230
Salt Lake City, Utah, U.S. (682,400)	163,034
Salvador, Brazil (2,050,000)	1,804,438
San Antonio, Texas, U.S. (968,200)	786,023
San Diego, California, U.S. (2,098,500)	875,538
San Francisco, California, U.S. (4,683,200)	678,974
San José, Costa Rica (670,000)	241,464
San Juan, Puerto Rico (1,775,260)	424,600
San Salvador, El Salvador (920,000)	459,902
Santiago, Chile (4,025,000)	425,924
Santo Domingo, Dominican Rep.	1,313,172
São Paulo, Brazil (15,175,000)	10,063,110
Sapporo, Japan (1,900,000)	1,542,979
Saratov, Soviet Union (1,170,000)	918,000
Seattle, Washington, U.S. (2,077,100)	493,846
Seoul (Sŏul), South Korea (14,100,000)	9,639,110
Shanghai, China (9,300,000)	7,100,000
Shenyang (Mukden), China (4,290,000†)	3,840,000
Singapore, Singapore (3,000,000)	2,631,000
Sofia (Sofiya), Bulgaria (1,199,405)	1,114,962
Stockholm, Sweden (1,449,972)	663,217
Stuttgart, Ger. (1,925,000)	565,486
Surabaya, Indonesia	2,027,913
Sverdlovsk, Soviet Union (1,575,000)	1,331,000
Sydney, Australia (3,364,858)	86,311
Taegu, South Korea	2,029,853
T'aipei, Taiwan (5,725,000)	2,507,620
Taiyuan, China (1,930,000†)	1,660,000
Tashkent, Soviet Union (2,370,000)	2,124,000
Tbilisi, Soviet Union (1,380,000)	1,194,000
Tegucigalpa, Honduras	597,500
Tehrān, Iran (6,400,000)	5,734,199
Tel Aviv-Yafo, Israel (1,670,000)	320,300
The Hague ('s-Gravenhage), Netherlands (770,000)	443,961
Tianjin (Tientsin), China (5,460,000†)	4,880,000
Tiranë, Albania	210,800
Tōkyō, Japan (27,700,000)	8,354,615
Toronto, Canada (3,427,168)	612,289
Tripoli (Tarābulus), Libya	858,500
Tunis, Tunisia (1,225,000)	596,654
Turin (Torino), Italy (1,600,000)	1,103,520
Ufa, Soviet Union (1,110,000)	1,092,000
Ulan Bator, Mongolia	488,200
Valencia, Spain (1,270,000)	738,575
Valparaíso, Chile (700,000)	265,355
Vancouver, Canada (1,380,729)	431,147
Venice (Venezia), Italy (415,000)	332,775
Vienna (Wien), Austria (1,875,000)	1,489,153
Vladivostok, Soviet Union	615,000
Volgograd (Stalingrad), Soviet Union (1,335,000)	988,000
Warsaw (Warszawa), Poland (2,323,000)	1,664,700
Washington, D.C., U.S. (3,221,400)	638,432
Wellington, New Zealand (350,000)	137,495
Winnipeg, Canada (625,304)	594,551
Wuhan, China	3,490,000
Wuppertal, Ger. (830,000)	374,217
Xi'an, China (2,390,000†)	2,050,000
Yerevan, Soviet Union (1,280,000)	1,168,000
Yokohama, Japan (*Tōkyō)	2,992,926
Zagreb, Yugoslavia	768,700
Zhengzhou, China (1,610,000†)	1,170,000
Zurich, Switzerland (860,000)	349,549

Metropolitan area populations are shown in parentheses.
*City is located within the metropolitan area of another city; for example, Kyōto, Japan is located in the Ōsaka metropolitan area.
†Population of entire municipality or district, including rural area.

x of Major Places on the Physical-Political Maps

ch entry in this index reference system consists of a ce-name, a political-division name, or a physical-feature ame; a map key; and a map page number. For specific instructions on the use of map keys, see page 19.

Each place-name is indexed to its city symbol on the map. Each political division, such as a state, is indexed to the location of its name on the map. Each physical feature, such as a river, is also indexed to the location of its name.

Following each name is the name of the country in which the feature is located. However, some physical features extend into two or more countries. In this case, the continent is listed.

In some entries, an alternate name is given in parentheses. This is the name used locally for that place, or a previously used name.

A small, or lowercase, letter in a map key means that place is keyed to an inset map rather than to the main map on the page. Two map keys are shown for areas that begin on one map and continue on another map.

A standard alphabetizing system is used in this index. If more than one name has the same spelling, place-names are listed first, political divisions second, and physical features third.

Index of Major Places on the Physical-Political Maps

ARCTIC OCEAN

75°

Beaufort Sea
QUEEN ELIZABETH ISLANDS

BROOKS RANGE
MACKENZIE MTS
Mt. McKinley
ALASKA RANGE
60°
Bering Sea
Gulf of Alaska

Arctic Circle
Hudson Bay
BAFFIN ISLAND
Baffin Bay
GREENLAND

ICELAND
No

45°
Labrador Sea

NEWFOUNDLAND

N O R T H
A M E R I C A

GREAT PLAINS

ROCKY MOUNTAINS

SIERRA NEVADA

APPALACHIAN MOUNTAINS

ATLANTIC

IB
PE

P A C I F I C
30°

Mississippi

Gulf of Mexico

SIERRA MADRE OCCIDENTAL
SIERRA MADRE ORIENTAL

HAWAIIAN ISLANDS
Tropic of Cancer
O C E A N

WEST INDIES
OCEAN
S

15°
Caribbean Sea

ISTHMUS OF PANAMA

LLANOS

0°
Equator

Amazon

S O U T H
A M E R I C A

A N D E S

P
O
L
Y
N
E
S
I
A

15°

SERRA DO ESPINHAÇO
ATLANTIC

GRAN CHACO
Paraná

P A C I F I C

Tropic of Capricorn

30°

O C E A N

OCEAN

Mt. Aconcagua
PAMPA

45°
FALKLAND ISLANDS

TIERRA DEL FUEGO
Cape Horn

60°
Antarctic Circle
Weddell Sea

75°
MARIE BYRD LAND
A N T

90° 180° 165° 150° 135° 120° 105° 90° 75° 60° 45° 30° 15° 0°

180° 165° 150°. 135° 120° 105° 90° 75° 60° 45° 30° 15° 0°